Warriors of Death

A man who joined the army at 16 by lying about his age, Charles Whiting became a well-known author and military historian through his academic prowess. His first novel, written while still an undergraduate, was published in 1954 and by 1958 had been followed by three wartime thrillers. Between 1960 and 2007 Charles went on to write over 350 titles, including 70 non-fiction titles covering varied topics from the Nazi intelligence service to British Regiments during World War II. He passed away in 2007.

Also by Charles Whiting

Hitler's Secret War
Paths of Death and Glory
Warriors of Death

Common Smith VC Adventures

The Baltic Run
In Turkish Waters
Death on the Rhine
Passage to Petrograd
Death Trap
The Japanese Princess
Hell's Angels

CHARLES WHITING

WARRIORS OF DEATH

CANELOHISTORY

First published in Great Britain in 1991 by Arrow

This edition published in the United Kingdom in 2022 by

Canelo
Unit 9, 5th Floor
Cargo Works, 1–2 Hatfields
London, SE1 9PG
United Kingdom

A CIP catalogue record for this book is available from the British Library.

Print ISBN 978 1 80032 655 2
Ebook ISBN 978 1 80032 654 5

Look for more great books at www.canelo.co

Printed and bound in Great Britain by Clays Ltd, Elcograf S.p.A.

1

A new man, the storm soldier, the elite of Central Europe. A completely new race, cunning, strong and packed with purpose... battle proven, merciless to both himself and others.

Ernest Juenger
German combat soldier and poet

INTRODUCTION

I have eaten your bread and salt.
I have drunk your water and wine.
The deaths ye died, I have watched beside,
And the lives ye led were mine.

Rudyard Kipling

'There has been a change of plan,' the little *Herr Doktor* said, as I stood there on the platform waiting for the train to Hamburg.

The previous day the *Herr Doktor* with his cropped blond hair had advised me to take the morning train to Hamburg, where friends of the man I wanted to see would pick me up at the *Hauptbahnhof*. Now appearing so surprisingly this cold morning, he said *we* (apparently he was going with me now) were not going to Hamburg. Instead, we would travel to Harburg on the opposite side of the River Elbe. I understood, didn't I? The man I was going to see was still wanted in Western Germany – or at least he couldn't enter the country legally – and we didn't want any trouble with the police, did we? I agreed we didn't.

An hour later, we were in Harburg, where we were picked up swiftly outside the station by a black BMW, which did not have the local licence plates. The driver, who did not introduce himself – something unusual in a very formal West Germany – circled the area for about ten minutes until he was satisfied we weren't being tailed before he dropped us off at a nondescript flat in the residential area.

It was full of big middle-aged men, some, judging by their accents and clothes, not German, and they all looked wary. There was whisky and schnaps, bottles of the stuff, rapidly disappearing down their throats, and it was only ten o'clock in the morning. Finally, whoever was in charge seemed satisfied that everything was safe and we set off in a small fleet of cars, one of them lagging behind to check if we were being followed.

Now I learned the reason for the presence in Germany of the man I wanted to see. In Madrid, where he had fled in 1948, his doctors had diagnosed a tumour on his spine. It could be removed, but the operation was tricky. If it went wrong, he could be paralysed for life. His doctors advised him that the best place to have the operation carried out was in Germany, despite the risk he ran there of perhaps being arrested.

Once the Allied Supreme Commander, General Eisenhower, had called him 'the most dangerous man in Europe'. Now his great frame lay flat on a hospital bed in a room filled with his former soldiers, who had come from all of Western Europe to guard him while he was in Germany. He was obviously a very sick man. He had lost a great deal of weight, his dark eyes were faded and his skin had a yellow, unhealthy look. But his face, criss-crossed with the duelling scars of his youth, still had the bold, challenging look that I remembered from his wartime photographs.

'Skorzeny,' he said, and offered me his hand in the Viennese fashion, while one of his men stared fixedly out of the window at the ground below, as he might have done all those years before when they had crash-landed their glider on the Gran Sasso to abduct the Italian dictator, Mussolini.

Thus I met the first of those legendary – some would say infamous – colonels who had once belonged to Adolf Hitler's own bodyguard regiment, *die Leibstandarte SS Adolf Hitler.*

In the years to come, I met others. There was Jochen Peiper, once the youngest colonel of them all. For years after the war, he had lived under the sentence of death, his trial so controversial that a Pope, a US President, a West German Chancellor and that notorious Junior Senator from Wisconsin, Joe McCarthy, became involved in challenging its verdict.

When I met him, Peiper was approaching sixty. His neck was scrawny and he had to use spectacles to read. But he was still as slim and as vital as he had been when he had led his regiment into the Ardennes back in 1944, panicking a whole army and forcing a US army commander to run for his life. His speech was still heavy with tough old soldier's phrases of that time – 'heaven, arse and cloudburst… I could have jumped in his face with my naked arse… They should have castrated him with a broken bottle…'

But for all his vitality, he was a broken man. 'I'm a fatalist today. The world has branded me and my men as the scum of the earth. They see us as German gangsters – Al Capones, the lot of us – with a revolver under each armpit and a tommy gun in our hands.' He was doomed, too, and he knew it. 'I'm sitting on a powder keg, you know. They've all tried to get me. One day someone will come along with a new "story" about me and the powder keg will explode under me. Then it'll be all over at last.'

It would be sooner than the bitter old man knew. Six years later, he would be attacked in his lonely retreat in eastern France and murdered, but Peiper would die as he had lived when a young man – with a gun in his hands…

There was Colonel Frey, too, immensely tall and fit even in his seventies, his face still purple and scarred from the horrible wound he had suffered three decades before. Rather than surrender to the Americans, he had taken off on his own. Penniless, in shabby civilian clothes and with little food, he had walked the whole length of France and Spain. When questioned by the locals, he told them he was an American, though he spoke only a few words of English and looked to even the most casual observer exactly what he was – a colonel in the SS on the run. But he'd made it. Thereafter he spent fifteen years of self-imposed exile in South America. For him, a colonel in the *Leibstandarte* did not surrender.

There was Colonel Gerd Bremer, too. In 1944 he had been the youngest battalion commander in the SS and one of the few survivors of the debacle in France. He also chose exile. With his own hands he built a house for rental in Spain as a means of making a living. Over the years he constructed more, building a strange, secluded, fortress-like holiday camp.

There, forty-odd years on, he parades his 'last command' on every 1 May, Labour Day. His 'last command' consists of two Spanish cleaning ladies and the odd-job man. As the *jefe coroner* appears, the radio on his battered old car blasting out wartime German marches, they come to attention, presenting their mops and brooms, broad grins on their faces. Then Bremer, who once paraded for Hitler with hundreds of other black–clad giants before the war, can order the 'march past' of his last command to commence…

These were the survivors, the 'old hares', as they call themselves. In 1944 their old commander, General Sepp Dietrich, had calculated that there were only thirty left of the original thirty thousand men he had taken to war in 1939. Somehow these men had survived the war, exile, and imprisonment to testify to that black time when they were the terror of Europe, Hitler's own Praetorian Guard.

They had been the elite of the elite, the premier SS division. Formed right at the beginning of that 'New Order', which its master Adolf Hitler had boasted would last a thousand years, they had been a nucleus of a private SS army, which in the end was a million strong. But no other SS division could ever match them in their courage, boldness and arrogant, bitter ruthlessness. The 1st SS Panzer Division, *die Leibstandarte Adolf Hitler*, was in a league of its own.

Their badge was the silver death's head, their flash the double runic 'S' of pagan Germany. Wherever they appeared in a battle – and they fought almost constantly for five years and eight months – they were feared and respected. Captured Russian Corps Commander General Artemenko is reported to have said that the Red Army 'breathed a sigh of relief' whenever they were taken out of the line. A Canadian battalion commander said of them: 'The only guys who really earn medals in this war are those SS birds. Every one of them deserves the VC. They're a bad bunch of bastards, but are they ever soldiers! They make us fellows look like amateurs.'

In 1944 as their tanks rumbled into Belgium to meet the new challenge, which would come from the sea, their commanders eager for some desperate glory, they sang that bold song of theirs:

SS marschiert, die Strasse frei.
Die Stunnkolonnen stehen.
Der Tod ist unser Kampfgenosse.
Wir sind die schwarzen Scharen[1]

One year later it was all over. Nearly half their number had been killed in action. Those who survived those bloody battles in France, Belgium and Hungary were suddenly wanted men, branded as war criminals, outlawed in their own country and in every other land in Europe. They had fallen from being the idolised heroes of Hitler's Third Reich to become the scum of the earth: rogues who had brought only disgrace and shame to their fatherland.

By the summer of 1945 *die Leibstandarte SS Adolf Hitler* no longer existed. After their master's suicide, the survivors had slunk away like grey rats into the sewers and tunnels of a dying Berlin. Slowly, over the years that followed, the infamous legend of those ruthless, black-clad young men who had once sworn an oath of loyalty to the death of their evil master, Adolf Hitler, faded into history.

By the sixties, the booming West Germany of the 'economic miracle' had virtually forgotten those men who had once carved out Hitler's empire for him: an empire with three hundred million subjects stretching from the Channel to the Urals, greater even than that of the Romans.

Now, thirty years on, times are changing rapidly. Within this present decade it seems likely that the Soviet Union will break up and there will be a reunified Germany – 'the Fourth Reich', following that unholy one, which died violently some fifty years ago, will have been created. It will have some eighty million citizens, the same number with which Hitler started his march to the domination of Europe. Then this rich, talented nation, enjoying a new economic miracle, thanks to demand from its new eastern half, will have replaced the Soviet Union as the new superpower in Europe.

What then? Will those old flags be waved once more? Will German streets echo and re-echo to that old, harsh command, '*Eins, zwei, drei – Ein Lied!*'[2] followed by the lusty bellow of a thousand throats bursting into one of the old marching songs? Will the 'warriors of death' march yet again…?

PART ONE

THE RETREAT

Though we observe the Higher Law
And thought we had our quarrel just
Were I permitted to withdraw
You wouldn't see my arse for dust.

Anon

1. 'WHEN AND WHERE THE LAST DICE WILL BE CAST, I CANNOT SAY'

It was midnight, Monday, 31 July 1944. The moment of truth had arrived. Obediently, the seven German staff officers, led by the chief-of-staff, Colonel-General Jodl, trooped into the charred map room. Jodl, as bleak-faced as ever, still wore a thick bandage around his head. For in this same room, eleven days before, his own comrades and fellow staff officers had exploded a bomb, which they hoped would kill the Fuehrer. He had been wounded in the attempt, but the Fuehrer had escaped with his life. Now for the first time since the dastardly *attentat*, the Fuehrer was going to address his staff on the events currently taking place in far-off France.

Adolf Hitler, the man who had once commanded the destinies of three hundred million Europeans, was ashen and shrivelled. As he came slowly into the map room, supported by one of his gigantic SS orderlies, he dragged one foot and held his left hand in his right one to hide the shaking. The explosion of the bomb had had its effect. But the Fuehrer was eating again and, due to his vegetarian diet and the sixty pills a day he took to combat gas and overweight, he was breaking wind constantly, as he had always done in the past.

The Fuehrer indicated that the staff should be seated. The only creature he really loved in this world, *Blondi*, his Alsatian bitch, crouched at his feet. Now a heavy night silence fell on the room, broken only by the crunch of the sentries' heavy boots on the gravel outside – and Hitler's own farting.

This was the moment of truth. Hitler was going to make a definitive statement on the war in the West. On this hot sultry' July night, Hitler was no longer the visionary war lord who had always conducted his campaigns on hunches and his own fevered intuitions. Now, for once, he was going to face up to facts in an almost detached, objective manner.

'Jodl,' he commenced, addressing his clever, calculating chief-of-staff, 'if we lose France as a theatre of war, we forfeit the starting point of the U-boat war. In addition, we receive from France many things which are vital to our war effort, including the last tungsten we can hope to get.'

The Fuehrer's old, piercing, almost hypnotic look had long vanished. Nowadays those eyes, which had once mesmerised the most cynical and wordly of his generals, were watery and yellow. That harsh snarling Austrian voice had become weaker, too. It no longer frightened, impelled, bullied.

But to Jodl, the Fuehrer's first words were clear enough all the same. They indicated that, for the very first time, Hitler had begun to realise that the great struggle would *not* be decided in the East, as Hitler had always believed up to now, but in the West. He waited attentively, his cunning eyes revealing nothing.

'We must be clear in our minds,' Hitler continued, 'that a change for the better in France would be possible only if we could gain superiority in the air – even if only for a brief period of time. Yet I am of the opinion that we must – no matter how bitter this may be – preserve our new *Luftwaffe* units inside the Reich to employ them as a very last resort.'

Jodl nodded his bandaged head in approval. In France the enemy air forces dominated the whole battlefield. Nothing, man or motor, could move in daylight without running the risk of being blasted to pieces by one of those damned enemy *jabos*[3]. But something had to be done in Normandy before it was too late, as the Fuehrer had obviously realised at long last.

Hitler licked his cracked, parched lips. 'When and where the last dice will be cast,' he said, face thoughtful, brow wrinkled under that dangling lock of dyed hair, 'I cannot say...' Hitler's voice faded as he let his staff officers absorb those words: *The last dice!*

–

Even as Adolf Hitler spoke to his staff in far-off East Prussia, the dice were already being cast in France. On this hot Monday morning, Hitler would be forced to make his overwhelming decision upon which the fate of the *Wehrmacht* in Occupied France depended.

There on the coastal road between St Sauveur and Lendelin, the General whom the US Press had nicknamed 'Ole Blood an' Guts' Patton ('yeah,' his soldiers quipped bitterly, *'our blood – and his guts')* watched impatiently as his armour rolled towards Brittany.

He was attended only by his deputy chief-of-staff, Colonel Harkins, later the officer who would embroil America in the hell of Vietnam. Harkins kept looking at his wristwatch. At midday, Patton's Third Army would become operational. Then, over the next seventy-two hours, Patton would feed seven whole divisions, perhaps some 150,000 soldiers, down a *single* road over a *single* bridge to debouch from the stalemated front in Normandy into the wide-open spaces of Brittany.

Harkins knew it was going to be a tremendously risky undertaking. Understandably, Patton was worried. After being relieved of his command back in Sicily in '43 for having slapped a GI he thought was 'yellow', Patton could not make any mistakes with his new command, the Third Army. The tall, immaculate, silver-haired Commanding General was fifty-nine years of age and Washington wouldn't give him a second chance.

Once, viewing a battlefield heavy with shattered vehicles and dead Germans, Patton encompassed it with a sweep of his outstretched arms and exclaimed to an aide, 'Just look at that! Could anything be more magnificent? Compared to war, all other forms of human endeavour shrink to insignificance.' His voice had shaken with emotion. '*God, how I love it!*'

Now Patton was taking a calculated risk, for if the Germans cut off this road – and they were only a score of miles away – his army might well be trapped.

But if Patton was worried and impatient, his ugly black-and-white pooch, Willie, inherited from a dead RAF pilot, remained sanguine. After engaging in a slight, amorous dalliance with a local French lady dog, which had appeared seemingly from nowhere, undeterred by the rumble of the armour thundering by, Willie now proceeded to scratch away at the earth near his master's feet. Slowly, he began to reveal the waxen yellow face of a dead German soldier who had recently been hastily buried there.

Harkins took his gaze from the dead man and flashed a glance at his watch. It was exactly twelve noon. Hurriedly, he produced the bottle of what an aide had called 'choice three-star' brandy to celebrate the activation of the US Third Army. But the brandy wasn't that choice. In fact, Harkins thought it rotgut. Patton was too nervous anyway. 'We tried to drink it,' he recorded later, 'but we gagged.'

It didn't matter. The dice had fallen now. The armour of Patton's Third Army was racing all out for Brittany along that single road. The time had come for Hitler to react while there was still a chance to save the *Wehrmacht* in France.

—

By mid-afternoon, Hitler had learned where the dice had fallen. Poring over a map of France with Jodl, he snorted: 'Just look at that crazy cowboy general… driving down to the south and into Brittany along a *single* road and over a *single* bridge with an entire army! He doesn't care about the risk and acts as if he owns the world! It doesn't seem possible.' He shook his head in wonder.

Both Hitler and Jodl had not a particularly high opinion of Americans as soldiers. They felt that the '*Amis*', as they called the Americans, relied too much on their lavishly supplied machines – tanks, artillery, planes – to do their fighting for them. Man for man they were no match for the German soldier. Still, they knew of Patton's reputation as the boldest armoured commander in the Allied camp. They had already seen what the 'crazy cowboy' General could do the previous year in Sicily. There he had driven his men ruthlessly. Now it was imperative to stop Patton before he turned the left flank of the German army in France and brought about disaster.

Although on the night before Hitler had declared to his staff that the *Wehrmacht* in France was not in a position to carry out an attack and would have to stay on the defensive 'because mobility – a war of movement – is impossible for us', now he changed his mind. He saw the fatal flaw in Patton's attempt to turn the *Wehrmacht's* left flank. His whole thrust depended on the possession of a mere sixteen-mile stretch of the coastal road along which he was moving all his armour. Surely Patton had overreached himself this time.

Hitler thought so, and Jodl did as well. Admittedly the enemy had air superiority in France at present, but as yet *Reichsmarschall* Hermann Goering, the head of the *Luftwaffe*, had not committed his fighters based on the fields around Paris. If they were committed, then he, Hitler, could throw in his reserves: seven whole panzer divisions, including four SS ones. And one of those was his own personal bodyguard, *die Leibstandarte Adolf Hitler*, the 1st SS Panzer Division. Why, it alone, the elite of the elite, might well be capable of slicing through the enemy's front line and covering the handful of kilometres to that single coastal road, which this morning had become the most important stretch of roadway in the world!

As he pondered the idea, Hitler's eyes sparkled with some of his old restless energy. For two months now, he had been waiting for an opportunity like this, ever since the Allies had landed on the beaches on 6 June 1944. Now 'the crazy cowboy' General had given him a golden chance. This could be the great turning point in the battle for France. Once, in June 1940, his *Leibstandarte* had helped to send the British scurrying for the beaches, throwing them out of France for four long years. Now they might be able to do it again. Hitler slammed his right fist into the palm of his left hand at the thought. This could be… *a second Dunkirk!*

Ever since the bomb attempt on his life, Hitler had not trusted his aristocratic senior generals of the *Wehrmacht*. Contemptuously, the ex-corporal called them '*die Monokelfritzen*', 'the monocle Fritzes', due to the fact that many of them affected a monocle. Some of the worst, most dastardly conspirators against his life had been apprehended in France, and now he was certainly not going to reveal his plans for dealing with Patton to the surviving '*Monokelfritzen*' in that country. For all he knew, they might even betray his intentions to the enemy.

Instead, he and his staff, under Jodl's supervision, working from large-scale maps of Normandy, planned to concentrate the seven panzer divisions in the area of the French village of Mortain. Once the signal was given, the massed armour, protected by Goering's fighters, would bull their way through the American line, which was held by a single division – the 30th US Infantry – and race for the coastal road.

Although the Commander-in-Chief West, Field Marshal von Kluge, would remain in nominal control of the great surprise attack, the actual execution would be carried out by two SS commanders, Colonel-Generals Dietrich and Hausser. Both of them were hard-bitten frontline soldiers whom Hitler trusted implicitly, and both would command SS formations. The *Wehrmacht* under the *Monokelfritzen* had let him down badly in France. This time it would be his own SS, headed by the *Leibstandarte*, which would give him the victory he needed. *They* wouldn't let him down!

'The plan came to us at the headquarters of the Commander-in-Chief West in the most minute detail,' von Kluge's chief-of-staff recalled after the war. 'It set out the specific divisions that were to be used and how they were to be pulled out of the line as quickly as possible for this purpose. The sector in which the attack was to take place was specifically identified and the very roads and villages through which the assaulting forces were to advance were all included. All the planning had been done in Berlin... and the advice of the generals in France was not asked for – nor was it encouraged.'

Naturally, Field Marshal von Kluge did not like being told what to do in such specific detail. A plan like this, dictated from Hitler's HQ, made him into a mere *Befehlsempfanger* – a recipient of orders. Nor did he like the date that Hitler had set for the great surprise attack, now code-named 'Operation Liege'. In his opinion, it was too late. With Patton's two armoured divisions thrusting into Brittany, followed by five infantry divisions, every hour was vital.

He called Jodl and said: 'We've got to strike at once! The enemy is getting stronger every day. He's already got an entire army through the Avranches gap.'

Jodl's reply showed just how remote the Fuehrer's HQ was from the realities of the front in France. 'Don't worry,' he appeased the Field Marshal, 'don't worry about the Americans who have broken through. The *more* there are through, the *more* will be cut off!'

Von Kluge, an able soldier (behind his back his soldiers called him 'Clever Hans'[4]), had become weak over the years, even spineless. He had been bribed by Hitler with large money gifts and he had been promised a large estate after the successful conclusion of the war. He was afraid, too, of what the Gestapo might do to his family in the Reich, if he were discovered to have been associating with those who had planned to kill the Fuehrer. He dropped his objections and decided to do as he was ordered without any further complaint.

Colonel General Sepp Dietrich was a different proposition. He did not keep 'a leaf on his tongue', as the Germans said. He didn't approve of the plan and he was going to let those fine gentlemen at Hitler's HQ know it, even if it did cost him command of his Fifth Panzer Army. Sepp Dietrich, the illegitimate son of a Bavarian farm servant girl, had known Hitler almost since the start of the 'movement'. After serving in the artillery in World War One as a sergeant, he fought with one of the post-war free corps and did all kinds of odd jobs in the crazy Germany of the twenties until he joined the new SS in 1928 and became Hitler's chauffeur and bodyguard. Five years later, the ex-NCO had been given the task of organising Hitler's own personal household troops, *die Leibstandarte Adolf Hitler.*

Short and burly and personally brave, he was not particularly bright. Field Marshal von Rundstedt thought him 'decent but stupid'. Another SS commander, General Bittrich, explained he had once spent half an hour trying to teach him how to read a map, but in the end he had given up. 'Dietrich just couldn't manage.'

By 1944, Dietrich had a mistress, was drinking too much, and was in above his head commanding a whole army, the Fifth. At the same time, he was not afraid of Hitler, as were most of the *Wehrmacht* commanders, and he still remembered his old loyalty to the *Leibstandarte*, the unit he had founded so long before. '*Meine Junge*' he called its men, though those 'boys' who had once nicknamed him 'Papa' when he commanded the division were all long dead, vanished in the snows of Russia.

Now he was being asked to throw the *Leibstandarte* into another battle, which he thought was hopeless, and he protested violently. He did so 'for over an hour', as he told his interrogators after the war. He protested 'about the impracticability of such an operation. I used every argument in the book. There was not sufficient petrol for such an attack. If three armoured divisions were sent west, it would be impossible to hold Falaise [the key to the defence of the front where the British and Canadians were currently attacking]. It was impossible to concentrate so many tanks without inviting disaster from the air. There wasn't sufficient space to deploy so large an armoured force. The Americans were far too strong in the south, and such an attack was only wedging one's way tighter into a trap rather than safely getting out. To each of my arguments von Kluge had only one reply, "*It is Hitler's order!*"'

Reluctantly, the burly little SS General concluded: 'There was nothing more that could be done. I gave him what he wanted.' Dietrich should have fought harder. Now the stage was set for a tragedy.

In the final years of World War Two, any sharp-eyed visitor to one of the major US headquarters in the European theatre of operations might have spotted them: a truck, a handful of camouflaged tents, perhaps a van bristling with aerials, all tucked away discreetly in an orchard or behind a barn. And strangely enough, the handful of men clustering around the vehicles and tents would not be wearing the round helmets and olive drab of the US Army, but the sky blue of the Royal Air Force. 'What,' the observant visitor might have asked, 'were RAF men

– and mostly of low rank to boot – doing at an American headquarters where bird colonels were a dime a dozen?'

'There was a little truck hidden among the trees,' a US Army Air Corps officer, Lewis Powell, noted in North Africa in 1943, 'with people occasionally going to and fro. I thought it was a Direction-Finding Unit.' That was exactly what grey-haired, reticent spymaster 'C', otherwise Sir Stewart Menzies, head of the SIS, wanted such nosey individuals to believe. It was as good a cover as any.

At the European headquarters of General Bradley, the US forces' overall ground commander in Normandy, the frustrated HQ clerks and typists, unable to make out the identity of these standoffish limeys in their midst who seemed to have access to the Commanding General whenever they damned well liked, christened them 'the secret limeys'.

These secret limeys were, in fact, members of the SLU, or Special Liaison Unit. Their title, for obvious reasons, gave no clue to their real function, which was to be the transmitters between London and the HQ of a secret that warranted a new classification – 'the Ultra Secret'. For these low-ranking RAF men and women bore with them the most important Allied secret of the whole war: one that hundreds of men and women kept for decades after it was all over, until their former chief, Group Captain Freddie Winterbotham, living in that remote Devonshire farmhouse of his, with its leaking roof and dilapidated outhouses, finally revealed it to an astonished world in 1974.

–

Throughout World War Two, Hitler and his security chiefs believed implicitly that they had the most secure enciphering system for radio communications in the whole world. With that typical German stubbornness, they were convinced that no one could break their codes, for they possessed an enciphering machine that was unbreakable.

It consisted of a machine like a bulky typewriter in a varnished wooden case. Its letters were arranged like a typewriter's, but there the similarity ended. The keyboard had no numbers or punctuation marks, and on the deck behind the board the twenty-six letters of the alphabet appeared in three rows in alphabetical order. When the military operator punched a letter on the board, one of the letters on the deck lit up. But it was never the same letter the operator had just punched.

As the keyboard operator punched the letters, an assistant wrote down the letters that appeared on the deck. These seemed to be a random jumble, with no meaning to him. Then he transmitted the string of letters in Morse over the radio. Equipped with the same type of machine, the Enigma, as it was called, at the other end, the recipient typed the jumble on to his own keyboard, whereupon they appeared on the lit deck in the form the original operator had typed them – and made sense.

Naturally, the Germans knew that the radio message in Morse could be intercepted. In theory, it could also be decoded if the interceptor was also equipped with an Enigma. But even then the interceptor would have to know the particular machine setting the German operator had used that day, and there were literally millions of possible settings. Indeed, by 1944, the Germans were changing the settings at least once a day. In short, the German security services believed their code, sent from the Fuehrer's HQ to all major commands using the Enigma, was uncrackable.

But it wasn't!

Ever since the Poles had first stolen one of the German Enigmas back in the mid-thirties, they, then their allies the French, and finally the British, had been working feverishly on a means of outwitting the machine. By early 1940 they had done it. Working from Bletchley Park, a Victorian Gothic mansion in Buckinghamshire, fifty miles northwest of London, British scientists, mostly former Oxbridge dons, had linked together six Enigmas to form a kind of primitive early computer, known as the 'Bombe' or the 'Green Goddess'.

Set at the end of Hut Six, a rusting Nissen hut in the grounds of Bletchley Park, the strange-looking device was used to discover which of a million keys or variations of them were being used by the German operator in any message picked up by radio interception. Once that had been established, the difficult and laborious task of decoding commenced. When this task had been completed, the message was taken to Hut Three, where it was recoded and sent by radio (or even by hand, if it was going to the Prime Minister, who had an avid interest in this Ultra information, as it was code-named) to the major headquarters concerned.

Here the head of the British SLU unit was responsible for passing on the Ultra as quickly as possible to those commanders who had been let into the great secret, and then ensuring that the green 'flimsy', as the top-secret message form was known, was destroyed within twenty-four hours.

Thus it was that, thanks to the 'Bombe' and the efforts of those elderly Oxbridge dons in their tweed jackets and baggy grey flannels, Group Captain Winterbotham could inform General Bradley on 3 August 1944 that a German counter-attack was in the offing. The sharp-eyed ex-pilot, who had worked for the SIS since 1929 and had once engaged in spying inside Nazi Germany himself, was plagued by one problem, however: When would the great 'surprise' attack come?

He knew from the Ultra intercepts coming from Hut Three that a series of angry signals were going back and forth between Field Marshal von Kluge and Hitler about the exact timing of the operation. Winterbotham also knew that von Kluge was having difficulty, just as Dietrich of the SS had predicted, in assembling the armour he needed. Vigorous attacks on the British-Canadian front were pinning down two SS divisions, including the *Leibstandarte*. But as Winterbotham, a tall, lean man, who had met Hitler personally during his spying career in Germany, said later: 'I put my money on Hitler.' He knew whatever difficulties von Kluge made, Hitler would have his way.

As another three days passed and Hitler had still not approved a final date for the great attack, von Kluge started to get cold feet about the whole operation. In Bletchley, the decoders, working all round the clock, followed the von Kluge-Hitler drama conducted over the air waves. Churchill insisted on being kept up to date. He would spread the green flimsies all over the floor of his office and try to work out what Hitler's intentions were. In France, General Bradley, noting the constant build-up of German armour on a front held by a single infantry division, started to worry. Patton, galloping off deep into Brittany, intent on capturing the key Breton ports – some of them two hundred kilometres from his starting point – seemed totally unconcerned about the danger to his flank.

On the fourth, he visited Patton personally and relayed his worries to the flamboyant commander of the Third Army. Patton told him not to worry. Throughout the fifth and sixth of August he kept warning Patton about advancing too deep into Brittany. After all, the whole Third Army could be cut off if anything went wrong and the Germans managed to sever the road link between Normandy and Brittany.

'Ole Blood an' Guts' Patton, all nervousness and hesitation vanished now, pooh-poohed the stolid, ex-infantryman Bradley's warnings. He told his boss: 'I don't think you've anything to worry about, Brad … The Kraut's only bluffing to cover his withdrawal.'

Von Kluge tried one last time. He signalled Hitler: 'Apart from withdrawing the essential defensive armoured divisions from Caen [where the British were exerting very strong pressure on the German front], such an attack, if not immediately successful, would lay open the whole attacking force to be cut off in the west.'

Hitler dismissed the objection. The attack was on. The massed SS armour would attack at dawn on 7 August. Immediately, Churchill was informed. Montgomery too. Eisenhower, the Supreme Allied Commander, warned Bradley to prepare for the shock to come.

Bradley had done the best he could. He had prepared a defence in depth, but naturally he had not been allowed to betray the great secret of Ultra by informing his subordinate commanders what was really coming their way. All he could do was to 'regroup' some of his infantry divisions, telling the divisional commanders that they were being moved to a quieter front to give them a little rest.

Over the last three weeks, seven of his infantry divisions had lost more than 40,000 men in the bloody slogging match through the Norman *bocage* country, where they had been forced to fight for every hedgerow. Accordingly, their commanders were glad of any kind of rest for their men, whatever the front. They didn't ask too many awkward questions. So Bradley, lantern-jawed and bespectacled, looking more like a village schoolteacher than a general, waited tensely for what was soon to come his way.

On the afternoon of 6 August, SS General Hausser – 'the ugliest man in uniform I have ever seen in all my life,' Patton said of him later, after he had been captured by the Third Army – prepared a last message for his young SS fanatics soon to be thrown into battle. Like von Kluge, Hausser, who had lost an eye before Moscow and affected an eye-patch, thought Hitler's counter-attack had come too late. All the same, he knew it was imperative to bolster up the morale of his men, who were being sent to an almost certain death in an operation that he thought had no chance of success.

'On the successful execution of the operation the Fuehrer has ordered,' he told his men in his final order-of-the-day, 'depends the outcome of the war in the West and with it, perhaps, the outcome of the war itself.

'Commanders of all ranks must be absolutely clear as to the enormous significance of this fact. I expect all corps and divisional commanders to ensure that all officers are aware of the unique significance of the whole situation.

'Only one thing counts: unceasing effort and determined will to victory.

'For Fuehrer, folk and fatherland!'

On that same day, fewer than eighty kilometres away from the headquarters where Hausser penned that final message to his troops, Bradley stood facing the commander of his 9th US Tactical Air Corps. He was youthful-looking General 'Pete' Quesada, who affected a battered cap set on the back of his head in the style of his young gung-ho pilots and who was not too keen on shaving every day.

In his hand, Bradley held the latest green flimsy from Bletchley. It gave Bradley the information he had been waiting for eagerly all week: the exact date of the German attack. It was to be at dawn on Monday, 7 August 1944.

Now Bradley was relieved, and it showed in the big grin he gave Quesada as he relayed the news. The Air Corps General, whose planes would soon wreak havoc on the Germans, returned the grin and said simply: '*Brad, we've got 'em…*'

2. 'MARCH OR CROAK'

Punctually, just before midnight on 9 November 1933, Hitler, the new German Chancellor, accompanied by *Reichsfuhrer SS* Himmler, arrived on the scene. Here in Munich, ten years before on this day, Hitler had attempted to seize power and had failed. The result had been a five-year sentence in jail. Now that was long behind him and he was the ruler of the 'New Germany', head of a Reich that he boasted would last one thousand years.

But Hitler knew his New Germany would depend upon the loyalty of his Party soldiers and not those of the regular army. Indeed, Hitler realised his own private army, however small – an army made up of young men dedicated to the National Socialist creed – would have to be prepared to fight – and, if necessary, die – for their Fuehrer. That was why he was here.

Now as he drove slowly across the great square, illuminated by thousands of Party members bearing flaming torches, over the road the chimes of the *Theatinerkirche* rang out the last stroke of midnight. It was the signal.

Gruppenfuhrer Sepp Dietrich marched to the head of the black-clad giants, bodies rigidly to attention, young faces impassive and hollowed out to a death's head in the flickering light of the flares. He snapped to attention and bellowed: 'My Fuehrer, your *Leibstandarte* is present and correct with 835 SS men to take the oath of allegiance.'

Hitler acknowledged with a flip of his right hand and stared momentarily at the men who would become his Praetorian Guard. This night they numbered fewer than the size of a battalion in the regular army. One day, however, they would grow to become a million strong, twenty-nine divisions of them, among their ranks not only Germans, but citizens of every European country, including those of his future enemies, Britons, Americans, Frenchmen, Belgians, Dutchmen. These 835 were the forerunners of the New Order's European Army.

But that would be in the future. Now, accompanied by the Flag of Blood, the one that had been dipped in the blood of the Party's martyrs who had died under the fire of the troops back in 1923, Hitler went down the ranks of his *Leibstandarte* slowly, as each SS man took the oath, fingers resting on the *Blutfahne*.

'We swear to you, Adolf Hitler, loyalty and bravery,' they chanted in their hoarse young voices. 'We promise you and all those whom you place in authority above us obedience to the death…' The words echoed and re-echoed across the square: '*obedience to the death… obedience to the death… death…*' The premier regiment of the Armed SS, one day to be cursed and feared as the 'scourge of Europe', had come into being…

During the years that led up to World War Two, this private army was generally regarded inside and outside the Third Reich as a guards battalion, intended only for ceremonial duties, drilled to the standards of the British Brigade of Guards. Indeed, the black-uniformed men mockingly called themselves 'the asphalt soldiers' because they seemed always to be goose-stepping down the asphalt roads of the German capital.

In fact, the training of the *Leibstandarte* was radically different from that of the regular German army. In its ranks the old military courtesies disappeared. It was no longer '*Herr Hauptmann*', simply *Hauptmann*, and officers were no longer addressed in that curious oblique form that dated back to the eighteenth century, 'Would the *Herr Hauptmann* deign to regard this...?' Officers and men played sports together, and if a corporal was a better foot-baller than the colonel, well, then the corporal became the team captain.

Emphasis was on physical fitness and endurance. Field-craft played a major role. Training was realistic, with live ammunition being used all the time instead of blanks, as was customary in the regular army. Later, when tanks make their appearance, for example, soldiers were given shovels and told to dig themselves in. Then a platoon of tanks was driven over their foxholes. It was just too bad for the recruit who had not dug a deep enough hole.

The man behind their training was General Berger, known behind his back as the 'Duke of Swabia'. He aimed at creating a formation that would not be thrown into battle to be slaughtered as the infantry had been in World War One. His concept of the SS man was adopted from the English military theorist Liddell Hart, the 'hunter-poacher-athlete' type. He would be an indi-vidualist who knew how to look after himself, without orders from a superior, and who would not throw his life away purposelessly.

There was one other aspect of the *Leibstandarte*'s training that differed from that of the German regular army: ideological indoctrination in National Socialism. Much of it was heavy-handed, dull stuff, dreary disserta-tions on racial purity, the evilness of the 'eternal Jew' and the greatness of 'Aryan' blood – all subjects dear to *Reichsfuhrer* Himmler's pedantic schoolmaster's heart. But some of it rubbed off, especially the emphasis on German hardness on oneself – and the enemy. As Himmler expressed it to senior SS officers during the war: 'We must be honourable, decent, loyal and comradely to bearers of our own blood, *but no one else!*' It was a doctrine that one day would make the silver SS runes and death's head badge of the *Leibstandarte* the terror of Europe.

–

The *Leibstandarte* underwent its baptism of fire in regimental strength in Poland in September 1939. The average age of its officers was twenty-five and that of its men nineteen. There, the *Leibstandarte*, fighting under Army command, suffered higher casualties than any other unit in the whole *Wehrmacht*. Later, when one of its officers boasted of these casualties to an Army General, the latter snapped, 'I'm an officer, *not a butcher!*'

But Sepp Dietrich had no reasons to be worried about his losses. His regiment had taken all their objectives, despite its casualties, and young men all over Germany were fighting for the honour of belonging to the *Leibstandarte*. As one of them, future German TV personality and current head of the new West German Republican Party, Franz Schoenhuber, recorded recently: 'I couldn't believe it. They wanted me, the elite of the elite.'[5] The wearing of the *Leibstandarte SS Adolf Hitler* armband was the visible proof that one belonged to the guards, had become a Praetorian. These men believed in the creed of the '*garde napolienne*': 'The guard dies, but it never surrenders.'

By May 1940, the *Leibstandarte* was up to full strength again and had been re-equipped as a motorised regiment. In that month, these SS athletes, not one of them under five foot ten, surged through Holland, Belgium and France, impelled by a kind of blind fury, which made them arrogantly disdainful of losses as long as they took their objectives. That month, not only did a member of the *Leibstandarte* win the first Iron Cross of the campaign, but another succeeded in shooting General Student, the German airborne commander, two hours *after* the cease-fire had been sounded in captured Rotterdam.

But then Sepp Dietrich's *Leibstandarte* had never shown much respect for the *Wehrmacht* and the Army commander under whom the regiment had fought up to now. During the pursuit of the British Expeditionary Force towards Dunkirk, for instance, Dietrich was ordered to make an assault crossing of the As Canal. Once he had broken the resistance there, he was then to capture the town of Watten. But, at the very last moment, the assault was called off by the army to which the regiment belonged. Dietrich simply ignored the order. A handsome young company commander, Jochen Peiper, who one day would become the most famous – and infamous – member of the *Leibstandarte*, was detailed to assault the canal. He did so and won the Iron Cross for his bravery that day. In due course, totally against orders, Watten was taken, too.

Some time afterwards, however, while driving for the next French town, Wormhoudt, success eluded the *Leibstandarte*. Suddenly, that spirit of arrogant confidence with which the regiment had fought the campaign up to now vanished. It was replaced by one of savage ruthlessness. As always, Dietrich was at the front of the advance. He was driving in his Mercedes, together with his adjutant, Max Wuensche, when the car was struck by a British anti-tank shell. The driver slumped dead over the wheel in the same instant that the car's shattered engine went up in flames.

Hurriedly, the two officers baled out. They flung themselves into a nearby ditch, smearing themselves with wet mud as the flames seared the length of the ditch. Time and time again, Dietrich's men tried to rescue their commander, whose forty-eighth birthday this day was. But always they were driven back by British machine-gun fire.

Now the mood of the *Leibstandarte*'s rank-and-file turned ugly as the rumour swept the regiment that 'Papa' Dietrich had been treacherously killed by the 'Tommies'. On that 28 May, the *Leibstandarte* started to shoot their prisoners, the odds-and-sods of the Royal Warwickshire Regiment, the Cheshire Regiment and the Royal Artillery who had fought them to a standstill all that hot day.

Four years before, Sir Stafford Cripps, a prominent figure in the Labour Party, had told a working-class audience in Stockport that he disagreed with the party's decision to rearm. It wouldn't be a bad thing, he told his listeners, if Germany defeated Britain in any future war, for it 'would be a disaster to profit makers'. He meant the capitalist Tories. Now these unfortunate representatives of the working class in uniform were going to see the true face of National Socialist Germany.

As the prisoners, many of them wounded, were herded into a barn, Captain Lynn-Allen protested to one of the SS men. He said, 'I wish to complain that there are wounded men inside and there is not room enough for them to lie down.'

The SS men snorted. 'Yellow Englishmen, there will be plenty of room where you are going.'

Stubbornly the Captain said: 'I am not satisfied.'

The SS men flushed with anger. He reached for the stick grenade stuck down the side of his boot. Ripping out the pin, he lobbed it into the barn.

Men went down everywhere. As Captain Lynn-Allen shouted to the soldier next to him, Private Evans, who had just been wounded, to 'run for it, *quick*!' the Germans opened fire.

The two of them dodged the bullets and dropped into a pond some two hundred metres away. 'Get down,' the officer hissed, 'and keep your arm out of the water!'

It was no use. The men of the *Leibstandarte* had spotted them. One opened fire. A terrified Evans twice heard the ghastly *thwack* as slugs struck the officer in the head. He groaned, 'Oh, my God!' and disappeared beneath the green scummy surface of the pond.

Now the sobbing, wounded nineteen-year-old private listened to the rattle of gunfire and the screams of his comrades as they were slaughtered in cold blood. But he was not the only one to survive the massacre. Private John Lavelle, who had been wounded in the foot, was outside the barn peering through a crack in the woodwork as the SS began tossing in grenades. He saw Company Sergeant Major Jennings and Sergeant Moore throw themselves on to the first of the deadly devices to protect their comrades. To no avail. Men went down everywhere.

Suddenly the slaughter ceased – for a while. In the loud echoing silence, Lavalle heard a harsh voice command, '*Raus!*' and then in English, 'Five men outside!'

Inside the barn, someone said: 'Come on, if we've got to go, we've got to go.'

Tamely, like sheep being led to the slaughter, the first five prisoners ventured outside to face a rough-and-ready firing squad. One of them asked for a last cigarette. The request was refused. The next moment the five were mown down.

Now the SS demanded another five. Pandemonium broke out inside the barn. The SS didn't hesitate. They poked machine pistols through the door and began firing. Men went down on all sides. Someone screamed in agony: '*Shoot me… shoot me!*' Another cried: 'What a bloody way to die!' A third stammered the Lord's Prayer until he was hit.

In the end, five men survived, with more than ninety being slaughtered in cold blood. Eight months before they had marched to France so light-heartedly, boasting about the washing they were going to hang on the Siegfried Line – 'if the Siegfried Line's still there, mother dear'. Now they had been confronted with the harsh, brutal realities of total war, and *die Leibstandarte SS Adolf Hitler* had committed its first recorded atrocity…

On 22 June 1941, the *Leibstandarte*, now in divisional strength, first marched into Soviet Russia. In all the *Leibstandarte* would be sent to Russia four times, and four times it would return exhausted, decimated, brutalised, the survivors virtually walking skeletons. That first time the premier division of the SS penetrated an amazing thousand kilometres by November 1941. Finally, the 'Ivans', as they called the Russians, stopped them on the River Don. The headlong dash across the winter steppe against the demoralised Red Army had come to an end.

Now came a bitter slogging match, not only against the Ivans, but against those two Russian Generals who had beaten the great Napoleon – General Winter and General Frost. Food was in short supply. For weeks on end, the men saw no bread and precious little meat. The weekly ration of sausage was down to 150 grams. With none of the special winter clothing needed for this kind of killing climate, the *Leibstandarte* fought in temperatures of twenty below zero in their summer uniforms. Engines wouldn't start if they were not primed at ten-minute intervals all night. Sights in cannon and rifles clouded over because the SS did not have the special Arctic greases to keep them clear. Men's ears and noses froze, went purple and came off in their hands. The soldiers went down like flies with trench-foot, exposure, lung complaints and scurvy, a disease unknown in Germany since the Middle Ages.

Even the volunteers of the *Leibstandarte* couldn't stand those terrible conditions. They started inflicting wounds upon themselves – a rifle bullet fired through a sandbag at a toe, the sandbag preventing the tell-tale blackened skin of a self-inflicted wound; diesel oil rubbed into the chest to cause an incurable form of skin disease; toes soaked in water and bared to the frost at night to sham frostbite. There were even cases of men actually deserting to the Ivans. Now the young soldiers lived in a kind of limbo; the front had its own morals, its own jargon, its own verities. Here their world was divided into that of the 'front swine' (themselves), the ones at the sharp end, and the safe comfortable world of the 'rear echelon stallions', with their 'grey mice' (female auxiliaries) who more often than not acted as 'field mattresses' (mistresses) for the high-ranking quartermasters and staff officers, who would surely die of old age in bed.

Here at the front, they thought they had been forgotten by the homeland, as one of the 'old hares' (veterans), Captain Gert Bremer, all of twenty-three years of age, would maintain to his comrades during those long sub-zero nights while they waited for the Ivans to attack yet once again. 'We've been out here so long that they won't let us back into the Reich without a course in reeducation. We're wild men, not safe to be let loose on those unsuspecting civilians back there.' And he would add in Russian, for they all sprinkled their conversation liberally with Russian words by now, '*Ponemyu!*' (understood). And they would grin wryly, although they had heard Bremer's story often enough in the past. For it was true. They *had* been in Russia so long that they believed they had been forgotten by the homeland…

-

At 1500 hours on 4 July 1943, the 167th anniversary of American Independence Day, Hitler launched the Battle of Kursk in southern Russia. It would become the greatest tank battle in history and it was Hitler's last attempt in Russia to break the deadlock before the Western Allies landed in Europe and he would be faced with a two-front war.

Hitler's aim was to eradicate the Kursk salient. Named after the principal town of the area, the salient stuck out like a clenched fist into the German front. Its length was 400 kilometres, but at its base it was only 110 kilometres across – an ideal distance for one of those celebrated German armoured pincer movements. Cut off the salient, Hitler reasoned, and the Russians would lose hundreds of thousands of men and much equipment. This might convince the Red Army to postpone its own summer offensive for months to come, and by then Germany would be strong again and able to deal with any Western Allied landing.

As Hitler himself explained in his order to the assault force, made up of 900,000 soldiers, armed with 10,000 cannon and 2,700 tanks, supported by 2,650 planes: 'This offensive is of decisive importance. It must be carried out quickly and shatteringly. It must give us the initiative for the spring and summer of this year.'

As always, the *Leibstandarte*, which had lost forty-four per cent of its strength in its recent attempt to retain the city of Kharkov against everything the Red Army could throw at it, was in the forefront of the great attack. Under its new commander, SS General Wisch, nick-named 'Teddy', it was to break through the Russian front in the south and then drive north hell-for-leather to link up with the other arm of the German pincer, which was reaching south. But the opposition was going to be formidable. To stop the expected assault, the Red Army had massed 1,337,000 soldiers, equipped with 20,000 cannon and 3,306 tanks, supported by 2,500 planes. The Battle of Kursk would be a clash of Titans...

At three o'clock in the afternoon of that fateful 4 July, the tank commanders of the massed panzers waved their signal disks. Tank engines burst into noisy life. The air of the steppe was suddenly flooded with petrol fumes. '*Panzer – marsch!*' the red-faced, sweating tank commanders yelled above the racket, and as the gull-winged Stuka dive-bombers came roaring over the front to deal with the opposition, the hundreds of metal monsters started to waddle forward into the battle.

Like a solid steel battering ram, the tanks of the *Leib-standarte* smashed into the positions of the Russian 52nd

Guards Rifle Division and shattered them. With the words of Hitler's order ringing in their ears, '*the victory at Kursk must be a signal to the world*', the young SS men advanced with their old arrogant elan. By early evening the *Leibstandarte* had captured all their initial objectives and the Russians were running.

Frightened into action by the thought of impending disaster, Nikita Khrushchev, the roly-poly future head of the Soviet state and currently chief political commissar in the area, hurried to the Soviet guards' HQ. to lay down the law. 'The next two or three days will be terrible,' he declared. 'Either we hold, or the Fritzes will take Kursk. They are putting everything on one card. It's a matter of life or death for them. We must take care to see that they break their necks.' The dejected guards commanders knew what that meant. If they didn't stop the Germans, it would be the Gulag for them or – even worse – a NKVD bullet at the base of the skull!

On and on the Tigers of the *Leibstandarte*, massive 57-tonne monsters, rumbled at a steady ten miles an hour. On the burning horizon fiery red and green flares, summoning help, descended like fallen angels. Apart from the rumble of the massed tracks over the steppe, the firing had virtually ceased. Perhaps the Ivans were withdrawing yet again? Now the Tigers advanced in ominous silence.

Watching them, one Russian observer noted: 'The battlefield seemed too small for the hundreds of armoured machines. Groups of tanks moved over the steppe everywhere, taking cover behind isolated groves and in orchards, but coming forward all the time.'

Suddenly, one solitary multi-coloured flare hissed into the leaden dawn sky to the front. It was the Russian signal. Bursting out of their cover, hundreds of squat T-34 tanks hurried forward to take up the gauntlet of steel. From their hidden, well-camouflaged positions, fire spat from the muzzles of a thousand Russian antitank guns. A myriad white blobs hurtled towards the Tigers – armour-piercing solid shot.

At top speed, the much faster, but much lighter Soviet T-34s crashed into the German monsters. In an instant, a furious melee commenced. Within minutes, both sides started to suffer heavy losses: tanks shuddering to a sudden stop, burning furiously, their crews writhing in blue petrol flames in the charred grass as the cruel, merciless fire rose higher and higher; tanks with their shattered tracks strung out behind them like severed limbs, at the mercy of the Russian infantry; tanks backing out of the battle, shooting blinding white smoke to cover their retreat.

As the Soviet *Official History* describes the scene: 'The Tigers, deprived in close combat of the advantage of their powerful guns and thick armour, were successfully shot up by the T-34s at close range. The immense number of tanks was mixed up all over the battlefield and there was neither time nor space to disengage and reform the ranks. Shells fired at close range penetrated both the front and side armour of the tanks... There were frequent explosions as ammunition blew up while tank turrets blown off by the explosions were thrown dozens of metres away from the twisted machines...'

Above the embattled *Leibstandarte, Luftwaffe* Colonel Rudel's Stukas fell out of the sky like hungry black metal hawks. The mobile Soviet flak took up the challenge. The sky was peppered grey-brown with exploding shells. The Stukas hurled through the network of smoke, their pilots seeming to bear a charmed life. Sirens howling, their faces pressed flat by the G Force, they hurtled through the barrage. At the very last moment the pilots jerked back their sticks, most of them blacking out momentarily as they did so, as a myriad deadly black eggs fell from their blue-painted bellies.

But even with the aid of Rudel's tank busters, the *Leibstandarte* could only advance by the metre now, as Russian resistance thickened hourly. Now, with the Russian commanders desperate and knowing that their own heads were at stake if they failed, no quarter was given or expected. A battery of the *Leibstandarte*'s flak regiment was caught in an ambush and overrun before they had a chance. By now the blond giants knew what to expect if taken prisoner. At Charkov, the green-capped MKVD troops had slaughtered all their *Leibstandarte* prisoners and thrown them down a well before fleeing the city. Seriously wounded men of the *Leibstandarte* preferred to shoot themselves rather than fall into Russian hands.

This time it was no different. The captured members of the overrun battery were paraded before their captors and each one was asked his age. Thereupon every SS prisoner over the age of eighteen was shot in cold blood. One aged seventeen survived to tell his tale after he was released from the Gulag in 1949.

Young Major Jochen Peiper, the rising star of the *Leibstandarte*, was ordered forward to help break the impasse. But this time that bold young tank commander was out of luck. The Russians broke through to his rear. Peiper reacted immediately. He broke off his attack and successfully achieved that most difficult military tactic, turning his command around to face an attack from the rear. But now the Russians attacked from both flanks as well. Peiper, as daring and fanatical as he was, knew he was beaten. He ordered what was left of his command to withdraw.

Peiper's situation was similar to the one facing General Hausser, commander of the corps to which the *Leibstandarte* belonged. By now he had lost more than three hundred tanks. Everywhere his tank recovery crews were frantically patching up battered tanks on the battlefield or dragging them back to the workshops, where the bloody remains of the dead would be hosed out with water jets before the repair job could commence. His losses in men, too, were high. Already the *Leibstandarte* alone had had 474 soldiers killed and three times that number wounded. Hausser knew he couldn't continue much longer at this rate; the butcher's bill was simply too high.

But as Hausser fell into a troubled sleep that July night, worried by the thought of how many 'runners' he might have for the next day's battle, the Battle for the Kursk Salient was already being called off. Three days before, just as Hitler had anticipated, the Western Allies had returned to Europe. They had landed on the island of Sicily at the toe of Italy and, as a gloomy Hitler explained to his staff, 'Thanks to the miserable leadership of the Italians, it is as good as certain that Sicily will be lost. Maybe Eisenhower will land tomorrow on the Italian mainland or in the Balkans. When that happens, our entire European south flank will be directly threatened.' Hitler's last great counter-attack in Russia was over…

–

By the spring of 1944 when the premier SS division returned to the West to await the Allied invasion of France, it was no longer the *Leibstandarte* that had helped to achieve the great victory of 1940 over the French. Russia had seen to that.

Those fanatical blond giants, devoted to their Fuehrer and the National Socialist cause, had long perished in the snows of Russia. Now the *Leibstandarte*'s men were no longer all eager volunteers. Its ranks now included culls from other arms of the service, unwilling 'selectees' from the *Luftwaffe* and the German Navy. There were conscripts, too, and often unwilling conscripts at that.

By early 1944, the *Leibstandarte* was accepting entries into its hallowed ranks from a dozen different European countries, including even that 'decadent' enemy of four years before, France. From all over Europe they came, believing the lies of the recruiting posters pasted up in their boring provincial towns. For them the SS runes and the silver death's head badge meant glory and high adventure, fighting for a 'united Europe' against the 'sub-human Jewish Bolshevik hordes'.

In their training schools now, the concept of a 'Greater Germany' was played down. Instead, the concept of a 'Europe united against Communism' was the order of the day. Thus even nationals of those countries at war with Germany – Belgium, Holland, Norway, Denmark, etc. – could join without feeling they were traitors to their native land. For they were fighting not to defend Germany, but to preserve European freedom and independence from the clutches of the rapacious Russians.

Dutch officers now taught German cadets. An American SS officer attempted to recruit British POWs from their camps – and succeeded. Officers and NCOs of the *Leibstandarte* trained men of the SS Division *Charlemagne*, made up of French volunteers, many of whom had fought against the *Leibstandarte* back in 1940. Now everything was

'European', a forerunner of what was to come a decade later.

But if the *Leibstandarte* was no longer what it had been in that year of great victories when it first fought in France, it was still officered by the veterans. For like all old sweats, these 'old hares' had learned to survive. That summer, Dietrich, the *Leibstandarte*'s founder and first commander, maintained that only thirty men of the 30,000 who had once served under him were still alive after four years of total war. But among those thirty (if Dietrich's figure was correct – and by now he was drinking nearly a bottle of cognac a day) there were those officers who would set their indelible stamp of the re-formed division.

The ranks of the division might well be filled with reluctant ex-sailors and airmen, conscripts from the Reich's Hitler Youth, and young adventurers from all over Europe, some of whom could not really compre-hend in full the orders given to them in German ('Booty Germans', the others called them cynically behind their backs); but their senior commanders still retained that old SS arrogance and bold drive.

There was 'Teddy' Wisch, their divisional commander, who had been one of the original founding members of the division, one of the first 117 SS volunteers back in March 1933. He had worked his way through every rank in the division to become its commanding general. There was A. Frey, a giant of a man, face scarred with the terrible wound he had received in Russia, now a regimental commander. Another old hare. There were Diefenthal, Knittel, Sandig, all old hares; and, of course, there was Peiper, soon to be the youngest regimental commander in the whole of the million-strong SS, his skinny young chest heavy with 'tin' (their expression for awards and medals).

Russia had left its mark on these old hares, however. Naturally, they were immensely skilled in combat. They had been in battle for five years now and there was hardly an Allied commander who could match them in that kind of experience. They knew all the tricks of their deadly trade. But Russia had taught them more than just how to survive in combat. It had tempered and hardened them, even brutalised them. Now they could steel their hearts to the suffering, misery, death all around them. The objective *had* to be taken, regardless of the cost in human life.

Perhaps by now, whenever they thought about it, this elite of the elite no longer believed in total victory. Their enemies were too numerous – it seemed as if the whole world was now fighting against Germany. When they returned home on leave, they found their cities were in ruins. By night the RAF battered them and, by day, the 'Ami terror-fliers' did the same. That Reich which Hitler has boasted would last a thousand years was breaking up visibly. There was no denying that. War weariness was present everywhere – and the Generals were already plotting to assassinate the Fuehrer. Even Dietrich, it was rumoured, was party to the conspiracy.

But these old hares had once sworn a personal oath of loyalty to Hitler – '*We swear to you, Adolf Hitler, loyalty and bravery... obedience to the death...*' – all those years before. They could not abandon him, now that his world was falling apart: that great idealistic concept that had once inspired all those thousands of young men they left behind in unmarked graves on the rolling, limitless Russian steppe.

There was another consideration, apart from loyalty, too. Most of them knew no other world than that of the *Leibstandarte*. Officers such as Diefenthal, Knittel, Sandig, Peiper had been mere boys of eighteen and nineteen when they had joined the regiment back in the mid-thirties. The *Leibstandarte* was their mother and father, their home, their family. What could they do with their lives if Germany were defeated and the division broken up?

Besides, there was always the threat of being handed over to the Russians if they were captured. How long would they, officers of Hitler's own Praetorian Guard, survive in the hands of the Ivans? Five minutes was the guess of most of them when they discussed the matter. Time and the facts were against them. In essence, these old hares of the *Leibstandarte*'s last year of existence had no other alternative but to fight to the bitter end.

Back home, the war-weary civilian cynics were already whispering the saying of that year, '*Lieber ein Ende mit Schrecken als ein Schrecken ohne Ende*' ('Rather an end with horror, than a horror without ending'). That wasn't for them. There could be only one motto, a kind of fatalistic rallying cry, for these old hares when the order came for the *Leibstandarte* to join the great counter-offensive planned to push the Americans back into the sea – '*Marschieren oder krepieren!*' 'March or croak!'

3. 'BUY COMBS, LADS, THERE ARE LOUSY TIMES AHEAD'

On that hot dry night of 6–7 August 1944, one could almost hear the heavy breathing of history. At dawn, the great counter-attack would commence and all of them, from SS Brigadefuhrer Wisch, the divisional commander, right down to the teenage Sturmmann, recently recruited from the embattled Reich, knew the coming battle would decide the fate of the German army in France.

Waiting tensely in the sunken lanes and roads leading to the front, which were packed with vehicles and assault infantry, fiddling with their weapons, smoking one cigarette after another, urinating constantly in the ditches, a sure sign of nerves, these young men of Adolf Hitler's own bodyguard knew that if they failed now, France would be lost. And if France went, it would not be long before the Allies would be beating on the door of the Reich itself. They *must* not; they could *not* fail! They *had* to win!

Thirty kilometres from where they waited for the order to march, Bradley was also awake, tense and nervous, wondering if he had got all his plans right. By now he had alerted four infantry and two armoured divisions to a coming attack, but in order not to compromise Ultra he had not yet told them the source of his information. Patton, however, still did not totally believe the seriousness of the attack. Bradley knew he had failed to convince him that this was an all-out German effort. Indeed, unknown to Bradley, Patton was noting in his diary that night: 'We got a rumor last night from a secret source that several panzer divisions will attack ... Mortain ... or Avranches. Personally I think it is a German bluff to cover a withdrawal, but I stopped the 80th, French 2nd Armored and 35th in the vicinity of St Hilaire, just in case something might happen.'

If Patton was not convinced, Winston Churchill was – *totally*. Bradley already knew he was flying over in the morning. Apparently, the reason for his visit to Bradley's HQ in that remote orchard was to enlist his help in stopping the Allied invasion of southern France as an irrelevancy, but Bradley suspected that the real reason was to view the total defeat of the German attack. Not that it was going to be easy.

The day before, Eisenhower had limped into his HQ – he had injured his 'football knee' yet again – and assured his subordinate that the US Air Transport Command could deliver 2,000 tonnes of supplies a day, if the Germans achieved 'a temporary success' on his front. Eisenhower, who was now chain-smoking sixty cigarettes a day and was obviously living off his nerves, had scowled. Bradley wondered whether Eisenhower was not as confident as he made out. Montgomery had not been too pleased either. Eisenhower would note later: 'I was in his [Bradley's] Headquarters when he called Montgomery on the telephone to explain his plan and although the latter expressed a degree of concern about the Mortain position, he agreed that the prospective prize was great and left the entire responsibility for the matter in Bradley's hands.'

A nervous Bradley wondered if he were not over-reaching himself. Until now he had always faced up to inferior German forces on the defensive. Here, for the first time he was going to tackle a full-scale armoured German attack. *Could he cope…?*

Now it was nearly dawn on this fateful Monday. To the front of Mortain, a low mist started to creep across the fields like a silent grey cat. The mist, cold and damp, muted the rumble of the guns to the north of the Germans, where the 'Tommies' were attacking yet again, as they had been doing stubbornly for these past two terrible months. Somewhere, a machine gun chattered aimlessly like an irate woodpecker. Over Mortain, flares exploded in the sky, trying to penetrate the mist, as if the *Amis* knew they were there, planning to attack.

Suddenly, there was the soft muted drone of an aeroplane engine. Angrily, NCOs ordered the men to douse their cigarettes. On the flak trucks, the gunners spun round their quadruple 20 mm cannon effortlessly. In the cupolas of their tanks, the young men in their black uniforms with the silver runes of the SS on their collars tensed. But the plane droned on. Finally, the sound of its motors disappeared into the distance. The mist had protected them. The *Amis* had not spotted them. They relaxed. Again they lit up while others went to urinate in the ditches, the liquid gushing out, hot, yellow and steaming. The minutes passed in leaden inexorability. A soft hush. A plop. The first green signal flare hissed up to the top of the mist. For a moment it hung there spluttering, bathing their upturned young faces in its eerie, unnatural light.

Abruptly, their inertia vanished. It was the signal! Everywhere along the whole length of the German front similar flares shot into the dawn sky. Hoarse cries cut the still air. Officers barked orders. NCOs ran heavily down the column in their clumsy boots – 'dice-beakers', they called them. Tank engines burst into noisy life. Blue smoke spurted from exhausts. There was the rusty squeak of tracks. The sweating drivers, entombed in their steel boxes, slammed through half a dozen gears. The huge Tigers and Panthers, which could outfight and outgun any other tank in the world, lurched forward. '*Panzer – marsch!*' the tank commanders cried feverishly. The great attack had commenced...

At his HQ, Bradley received his first visitor of that long fateful day. He was Henry Morgenthau, who would soon propose to President Roosevelt that Germany should be transformed into an agricultural country, as it had been in the eighteenth century. Then it would never again present a danger to the world. Now Bradley told Morgenthau: 'This is an opportunity that comes to a commander not more than once in a century, Mr Secretary.'

Outside, the telephones jingled urgently and messengers doubled back and forth bearing the messages of alarm, which were now beginning to flood into the headquarters.

Henry Morgenthau nodded his head and waited.

Bradley took off his steel-rimmed GI glasses and rubbed his eyes wearily for a moment before replacing them. Then he said: 'Mr Secretary, today we are about to destroy an entire German army...'

–

Surprisingly enough, although Bradley had known of the coming offensive for four whole days now, at first things began to go drastically wrong for the American defenders. Right from the outset, even before the Germans struck, Bradley had relied upon 'Pete' Quesada's ability to deliver a massive air strike, once the Germans attacked. Now at his 9th TAF HQ, Quesada fumed impotently. The ground mist did not prevent the Krauts attacking, but it *was* stopping his fighter-bombers and ground-attack aircraft from taking off.

Things were not much better for the two US corps artillery groups, which Bradley had intended should support the defenders. They could hear the four hundred-odd German tanks bearing down upon them well enough, but they couldn't locate them in the milky-white mist. Their forward observers were powerless to bring down defensive fire until the very last moment and then the FO men ran the risk of being ground to pulp under the broad, frightening tracks of the advancing Tigers.

Luck that Monday seemed to be on the German side. The lead panzers penetrated the link between the two US army corps defending the Mortain sector. A link line this was always a difficult place to defend at the best of times because, although the infantrymen at the link might only be a foxhole's distance away from each other, the headquarters of their respective corps could be miles apart. The rumbling Tigers and the much faster Panthers swept through, while the slow-moving corps headquarters failed to react. By six that morning, the leading tanks had covered four of the twelve miles that separated them from that vital coast road upon which Patton depended for his supplies.

The first major objective, Mortain, was taken. The US 30th Division, which later gave itself the nickname 'Roosevelt's Butchers', was badly hit. General Hobbs, its commander, ordered the division to withdraw slightly. A whole battalion was surrounded. But instead of surrendering, the survivors dug themselves in on the most prominent feature of the area – Hill 317. Here the seven hundred-odd GIs who had survived the SS's first frenzied assault would now slug it out with the enemy for four long days…

Bradley, knowing he couldn't do much at the front itself, drove off to Patton's HQ in Brittany and briefed him on the 'Mortain counter-attack', as it was now being called. He told Patton, who was as impatient as ever, that he should keep a corps in reserve 'just in case'. When Bradley returned to his own headquarters, Churchill, looking like a pink fat Buddha and puffing at a large cigar, was already there. The Prime Minister said: 'General Bradley, I came to tell you how magnificently we believe you are doing.' Bradley blushed.

If General Bradley had known what was happening at the front, he would not have been so sanguine. By three o'clock that same afternoon, the seven hundred men of the 'lost battalion' trapped on Hill 317 were in acute danger. Their CO reported that the Germans were within two hundred kilometres of the regimental command post. Rations had already started to give out, and to the rear US artillery began firing shells containing supplies into the American-held perimeter, while GIs dug up the village gardens for potatoes and radishes overlooked by the thrifty Norman peasants who had now fled or taken refuge in their cellars. At Abbaye Blanche, another 150 men of the 30th Division held a vital crossroads, supported by a tiny, cross-eyed dog named Mobile Reserve. Indeed, the little dog was the only reserve the men had, for they, too, were cut off to the rear and no supplies were coming up to them. As one GI quipped: 'Well, if the ammo runs out, we'll stick ole Mobile Reserve on the Krauts!'

In fact, something *did* come up the road eventually in the shape of a very drunken GI. (How he managed to get so drunk in the middle of a battle, no one ever found out.) The looted Calvados had filled the drunk with plenty of Dutch courage. When another GI declined to take over a very exposed position, with the rusty rattle of tank tracks indicating that the German panzers were about to attack, the drunk volunteered to take over. 'Sure I'll go,' he said, and staggered forward. But when he attempted to fire both a machine gun and a bazooka missile launcher at the same time, the drunk was speedily withdrawn...

That Monday, another far more prominent American decided he'd better withdraw, too, before it was too late. Ernest Hemingway had driven up to the headquarters of the 22nd Infantry Regiment, belonging to the 4th Division. It was located in a handsome Norman castle, Chateau Lingeard, between Mortain and Juvigny. So far, the Fourth had not been involved in the new fighting and the headquarters were planning a party on the morrow to celebrate the twenty-fifth wedding anniversary of the CO, Colonel Lanham. There was going to be a cake and a roast goose, recently 'liberated' somewhere or other. Hemingway was invited to attend.

The thickset novelist, voted that August 'America's favourite writer', was never one to turn down an invitation to eat and drink. Now, strangely enough, he did. He said he'd have to return immediately to his base at Mont St Michel. At the time he gave no reason for his sudden decision, but later he told Colonel Lanham the reason he had done so was that 'the whole place stank of death'.

He was right too. Soon shells would be falling directly on the chateau, killing several staff officers and wounding Lanham himself. There would be no cake and roast goose with all the trimmings on the morrow, for the 4th Infantry Division stood directly in the path of advance of *SS Brigadegeneral* Wisch's *Leibstandarte*.

–

The *Leibstandarte* got off to a bad start. Making their way down a typical sunken lane of the area, still covered by the low-lying dawn mist, Peiper's column was alarmed by the sound of a fighter-bomber somewhere overhead. Without orders, the gunners manning a mobile flak wagon opened up – and struck lucky, despite the poor visibility. The American fighter-bomber staggered as if it had just run into an invisible wall. Bits of gleaming metal started to shred themselves from its fuselage. It began to screech down in its dive of death. With a great hollow boom of metal striking metal, it crashed directly into the lead tank. The drive forward was effectively stopped!

As vehicle after vehicle commenced piling up in the blocked lane, *Obersturmbannfuhrer* Peiper fumed. Why had he not had the foresight to put his combat engineers, equipped with wrecking equipment, at the front of the column for an eventuality such as this? But he hadn't, and in the future he would fail to do so once more – an oversight that would cost him dearly.

Cursing eloquently, Peiper ordered the whole column to begin reversing down the tight lane – it was too narrow for the big mental monsters to turn safely without getting stuck. 'Heaven, arse and cloudburst,' he swore, it was going to take hours. It did.

While the leading column of the *Leibstandarte* remained stalled, its running mate of the *Wehrmacht*, General von Luettwitz's 2nd Panzer Division, was making good progress. It had penetrated deep into the new corridor leading to the coast, and von Luettwitz, a gross man who was one of those '*Monokelfritzen*' whom Hitler so detested, told himself that soon he would be through to the coast. Then Patton would be cut off with his whole army. Everything, however, depended upon the weather.

'Bad weather is what we need, *Herr General*,' his chief-of-operations had told him that dawn, 'then everything will work out all right.' Now, as his panzers rumbled forward, von Luettwitz kept glancing at the mist lying over the battlefield. Was it possible? *Was the damned mist really beginning to clear?*

But, for the moment, the weather still favoured the attackers. Above, scores of Allied planes droned back and forth, trying to spot them. But the clear white soup continued to protect the Germans, and the angry, frustrated airmen were forced to return to their bases with no kills to report.

With Peiper stalled, *Brigadefuhrer* Wisch threw in the tough young assault infantry of his *panzergrenadier* regiment. They attacked and captured the little township of Saint Barthelemy. Hurriedly, the triumphant SS grenadiers looted the American positions and pushed on in their half-tracks and personnel carriers, gobbling down Hershey bars and puffing at Lucky Strike cigarettes, which, unlike their own weak, wartime smokes, made them feel dizzy. Now here and there on the heights where the mist was already beginning to disperse quickly, they could see that key road and, beyond, the sea shimmering in the first rays of the August sun.

Down on the low ground, with the mist still covering him, Peiper, with a handful of the tanks that had reversed down the lane, was pushing on. The rest of his command would follow in due course. It was an action typical of Peiper and the old hares of the *Leibstandarte*. They were renowned for their arrogance, boldness and disregard of conventional military tactics. Any other commander would have waited for the whole of his force to assemble before making a major thrust.

Besides, Peiper relied on the psychological impact of his Tigers on the *Amis*. He knew of the unreasoning 'Tiger phobia', which had swept through the Allied forces in Normandy after just three Tigers, under the command of Captain Michel Wittmann, a former officer of the *Leibstandarte*, had destroyed virtually a whole British brigade outside Caen. Wherever a Tiger appeared, the Allies usually threw away their weapons and ran. But not this day.

Some two hours after Peiper had set off again, driving hell-for-leather for the coast, a dark metallic shape loomed up on the road to the column's front. There was no mistaking the outline. It was an *Ami* Sherman tank! The Sherman weighed half that of the Tiger and it was outgunned and under-armoured, but it took up the challenge all the same.

The Sherman's gunner fired. The white blob of an armour-piercing shell hissed flatly down the road at the lead German tank. At that range the US gunner couldn't miss. The Tiger reeled as it was struck. The solid-shot shell gouged a gleaming silver scar on the Tiger's turret. The next moment it was howling off as harmlessly as a golf ball. Then the Tiger's great 88 mm cannon belched fire. The Sherman staggered as if struck by a great invisible fist. A moment later its vulnerable petrol engine exploded in flame and an intense, all-consuming blowtorch of angry fire seared its deck, instantly melting its paint so that it bubbled and crackled like the symptoms of some loathsome skin disease. No one got out.

But now more and more Shermans were rumbling up to face the Germans, hurriedly moving into the hull-down position so that only their turrets were visible to the attackers. Peiper cursed. These *Amis* weren't going to run away.

Peiper had blundered head-on into the 3rd US Armored Division. It was commanded by a martinet who had once served under Patton himself and who tolerated no weakness in himself or his subordinates. General Maurice Rose, commander of the 3rd Armored, was a veteran who, despite being the son of an East European rabbi, had risen from private to general in a prejudiced pre-war US Army. Now, if Maurice Rose (who would be killed in battle eight months later deep in the heart of Germany) had his way, Hitler's precious *Leibstandarte*, the symbol of everything he hated, would never reach the coast...

–

By mid-morning, the mist had cleared away everywhere in that part of France and the sun shone brightly from a perfect blue sky. Pete Quesada was jubilant and Bradley could heave a sigh of relief. Everything would be all right now. The dive-bombers, already airborne, did not wait for the order to attack. Below them were fat tempting targets everywhere, and not a Kraut fighter in sight.

At tree-top height, the Mustangs and Thunderbolts of the 9TAF, supported by the Typhoons and Spitfires of the 2nd British Tactical Air Force, came zooming in, machine guns and cannon pounding away, deadly black eggs tumbling from their wings. 'The [enemy] planes came down in hundreds,' von Luettwitz recalled afterwards, 'firing their rockets at the concentrated tanks and vehicles. We could do nothing – and we could make no further progress.'

'Suddenly through the mist I saw a large formation of what appeared to be enemy tanks and transport vehicles,' a Rhodesian wing commander on reconnaissance told the BBC correspondent Stewart Macpherson that August day. 'I went down closer and had another look. This time Jerry was a bit touchy and set off some flak. It was a bit rough, but I got by – and there they were sitting there like ducks on a pond.' Hurriedly, the wing commander whistled up a squadron of rocket-firing British Typhoons.

'I have never seen Germans run so fast,' the wing commander reported as the 'Tiffies' (as the pilots called them) hurtled into the attack. 'Some ran to both sides of the road, some of them jumped for the hedges, others took off for the ditches; one pilot of my squadron said he watched some of them – *climbing trees*!'

But if the crews managed to escape, nothing could save their tanks. 'It was the sort of thing we've been waiting for and this time we really had him flat-footed,' the wing commander told the BBC man. 'When the first attack started, I'd never seen aircraft come in from so many directions in all my life. They poured down on both sides of me like rain. The Hun is a master of salvage, so to prevent him from tidying up any of his tanks that were hit, we kept burning them up all afternoon and evening. He can't salvage tin cans!'

By one o'clock that afternoon Bletchley picked up a signal from a horrified *Brigadegeneral* Wisch. 'First SS Panzer Division has had no previous experience of fighter-bomber attacks on this scale,' he reported to corps HQ. Two hours later Bletchley received another signal, this time from General Hausser, informing Hitler's HQ: 'The actual attack has been at a standstill since 1300 hours owing to the employment by the enemy of a great number of fighter-bombers and the absence of our own aircraft.'

Hitler reacted angrily. He called *Reichsmarschall* Hermann Goering, known behind his back as 'Fat Hermann' due to his enormous girth, and demanded an explanation. The head of the *Luftwaffe*, who painted his face and nails and sniffed cocaine, explained his planes could not get off the ground because enemy fighters hovered over their fields everywhere.

'Goering,' Hitler snorted in disgust, 'the *Luftwaffe* is doing nothing! *Nothing!* And it's your fault... you're lazy!'

It was recorded that when the fat *Reichsmarschall*, who changed his uniforms, all of his own design, twenty times daily, heard these words great tears began to trickle down his plump, painted cheeks...

The fat commander's tears did not help the hard-pressed, stalled *Leibstandarte* as they slogged it out all that late afternoon with Rose's Shermans of the 3rd Armored and were battered by the constant air attacks of the dreaded *jabos*. More than once they tried to sideslip, to find an alternative route to the coast. But the enemy fighter-bombers soon found them, and their losses were mounting very rapidly. The attack was running out of steam.

Peiper's own command tank was hit by a bomb. Years later his young radioman recalled: 'There was a sudden great white flame. A tremendous hissing sound. Suddenly, frighteningly, I couldn't see anything. All I could hear were the screams of my trapped comrades. At first I thought we had been hit by a shell. Later I found it was a bomb. Someone – perhaps it was my commander – dragged me out and placed me on the grass. I still couldn't see. Then I fainted with the pain.'

Later, in hospital, the twenty-one-year-old radioman learned he had been blinded permanently. All the same, he would never think badly of the commander who had led him into his first – and last – battle that terrible August day. He would admire Peiper always.

–

By nightfall, a relieved Bradley knew he had virtually won. The attackers were stalled on all sides. He told his aide, Major Hansen, that the German assault was 'the greatest tactical blunder I've ever heard of. Probably won't happen again in a thousand years.' Bradley felt now that if Canadians attacking in the north could push into the French town of Falaise and, beyond, towards Argentan, and he could turn one of Patton's corps loose from Le Mans to link up with the Canadians at Argentan, he and Montgomery could trap the whole German army in Normandy. It would be a repeat of that classic encircling movement of the Battle of Cannae about which all generals dream.

But the success of that encircling movement, he knew, depended upon the Germans *not* withdrawing before the trap was sprung. But would the 'other feller', as Bradley liked to call the enemy, oblige him in this manner? Would Hitler see the danger and withdraw his men before Patton and the Canadians were in position? That was the sixty-four-dollar question...

Hitler fell right into Bradley's trap. Remote from the harsh realities of the war (unlike Churchill, Hitler never once visited a bombed German city, for example), Hitler had simply no idea of what was really happening on the Mortain front. There, the *Leibstandarte*, for instance, had already had scores of tanks knocked out of action, and Peiper, leading the van, was totally bogged down. Even now, with darkness falling and the *jabos* departed, he still could not break through Rose's 3rd Armored Division. Instead of ordering a general withdrawal while there was still time, Hitler commanded that another SS armoured division from Hausser's Seventh Army should be thrown into the fray to support the *Leibstandarte*.

Hausser despaired when he heard the order. For him it was a death blow, not only to the Seventh Army (his own command), but also to the entire *Wehrmacht* in the West. He knew how the Allies would react. They would attempt to encircle the *Wehrmacht* in Normandy, and that SS armoured division would have been invaluable in aiding any attempt to stop Patton joining up with the Tommies.

Hausser protested to von Kluge. The latter was at the end of his tether and he had toadied to the Fuehrer too long to protest energetically any more. He told Hausser baldly: 'It is the Fuehrer's order.' That was that. Reluctantly, Hausser ordered the SS panzer division to the Mortain front.

Bletchley picked up the news almost immediately. The information was transmitted to Bradley's HQ on the morning of the eighth. It left Bradley unmoved. Indeed, the first entry in the First Army's official diary for that day records that the General was expecting a visit from tough-guy actor Edward G. Robinson. That was really exciting news. Only then was the arrival of a new enemy division on the Mortain front mentioned.

Patton, too, was not stirred by the new German threat. He was too concerned with events in Brittany and the drive from Le Mans to Argentan. Soon he would be telephoning Bradley to inform him that he hoped to be linking up with the slow-moving British and cutting off the Krauts, quipping, 'We have elements in Argentan. Shall we continue and drive the British into the sea for another Dunkirk?'

Bradley laughed hollowly and told himself that 'Georgie' always had to have his little joke. Later he reasoned that Patton, who had always hated 'that little fart Monty', perhaps wasn't joking after all.

–

Now for two more days, while their Fuehrer threw good money after bad by reinforcing the stalled offensive, the *Leibstandarte* and the other SS panzer divisions fought stubbornly for the ground they had gained. They contested every patch of wood, farmhouse, barn, every sunken lane. All day long, hour after hour, till darkness brought a blessed relief, the defenders were hammered mercilessly by the Allied air forces. The enemy *jabos*, complete masters of the sky, despite Fat Hermann's tears and protestations, were able to hunt down German tanks, trucks, anti-tank guns, even individual soldiers, with impunity. Nowhere was it safe to move in the open during the hours of daylight.

There was a new danger, too, especially if you wore the black-and-white armband of the 'Adolf Hitler Bodyguard' on your sleeve – the French Maquis. Up to now, it had seemed to the average Allied serviceman that the French did not welcome them to France as 'liberators'. That had apparently been Aided propaganda for the four years before the invasion, the stuff of Hollywood B movies. Indeed, the Norman farmers, totally concerned with their Calvados and Camembert, had seemed to *resent* their presence in the province. Everyone from Montgomery down to Second-Lieutenant John Eisenhower, the Supreme Commander's own son, had noticed just how little enthusiasm the French showed for their liberators. As John Eisenhower wrote after visiting his father's HQ in France, 'The attitude of the French was sobering indeed. Instead of bursting with enthusiasm, they seemed not only indifferent but sullen. There was considerable cause for wondering whether these people wished to be "liberated".'

Now, however, the French, in the shape of the Resistance, seemed willing to take an active part in the battle against their German 'oppressors'. Suddenly they were everywhere in the battlefield: bold young men, armed with sten guns and weapons seized from the Germans, or with no arms at all, many of them naked to the waist in the burning August heat, with flowered sweat bands around their heads, eager to have a crack at the Boche.

In fact, many members of this resistance movement, steered from a still German-occupied Paris, were communists and had no interest whatsoever in helping the Americans. All they were concerned with was stealing as many German weapons as possible for the coming uprising. Within a week Paris would revolt in an attempt by the Communist Party to seize power in the French capital before de Gaulle arrived and set up a right-wing provisional government. Just as the Russian dictator Stalin was attempting to take over Warsaw and then Poland that August and present the Western Allies with a *fait accompli*, France's communists, on Moscow's orders, were trying to do the same in Paris. Now any isolated German soldiers, especially if they had automatic weapons in their possession, ran the risk of sudden death at the hands of the 'Free French Forces of the Interior'.

–

On the third morning of the counter-attack *Rottenfuhrer* (Corporal) Erwin Hirsch of the *Leibstandarte* was directing his self-propelled gun along the line of trees to his immediate front when a *jabo* swooped. Rockets, fiery-red and terrifying, hissed towards the lone armoured vehicle. One after another they harmlessly ploughed into the field nearby or sliced the foliage above their bent heads, showering them with heavy branches of oak and leaves. Suddenly the Skoda-built self-propelled gun shuddered violently and thick white smoke started to pour from the engine. The last rocket had hit them. As the *jabo* pilot hurtled back into the bright blue morning sky, executing a victory roll as he did so, Hirsch cursed, shook a fist at the departing pilot and hoped his bacon-and-egg breakfast choked him. Then he concentrated on getting the Skoda down to the hamlet that he had spotted below. The self-propelled gun was still moving – barely – but he had no idea how to make a running repair. He would have to get back to the workshops, if he could, and see what they could do. In the meantime, he wanted his young crew to be in the shelter of the Norman hamlet. At least there they stood a chance of not being shot up by the *jabos.*

Fifteen minutes later the damaged Skoda was hidden behind a barn, which seemed as abandoned as the rest of the little place, a straggle of white-painted houses huddled around a slate-roofed grey church. Now the corporal gave his men their instructions: 'Stay with the vehicle. No looking for loot. And keep your eyes peeled for partisans.' He gave his teenage crew a severe look and knew they'd do as he ordered. Even these greenhorns knew all about partisans, at least the Russian kind, who nailed priests to church doors and would cut a man's tail off and stick it in his mouth as soon as look at him. They'd stay within the thick steel protection of the Skoda all right. Grasping his machine pistol more firmly in his right fist, the *Rottenfuhrer* set off to find help.

Two hours later, the *Rottenfuhrer* returned in the big workshop half-truck, which they called the 'furniture van'. To his relief the Skoda was still where he had left it and the crew had managed to douse the white smoke that had been coming from its ruptured engine. All seemed well, yet as they came ever closer, the young corporal could feel the small hairs at the back of his neck standing erect. The hamlet was *too* quiet, and why weren't his crew reacting? The damned furniture van, packed high with equipment, was making enough racket as it clattered over the *pave* that led into the place.

A few moments later he discovered why. The Skoda was empty. The crew were not far away, however. He found them next to the hamlet's smithy, slumped on their knees, their hands tied behind their backs with barbed wire, and the back of each of their young skulls blasted into a red gory mess of caked blood and shattered bone,

4. CAULDRON OF BLOOD

On 14 August, Field Marshal Hans von Kluge disappeared for twelve hours. It was an amazing episode. The Commander-in-Chief of the *Wehrmacht* in the West was completely out of touch with his million-strong force, which was engaged in a life-or-death struggle, for half a day. It was as if Eisenhower had disappeared on D-Day and no one had known where to find him.

Later it was maintained by his fellow generals that his accompanying radio car had been destroyed by an Allied air attack and that this had prevented him contacting his HQ.

Hitler knew differently. He raged that von Kluge, whom he had made, was yet another traitor just like the rest of the '*Monokelfritzen*'! Von Kluge had sent away his escort and then gone to contact Allied patrols, accompanied only by his radio car; for it was the C-in-C's intention to lead the whole of the *Wehrmacht* in France into capitulation and go over to the enemy himself. The plan had miscarried, however, when his radio car had been inadvertently knocked out by an Allied *jabo* and he had been unable to make contact.

If that was the case, neither Montgomery nor Bradley mention the episode in their memoirs. All that Bradley ever said about von Kluge was a remark that day to his aide, Major Hansen: 'The German is either crazy or he doesn't know what's going on. I think he is too smart to do what he is doing. Surely the professional generals must know the jig is up.' To which Hansen replied dutifully: 'Hitler is your greatest ally, sir.' Bradley agreed: 'Yes, perhaps he is.'

At all events, when von Kluge did return to his HQ from his mysterious jaunt to the front, he knew the jig was indeed up. Earlier that day, Sepp Dietrich had warned him bluntly that any general, even an SS one, attempting to tell Hitler the truth ran the risk of being shot. Now von Kluge decided to run that risk. He called Jodl and asked permission to withdraw his battered divisions from the Mortain front at once. He was turned down on the spot, though Jodl, speaking for Hitler, conceded that von Kluge had permission to prepare strong withdrawal positions on the River Seine – just in case.

Then Jodl broke the bad news to the Field Marshal. The Fuehrer, von Kluge was told, had lost confidence in him. He was to return to East Prussia at once, 'to report'. Already Field Marshal Model was on his way from the Russian front to replace him. 'The Boy Marshal', as Field Marshal von Rundstedt, the doyen of the German Officer Corps, called him contemptuously, was the 'Fuehrer's Fireman'. He had stopped the rot in Russia four times already. He would do the same in France.

Sadly, von Kluge set off for the Reich. Perhaps he feared that he was going to be interrogated and tortured by the Gestapo in Berlin about his part in the plot to kill the Fuehrer. At all events, he knew he would not outlive the disgrace of the debacle in France, although it was not of his own making. There was only one way out. Just outside Verdun, beyond those grim chalk heights where he had fought as a young man in the First World War, he ordered his chauffeur to stop the car. He walked some way from it and then poisoned himself.

Behind him he left a long, carefully reasoned suicide note, which he asked should be forwarded to Hitler.

> *'When you receive these lines I shall be no more ... I am dispatching myself to where thousands of my comrades have already gone ... My Fuehrer, make up your mind to end the war. The German people have undergone such untold suffering that it is time to put an end to this frightfulness ... You have fought an honourable and great fight. History will prove that for you. Show yourself also great enough to put an end to a hopeless struggle when necessary.'*

The dead man's appeal fell on deaf ears. Two days before, Hitler had declared that '15 August was the worst day in my life'. All the same, he was not prepared to accord von Kluge's dying wish. Adolf Hitler had a Wagnerian vision of the ultimate end. It would be a *Goetterdaemmerung*.

The German people and the Germany Army had failed him, robbed him of the great achievements and great victories he had sought. Then, good, if he had to go down, he would drag the nation and the Army with him. There would be no peace. Germany would go down fighting!

–

On the same day that von Kluge swallowed cyanide, Field Marshal Model sprang into action. In appearance, the little burly Field Marshal was one of those '*Monokelfritzen*' whom Hitler detested, but of all Germany's field marshals he was perhaps the most sympathetic to the National Socialist cause.

Hated by his senior officers, whom he would sack at the drop of a hat, but respected by the rank-and-file, Model had a great deal of that SS arrogance and angry urgency about him. More than once, in moments of crisis in Russia, he had taken over infantry companies and led them into action himself. He pooh-poohed difficulties and rarely believed alarmist reports, especially when they came from staff officers. He always wanted to find out the true facts himself – from the sharp end, the front.

Once, when he was with a convoy stalled by deep snow, he sprang out of his staff car and, grabbing a shovel, started helping to clear the snow with the ordinary footsloggers. A little while later, meeting an officer who had sat in his car while the snow-clearing operation had been going on, he bellowed, red with rage, 'And you sat there while a German Field Marshal worked with a shovel, *Kamerad!*' With that he pulled off the unfortunate captain's epaulettes, reducing him to the rank of 'comrade', i.e. private. It was typical of Model.

Now he arrived at his HQ to find there was no water and no electricity and that von Kluge's staff were in the last stages of despair. Model soon changed all that, although he was still intent on carrying out the Fuehrer's orders. Without consulting Hitler, he ordered General Hausser to start a limited withdrawal to the River Orne. All the same, Model decreed: 'It's *south* of the Seine that we must make a stand. That is the Fuehrer's order, and I intend to carry it out… Meanwhile, I shall ask the Fuehrer's headquarters for further reinforcements. I must have thirty divisions, or at least 200,000 men.'

But this time, the Fuehrer's Fireman would not be able to put out the blaze. The conflagration had gone too far. For on that very same day, the British and Canadians at Falaise struck south and Patton's Third Army jumped off from their start-line at Argentan. Their aim was simple: to link up and trap the 100,000 miserable survivors of 'Operation Liege'. The end was near for the German Army in France...

–

For two months 'Panzermeyer', commander of the 12th SS Panzer Division Hitler Youth, had held the British and Canadians around Caen. General Kurt Meyer, nicknamed 'Panzermeyer', who had been an officer of the *Leibstandarte* till 1943, when he had been transferred to form the new Hitler Youth Division, had seen his 20,000 teenage volunteers savagely decimated day by day until, as the survivors pulled back to join the great retreat, he had only a final reserve of five hundred youngsters to hold up the victorious Allies. For three long days the five hundred held out against everything the enemy could throw at them. Finally, two of them slipped through enemy lines to report to Panzermeyer that the last-ditch-stand group had been annihilated. There was nothing left now to stop the enemy.

Panzermeyer ordered the remaining divisional radios to be destroyed. They would be needed no more. The Hitler Youth Division had ceased to exist. Now, with a handful of survivors, panic raging all around him, the hard-bitten thirty-six-year-old General, who spurned decoration and badges of rank and carried an ordinary infantryman's rifle, set off to find the Seventh Army Commander, General Hausser. He had heard that his old division, the *Leibstandarte*, still had a few tanks left. Perhaps he could convince Hausser to order a breakout with them before the enemy sprang the trap at Falaise and they were doomed.

The going was terrible. All that afternoon and right throughout the night, the young SS men on foot were subjected to the full weight of the enemy dive-bombers. As Panzermeyer recalled after the war: 'There was no use even attempting to take cover. We were helpless, stuck out in the open, presented to the enemy, as if on a silver platter.'

British fighter ace Wing Commander 'Johnnie' Johnson remembered: 'When the Spitfires arrived … the Typhoons were already at work. One of their favourite tactics against long streams of enemy vehicles was to seal off the front and rear of the column by accurately dropping a few bombs. This technique imprisoned the desperate enemy on a narrow stretch of dusty lane and since the transport was sometimes jammed four abreast, it made the subsequent rocket and cannon attacks a comparatively easy business.

'The tactics of the day were low-level strafing attacks with cannon shells and machine guns against soft-skinned targets, including all types of trucks, staff cars and lightly armoured vehicles. Here and there among the shambles on the ground were a few of the deadly Tiger tanks and although the cannon shells would have little effect against their tough armoured plate, a few rounds were blasted against them for good measure.'

Thus, as Panzermeyer struggled to fight Hausser, the impersonal, factory-like slaughter from the air continued, with one excited pilot reporting over his radio on the twentieth: 'One thousand plus… very little movement…

packed bumper to bumper… feeding main road from all side roads like herring bones.' By evening, another excited pilot directed on to that enormous traffic jam could report, '*Whole area burning!*' Below, all was panic-stricken chaos. Moving with what was left of the *Leibstandarte*, Karludwig Opitz recorded: 'Vehicles pile up. Cars, heavily laden with officers' gear, honk a way through the jam, twisting by lorries in their effort to make better time. Guns are abandoned and blown up. Heavy tractors stop for the lack of fuel; a couple of grenades in the engine and that's that. The huge Mercedes diesels of the workshop company are hit by rockets. The soldiers on the tanks cannot make out where these powerful ultra-modern machines can suddenly come from. The men have never seen them before. Christ, we should have had them earlier! Electric fitting machines, lathes, automatic welders, workshops on wheels, the very best transporters, capable of moving two tanks at once, searchlight trucks with antidazzle equipment for night driving. Lorry-loads of spare parts, dental trucks, a mobile film unit, dredgers… The fighters are having a field day. They hedgehop above the road, the engines screaming. Empty ammunition belts fall from them. Rockets, grenades, machine-gun bullets, bombs – everything is thrown at the stream of vehicles.'

This was a second Dunkirk all right, but this time it was the German Army that was at the receiving end.

–

After a day and a half of this terror from the air, Panzer-meyer and 150 of his boys met General Hausser at last. His empty eye socket covered with a black patch, he was squatting in a ditch, wearily studying a map with the aid of a monocle. A weary Panzermeyer reported in the German fashion, stiffly at attention, gaze fixed on some distant horizon. But before he could finish, a dive-bomber howled from the leaden sky. A salvo of bombs came hurtling down. The ground shook and trembled like a live thing. Red-hot pieces of shrapnel hissed through the air. Next to Hausser, his chief of staff, Colonel Count von Gersdorff, yelped with pain as he was hit.

Hausser continued to sit there, his lean, battered face revealing nothing, as men fell all around him. (His turn would come soon.) Finally, it was over and Hausser was able to tell Panzermeyer what he intended to do, if it was at all possible.

The plan had been hastily flung together and there had been little time to co-ordinate it with other units scattered over the Falaise Pocket, which the ordinary German stubble-hopper was now calling the 'cauldron of blood'. In essence, the *Leibstandarte* under General Wisch would lead a two-divisional attack, with what was left of the Army's tanks, perhaps a score at the most. The assault would be launched at the Allied line between the villages of Trun and Chambois with its *Schwerpunkt* at St Lambert, where the road and bridge across the River Dives were still in German hands. Once the breakthrough had been achieved, all the other shattered German form-ations still prepared to fight and chance their luck would follow, under the command of paratroop General Meindl, a tough, stocky veteran of the para-attack on Crete in 1941.

The plan offered a ray of hope to Panzermeyer, who was to attach himself and his 150 survivors of the Hitler Youth Division to Meindl's command. But he didn't know that his old comrade Wisch commanded exactly twenty tanks, two fewer than the strength of a single company; and that his infantry numbered three under-strength battalions. Things did not look too good for the bold attack, but then, in this last year of its existence, the *Leibstandarte SS Adolf Hitler* was going to have to get used to bold, desperate measures where there seemed little hope of success.

—

The *Leibstandarte* commenced its breakout attempt at dawn on Sunday 20 August. The panzer grenadiers in their camouflaged tunics, faces unshaven, pinched from lack of food and fatigue, eyes red-rimmed with the strain of the last week, pushed forward with some of that old confidence that had made the division unstoppable in the past. They overran the first of the British positions.

Swiftly, their initial success was radioed to the rear. Wisch rapped out his orders. The tanks started moving, breaking forth from their camouflaged hide-out, hoping they had caught the enemy on the hop, at least for a while. That wasn't to be. They had already been spotted by the British forward artillery observers. With a cataclysmic roar, the whole weight of the British Second Army's artillery fell upon them. The British had not been caught off guard after all.

To their front, great steaming black holes were gouged in the fields on all sides like the work of some monstrous mole. Mushrooms of evil, red-ringed smoke shot heavenwards. Burning-hot shrapnel, the size of a human fist, pattered against the turrets of their tanks like heavy tropical rain on a tin roof. The infantry mounted upon their decks were swept away as if they had been swatted. Here and there a tank lurched to a sudden stop, flame jetting from its ruptured engine or a great smoke ring ascending slowly from its open turret.

Within minutes, the *Leibstandarte's* attempt to burst out of the trap with tanks had come to a halt. Desperately, General Wisch tried to get his tankers moving again. To no avail. The enemy artillery bombardment was too fierce. Here and there some of the younger men were abandoning their tanks even before they had been hit. Furious and red-faced, Wisch tongue-lashed his men. But not for long. Suddenly he fell to the ground, whimpering with pain. He had been badly wounded. And that was the end of the *Leibstandarte's* concerted effort to break out and provide an escape route for the trapped survivors.

By midnight on that terrible day of sudden death and destruction, the two trapped armies, Dietrich's 5th Panzer and Hausser's 7th Infantry, had disappeared as recognisable formations. Senior officers and divisional commanders had lost control. Panic was in the very air and order had virtually disappeared in that blazing inferno of burning tanks and exploding munition trucks. Men were surrendering on all sides. 'Hundreds of men were coming towards me,' Corporal Wingfield of the 7th Armoured Division, the 'Desert Rats', remembered long afterwards. 'They were German. They were from the Falaise Gap. I never want to see men like that again. They came, shambling in dusty files. Every few yards there was a single British infantryman. Even that guard was unnecessary. The shuffling wrecks just followed the Bren carrier in the lead. They were past caring. The figures were bowed with fatigue, although they had nothing to carry but their ragged uniforms and their weary, hopeless, battle-drugged bodies.'

Now it was *sauve qui peut*, and up to individual officers to lead out bold groups of men who were not prepared to surrender when all seemed so hopeless, lost.

In particular, the officers of the *Leibstandarte* and the other trapped SS panzer divisions were determined to break out. They knew they faced long years of imprisonment behind the barbed wire of the enemy POW cages if they were captured, for they came under the automatic arrest clause as members of the now proscribed organisation, the Armed SS. As for the members of the French resistance who were making their appearance in every village and hamlet now, all armed to the teeth and with a very low boiling point indeed – well, they couldn't expect any mercy if they fell into their hands. They'd be shot out of hand like rabid dogs.

Now those who were preparing to break out started to gather in the neighbourhood of the village of St Lambert. Here there was a single road in German hands, and it led to the bridge across the River Dives, also in German hands, the only route out of the cauldron of blood. There was only one catch. The sole escape route was dominated by a small force of Canadians under the command of a Major Currie (who would win the Victoria Cross for his bravery at St Lambert). Currie and his men were directing artillery fire on anything that moved along that road, and so far the Canadians had beaten off any attempt to dislodge them from their positions.

The Canadian fire caused frightful carnage. Currie could do little against the handful of remaining German Tigers – their hides were too tough. But their artillery fire played havoc with the massed columns of horse-drawn transport trying to cross the Dives.

General von Luettwitz, whose 2nd Panzer had been the most successful of all the German armoured divisions during Operation Liege, recalled the horror of trying to cross the river. 'The crossing of the bridge over the Dives was a particularly ghastly affair. Men, horses, vehicles and other equipment that had been shot-up while making the crossing had crashed from the bridge into the deep ravine of the Dives and lay there jumbled together in gruesome heaps … Towering pillars of smoke rose incessantly from petrol tanks as they were hit, riderless horses stampeded, some of them badly wounded.' In the end, von Luettwitz decided he hadn't a chance of crossing there. Another crossing site had to be found.

It was the same kind of decision made by others who could not face the bloody carnage of that bridge. Panzermeyer, hiding near the shell-pocked structure, watched German soldiers being mown down mercilessly as they attempted to cross. As darkness fell, he could hear the sound of a heavy fire-fight from the village of St Lambert itself and guessed that some fortunate German unit had managed to cross and break through the Canadians. Panzermeyer was right. Currie was down to two hundred men, grimly holding on to the southern end of the village, unable to stop German armour breaking through. Twice he had been forced to direct friendly artillery fire on his own positions to frighten off the furiously attacking Germans.

It was here that Hausser crossed, blood streaming from a new wound in his face, lying on the deck of a *Leibstandarte* tank, machine pistol at the ready, while von Gersdorff organised a 'battle group' of exactly two tanks. The two last tanks of the *Leibstandarte* lumbered up the battle-littered, cratered village road and broke through.

Immediately what was left of the divisional transport burst from their hiding places and hurtled forward.

Suddenly they ran into a position newly occupied by the US 90th Division. Both formations were caught by surprise, but the SS reacted more swiftly. They opened up a wild fire, and the startled Americans began to throw down their weapons and surrender. But what to do with them? They couldn't take their new prisoners with them; their few remaining vehicles were jam-packed with survivors. The Americans were fortunate. They were disarmed and left where they were. They would live to fight another day. Not many of the escaping SS would.

A little later a young soldier of the *Leibstandarte* was shot and fell over the side of his vehicle as it fled up the road. On the body of the dead soldier, a letter destined for his relatives back in the Reich read: 'Our future looks hopeless and I think it is only right to tell you that most likely we will be taken prisoner. I know it will be hard on you, but I can't help it. At least, I have let you know how things are and when you get the notification that I am missing you will know that I am a prisoner.' Well, the young SS man had been wrong in his calculations. Now he lay in a ditch, a blond young man with a bloody face staring at the merciless blue sky of August with unseeing eyes...

–

Panzermeyer, with his Cossack servant Michel and a mixed bunch of SS men from the *Hitlerjugend* and the *Leibstandarte*, now knew, this last night of the cauldron of blood, that the only remaining escape route was to swim the River Dives. Thus, he led his men across a potato field, for the most part crawling down the furrows, with tracer zipping over their heads in a bright-glowing lethal Morse, heading for the water. To their right, St Lambert was burning brightly, and by the reflected glow Panzermeyer could see the high shapes of Tommy Sherman tanks everywhere on the roads. It was obvious the British were across the river. Time was running out rapidly. This was their last chance.

Meyer was first to slip into the water. It was pink-coloured, as if suffused by blood. Everywhere there were dead bodies in field-grey floating face downwards. Gritting his teeth and nudging them aside, the last commander of the Hitler Youth began to swim. His men followed. Five minutes later he was across, together with some two hundred SS men.

But they weren't out of danger yet. On the height to their front, the British and Canadians were dug in. They would have to break through the Tommy line now if they were going to make good their escape. In a whisper, Panzermeyer explained he was prepared to lead only those men who were armed. He would not be burdened by cowards who had flung away their weapons. His words encouraged his young SS men. Officers and men, they crawled around the fields on hands and knees, searching the German dead for weapons.

Half an hour later the breakout force was armed and ready. Panzermeyer, who knew the ground intimately from pre-D-Day training exercises, took the lead. Together with Michel, whom he had 'found' in Russia during his time with the *Leibstandarte* there, Panzermeyer crawled to have a look at the enemy positions on the height. As far as he could make out, they were occupied by two companies of infantry dug in in a thin line of foxholes.

'Surprise attack!' he announced to Michel. 'The Tommies won't expect us to rush them.'

Michel indicated the bloody bandage around his master's head. 'Bandage no good,' he whispered in broken German. 'I make another – later.' Panzermeyer understood. The bandage would stand out in the darkness. He allowed the Cossack to untie it. The blood started to trickle down his forehead once more.

Five minutes later, the assault force crawled ever closer to the enemy positions. On the roads to both sides of them, Sherman tanks were pounding the mass of the Germans still trapped in the pocket. They took no notice of Panzermeyer's men. Suddenly, however, a Bren-gun carrier appeared to their front.

Panzermeyer recognised it immediately. 'Duck!' he hissed. His men flopped to the ground. Had they been spotted? Panzermeyer's heart was beating like a trip-hammer. Nerves tingling electrically, they waited. Nothing happened. The British Bren-gun carrier turned and rattled away.

'NOW!' Panzermeyer yelled. Like ghosts rising from their graves, they sprang up and charged forward. The enemy were caught completely by surprise. Hardly a shot was fired, as the Tommies fell back in sudden panic.

'Look out!' Panzermeyer's chief-of-staff, Colonel Meyer, yelled. Panzermeyer, gasping for breath, blood streaming down his face, swung round. Fewer than thirty metres away there was the unmistakeable high silhouette of a Sherman tank. He had almost run right into it. He ducked behind a hedge and continuing running. But he was weakening badly. He couldn't keep up with the rest.

'You take over the lead, Hubert,' he gasped to his chief-of-staff. 'I'm… I'm beat.'

Meyer nodded his understanding and doubled away, leaving his chief, together with the Cossack.

'Only a hundred metres, Commander,' Michel said, taking Panzermeyer and supporting the wounded General. 'Only a hundred...' Gratefully, one of the most hard-bitten officers of the Armed SS, already branded a war criminal by the Canadians, allowed himself to be led to safety by one of those humble Russians whom once in the great days of the *Leibstandarte* he and his comrades had labelled 'sub-human trash'...

Now the victors came to view the carnage. Alan Moorehead, the veteran Australian war correspondent who had reported on World War Two from every British battlefield since 1940, was appalled by what he saw. Walking along the road from St Lambert, he came to an orchard. 'It is full of Germans – Germans beaten and numbed into senselessness. Like animals they seem to have no will of their own. They are all armed with machine pistols and rifles, but no one takes the slightest notice of them ... Over at the hospital it is far worse. The dead and the wounded lie together. Living or dead there is not much difference in the appearance of the men. Many hours ago life ceased to count for anything at all. The wounded keep dying, but quietly. They are all jumbled on top of one another and the stench makes it difficult for one to refrain from being sick. Outside a Canadian soldier is mercifully going round shooting wounded horses with a Luger pistol.'

Moorehead and the other correspondents, now sober and silent, came across a young Canadian officer. He explained: 'They kept coming up the road in bursts every three minutes. We shot the leaders of each group and captured the others.' Moorehead nodded his understanding and thought: 'I see the end of Germany here. This was their best in weapons and men, their strongest barrier before the Rhine. It has been brushed aside, shattered into bits. The beaten *Wehrmacht* is a pitiful thing.'

The German commanders thought the same. Standing at the bridges and pontoon bridges over the Seine, armed with pistols to prevent the panic getting even worse, the SS senior officers tried to re-establish some semblance of order among the rabble. It was hard. The beaten *Wehrmacht* had suffered fifty per cent casualties in the cauldron of blood over the past four terrible days. The men had lost, and were intent solely on saving their own skins. Even the SS, those who had survived the bloodbath, were at the end of their tether.

Sepp Dietrich, standing with his officers and watching the remnants of his divisions trickle across the bridges over the Seine, was shocked by their losses. In the case of the *Leibstandarte*, the division seemed to have not a single tank left and its two panzer grenadier regiments, usually three battalions in strength each, were down to a single battalion. As an effective fighting force, the *Leibstandarte Adolf Hitler* had ceased to exist.

While Sepp Dietrich waited for the *Leibstandarte* to finish filing its weary way across the river, the Allied dive-bombers came winging down from the sun yet once again. Panzermeyer, wounded, ragged, exhausted, staggered up to report to his former divisional commander and old comrade of ten years' standing.

At first, Dietrich could not recognise the scarecrow with the bloody bandage wrapped around his head, then he did and exclaimed: 'But we all thought you were dead, Kurt!'

It was too much for Panzermeyer. He broke down at last and burst into hot tears.

–

For a few days more, Hitler's Fireman, Field Marshal Model, thought he might be able to hold the Allies on the line of the River Seine to both sides of Paris. But he was out of luck. By chance, a small patrol of Patton's 79th Infantry Division came across an unguarded bridge at Mantes, west of Paris. At first the Americans couldn't believe the evidence of their own eyes. Not only were there no Germans on the bridge, but there were none on the opposite bank either. Was this some kind of trap? After all, they all knew the Kraut would try to hold the great French river.

Sergeant White and two other volunteers decided to chance it. They crossed the footbridge at the double and crouched. Nothing happened. There really weren't any Germans in the area. White waved for the rest of the patrol to follow him. They did, and the GIs cautiously probed the houses on the other side, bodies tensed waiting for the first burst of enemy machine-gun fire. None came.

Sergeant White made the decision that won him a medal from 'Ole Blood an' Guts' himself. 'Whatever you do, don't make any more noise than you have to,' he told his men, and ordered them to set up two heavy machine guns on the far bank. Then he had some mortars rushed up and prepared a perimeter defence just in case the Krauts did appear and attack.

The news that the first crossing of the Seine had been undertaken was rushed to Third Army's HQ. Patton drove down to see if it was true. He was overjoyed to find out that it was. Immediately, the 79th Divisional HQ was ordered, 'Get the 313th Regiment over the river!'

Two days later, on 23 August, on the Seine near Ponthierry, Corps Commander Walker, a roly-poly two-star General of whom Patton once said, 'He'll do well unless he blows up', took personal charge of a minor attack – which benefited only a group of French criminals whose prison he had just helped to 'liberate'. Afterwards, the tremendously fat Corps Commander happened to pass a unit of the US 7th Armored Division waiting on the left bank of the Seine. They had been ordered to help the attack on the prison, which was located on an island in the middle of the Seine, but had done nothing about it.

Now Walker took charge again. He ordered the 7th to cross by a causeway to the island and one of his aides to swim the river (under fire) to find out the state of the German defences on the other side. Hours later, Patton had his second bridgehead over on the other side of the River Seine.

By this time a straggle of units of the *Leibstandarte* under Captain Wahl, acting on his own initiative, had been holding up a whole US armoured division, the 5th Armored, while a couple of hundred of Panzermeyer's *Hitler Jugend* had actually staged a limited counter-attack. But these efforts were all in vain. The Americans were crossing the river and their running mate, the British Second Army to the east, was doing the same. The Seine Line, despite Model's assurances to the Fuehrer, simply could *not* be held. France had to be abandoned – *swiftly!*

On 3 September 1944, the fifth anniversary of the outbreak of World War Two, Model issued an order to his fleeing troops. The 200,000 men he had requested from the Fuehrer were simply not forthcoming. Now all he could do was to appeal to that old ingrained self-sacrifice of the German soldier, especially if he belonged to the SS.

SOLDIERS OF THE WESTERN ARMY! [the last appeal in France read] WITH THE ENEMY ADVANCE AND THE WITHDRAWAL OF OUR FRONT, A GREAT STREAM OF TROOPS HAS BEEN SET IN MOTION, SEVERAL HUNDRED THOUSAND SOLDIERS ARE MOVING BACKWARDS ... WE HAVE LOST A BATTLE, BUT I TELL YOU, WE WILL WIN THIS WAR!...

AT THIS MOMENT EVERYTHING ADDS UP TO THE NECESSITY TO GAIN THE TIME WHICH THE FUHRER NEEDS TO BRING INTO OPERATION NEW TROOPS AND NEW WEAPONS. THEY WILL COME. SOLDIERS, WE MUST GAIN THIS TIME FOR THE FUHRER.

Field Marshal Model

Now the question in the ranks of the *Leibstandarte* fleeing eastwards with the rest of the disorganised mob was: Could they gain time for the Fuehrer? *Or was everything already lost?*

5. 'I'M A GENERAL... NOT AN UNDERTAKER!'

'No human account could ever describe the hardship, the sacrifice, the misery the men of this division alone suffered,' one survivor of the *Leibstandarte* recalled long afterwards. 'No one who finished this retreat still alive will ever forget this Gethsemane because each village, each road, even each bush is seared into his brain with memories of terrible hours, insufferable misery, of cowardice, despair and destruction.'

But how the survivors had reached the Reich and were streaming across the border from Trier in the south to Aachen in the north, with the Americans hard on their heels.

There was no time to dwell on the dreadful events of the immediate past. It might be only a matter of days, even hours, before the Americans started crossing from half a dozen points in Belgium and Luxembourg and attacking the *Westwall*, which the Allies, for some reason known only to themselves, called the 'Siegfried Line'.

The surviving officers of the *Leibstandarte*, which now possessed no tanks, no guns and had been reduced to a handful of weary infantrymen of the panzer grenadier regiments, snapped into action. They wanted 'bodies' to fill their depleted ranks and equipment and they were not too fussy in their means of acquiring them. They posted themselves at the border crossroads, pistols drawn, and shanghaied any soldier who could not give a satisfactory answer to their questions. As one of them recalled after the war: 'In one instance, I was directing traffic into the divisional area. The Army men, not quite happy about being impressed into the SS, circled the area until they hit another road. Only this road led to the same junction where I stood. I redirected the Army men into the divisional area, rather amused by the merry-go-round. When antitank guns were needed, a fellow officer, with a few prime movers [transport vehicles] set up shop at a road crossing and waited for passing guns. When he found one whose crew was not quite certain about their destination or attachment, their horses would be unharnessed, their guns attached to the prime movers and suddenly the gun crews found themselves to be members of the *Leibstandarte*!'

Now while the *Leibstandarte* attempted to fill its ranks any way it could, draconian measures were applied to the rear to prepare the Reich for the battle soon to come. On 1 September 1944, all theatres, music halls, cabarets, schools of music, etc, were closed. All publishers were closed down save those publishing school books and the Fuehrer's own *Mein Kampf*. All university departments, save those training students for posts vital to the war effort such as medicine, were ordered to cease teaching too. By these harsh means, several hundred thousand men and women were released for war work and the armed forces. It was just the start of a *levee en masse*.

Goering's *Luftwaffe*, which had angered the Fuehrer so much during Operation Liege, was ordered to close all its pilot, navigator and radio schools. The men released, plus the ground crews who serviced their planes, were redirected to the infantry. They were organised immediately into battle groups under the command of an experienced Army officer. In one case, four hundred culls from the *Luftwaffe* were given exactly one day's infantry training and then thrown into battle.

It was the same with the German Navy, *die Kriegsmarine*. There weren't many capital ships left, but the crews of those that had survived were transferred to the infantry, as were U-boat crews for whom there were no longer submarines.

Everywhere throughout the Reich, the military depots, workshops, even convalescent hospitals, were combed for 'bodies'. 'Stomach Battalions', made up of men who suffered from severe stomach complaints due to illness or wounds and who were grouped together for special diets, were formed into a 'Whitebread Division' (thus named because they were fed on white bread instead of the usual black, hard German Army bread). It was sent to the front, too.

'Ear and Nose Battalions' followed. These were made up of men who had one or both ears missing or were deaf. In such battalions orders often had to be given in deaf-and-dumb language. Service with these battalions in the line could be dangerous, particularly at night. In one Ear and Nose Battalion two sergeants of the guard were shot on successive nights because deaf sentries shot first and asked questions afterwards when suddenly confronted by a guard commander appearing out of the darkness. Later, these battalions suffered high casualties from artillery fire because their members couldn't hear the shells coming.

When these desperate measures were announced publicly by Berlin, they all sounded very funny to the people in Britain and America, and the newspapers seized upon them as a wonderful story: 'GERMANY'S VOLK-STURM MADE UP OF OLD MEN, STOMACH CASES, CRIPPLES WITH GLASS EYES AND WOODEN LEGS'.

Up front, the GIs about to attack the Reich didn't think it amusing at all. As one of them told *Yank* magazine reporters that month: 'I don't care if the guy behind the gun is a syphilitic prick who's a hundred years old – he's still sitting behind eight feet of concrete and he's still got enough fingers to press triggers and shoot bullets!'

As yet, however, that formidable *Westwall* was in no state to shelter a 'syphilitic prick who's a hundred years old', or the first of the *Leibstandarte*'s units that were beginning to filter into the line there.

The *Westwall*, a line of fortifications that ran eight hundred kilometres from the border with Switzerland to the border with southern Holland, had been under construction from 1936 until building had been suspended in 1940 when German troops had broken through France's Maginot Line. Since that time it had been virtually abandoned, with the local farmers taking over the bunkers and in some cases turning them into chicken coops. In others, the bunkers had been locked up in May 1940 and their keys mislaid. All of the bunkers, however, were out of date and could not house Germany's latest cannon, such as the 75 mm and the feared 88 mm.

But aged Field Marshal von Rundstedt, who had been brought out of retirement by Hitler at this hour of Germany's greatest need, felt the *Westwall* could be used to stop the Western Allies for a while. 'I knew that there was no chance of winning the war,' he told his interrogators after the end of the conflict, 'but I hoped that if I held on long enough a shift in political events might save Germany from complete collapse.' He meant a breakdown of the Anglo-American-Russian alliance. Accordingly, the Field Marshal, clever and resourceful but much addicted to fine French cognac these days, gave out the order: 'Rearm and man the *Westwall*.'

On 10 September, 167,000 men and women, plus the same number of boys from the Hitler Youth and the Labour Service, were hurried from all over Germany to prepare the *Westwall* for the storm to come. As soon as the line was readied, the new 'People's Grenadier Divisions' – hastily re-formed divisions built around the ones shattered in France, and, filled with the culls, the new recruits released by this *levee en masse*, and the transfer from the *Luftwaffe* and the Navy – would be rushed into the bunkers to take over.

But already, two days after that order was given on 11 and 12 September, American patrols had begun to cross the German frontier at half a dozen different points, and the *Leibstandarte* would have to do its best to stop them, whether the *Westwall* was finished or not...

–

Ernest Hemingway, attached to the US 4th Infantry Division, was with its 22nd Regiment when it made its first attack on the Siegfried Line, defended by a handful of *Leibstandarte* men and a hastily organised army battle group.

As Hemingway wrote at the time: 'We passed the unmanned old-fashioned pillboxes that many unfortunate people were to think constituted the Siegfried Line... The next day we were past the second line of concrete fortified strong points that guarded road junctions and approaches to the main *Westwall* and that same night we were up on the highest of the high ground before the *Westwall*, ready to assault in the morning.'

Next morning, Hemingway watched as the regimental commander Colonel 'Buck' Lanham led the attack, describing it in typical tough Hemingway style: 'The Colonel came up the hill where they [his men] were all lying and he said: "Let's go get these Krauts! Let's kill the chickenspitters! Let's get up the hill now and get this place taken!"'

Soon afterwards the attackers came to a bunker held by the *Leibstandarte*. They were asked to surrender. They refused, although they were surrounded. Lanham ordered up his 'Wump gun', as Hemingway called it, a tank destroyer armed with a huge 155 mm cannon. Again Lanham forced one of their prisoners to ask the SS to come out. 'They wouldn't come. They wouldn't answer. So we pulled the Wump gun up to the back door just like the other time and yelled to them to come out and they wouldn't come. So we put in about ten shots from the Wump gun and then they came out – what was left of them. They were a sad and bedraggled lot. Every one of them was in awful shape. They were SS boys, all of them, and they got down in the road, one by one, on their knees. They expected to get shot. But we were obliged to disappoint them. There were about twelve who got out. As for the rest,' Hemingway indulged himself in that *Grand Guignol* type of description that he had adopted in his reports from the Spanish Civil War, 'they were blown to pieces and wounded all to hell. There were legs and arms and heads scattered all over that goddam place.'

Later, Colonel Lanham told him what they had just seen and experienced would be suitable for 'a screen treatment' because 'Ernie, a lot of time I felt as though I were at a Grade B picture.' Hemingway reflected, 'The only thing that will be probably hard to get properly [in the movie] is the German SS troops, their faces black from the concussion, bleeding at the nose and mouth, kneeling in the road, grabbing their stomachs, hardly able to get out of the way of the tanks.' In the end, however, Hemingway concluded that 'probably the cinema will be able to make this even more realistic...'

While one battalion of the *Leibstandarte* tried to hold the *Amis* in the *Westwall* another, *Kampfgruppe* Rink of the division's 1st Panzer Grenadier Battalion, was trying to do the same some sixty kilometres to the north at the old German imperial city of Aachen.

Young Major Rink, a veteran of the Russian front, was in an ugly mood when he arrived at the front in Aachen, which was besieged by three American divisions. A day or so before, his men had been conscripted to help clear up after a massive raid on the nearby town of Dueren. There he had seen 'women literally smeared up against the walls by the bombs... dead children everywhere in the ruins.' Now he and his men were prepared 'to castrate the Americans who did that – with the blunt edge of a broken bottle'.

The *Leibstandarte* battle group attacked immediately. They slung the *Amis* out of one of the city's suburbs that they had captured, and set them off running and flinging away their arms in unreasoning panic as they went. The cost was high. Rink's NCOs reported that night that out of the 274 other ranks and 32 NCOs who had gone into action, only 142 rank-and-file were left and 25 NCOs. The battle group had lost fifty per cent of its strength in a few short hours. But when the American Corps General Corlett heard that the *Leibstandarte* had turned up on the Aachen front, he turned to Leland Hobbs, the commander of the US 30th Infantry Division, which had last fought the SS division at Mortain, and exclaimed: 'If the *Adolf Hitler* are in there, this is one of the decisive battles of the war.'

In wasn't to be. For by now, what was left of the *Leibstandarte*, apart from Rink's men, were being quietly withdrawn from the front, together with the other SS panzer divisions. One by one the battered survivors were pulled out of the line to be replaced by the new 'people's grenadier divisions' and gradually disappeared from Allied Intelligence's daily order-of-battle. To Allied Intelligence there seemed nothing unusual in this. Why should armoured divisions be wasted defending fixed positions? That was the job of infantry, wasn't it?

Besides, most of them were supremely confident that the Germans were about finished. Why worry that Germany's premier division, the *Leibstandarte*, and all the rest of the SS panzer divisions seemed to have vanished from the front? Victory was in the air.

As September gave way to October and October to November, these senior Intelligence officers were still unconcerned. All right, the Germans had not cracked up in September as they had confidently predicted. Indeed, the enemy had fought savagely in Aachen and northern France and were now doing the same in the Hurtgen Forest – called the 'death factory' by the GIs – where whole battalions were being slaughtered. But to Allied Intelligence that only meant the Germans would burn themselves out long before the Allies ran out of troops.

As General Sibert, Bradley's chief-of-Intelligence, reported: 'It is now certain that attrition is steadily sapping the strength of the German forces on the Western front and that the crust of defense is thinner, more brittle and more vulnerable that it appears on our G-2 [intelligence] maps or to the troops in the line.'

It was the kind of unfounded optimism shared by most senior Allied Intelligence officers that autumn. They reasoned that continued German resistance depended solely on Adolf Hitler. Eliminate the Fuehrer and what was left of the battered Third Reich would collapse like a house of cards.

Indeed, in Washington the American Intelligence organisation, the OSS, forerunner of the CIA, was considering doing just that – kill Hitler. As one senior member of the organisation told the head of the OSS, General 'Wild Bill' Donovan, when it was learned that Hitler was to meet Mussolini at the Brenner Pass, 'Let's parachute a cadre of our toughest men into the area and shoot up the bastards! Sure it'll be a suicide operation, but that's what we're organised for.'

Another of Wild Bill's subordinates, a mild-mannered scientist called Dr Stanley Lovell, who was in charge of the OSS's department of 'dirty tricks', was nicknamed 'Professor Moriarty'. He suggested a more subtle approach. A vase containing cut flowers – and a deadly odourless gas – would be brought into the room by agents before the two dictators met. 'If they are in the room for twenty minutes,' he told his boss, 'the invisible gas will affect their bodies through their eyeballs. Everyone in the room will be permanently blinded. The optic nerve will be atrophied. A blind leader can't continue the war – at least, I don't believe he can.'

Thus, while senior Allied Intelligence men played their silly little games or shut their minds to the harsh realities of the front, a whole new German army was formed – the Sixth SS Panzer Army – which was commanded by no less a person than the founder of the *Leibstandarte*, Sepp Dietrich. The choice of an SS general and one as close to the Fuehrer as Dietrich *should* have roused the suspicions of the men in charge of Allied Intelligence. Unfortunately, in the light of the tragedy soon to come, they knew of neither the Sixth SS Army nor its new commander. They continued to make optimistic forecasts about the imminent collapse of the Third Reich, reasoning that if – and it was a big 'if' – anything untoward was to happen, the 'boffins of Bletchley' would warn them well in advance. Hut Three had been alerting them to each new German threat for years now. Why should there be any change in that situation in this, the last winter of the war?

–

By early December 1944, Allied Intelligence had finally established there was an army called the Sixth SS Panzer, which appeared to be 'the strategic reserve for the Fuehrer's HQ', and was made up of five panzer and one parachute divisions. But exactly where this new army was located was a matter of conjecture. Bradley's chief-of-Intelligence thought it was located north of Cologne in the Bielefeld area. The chief-of-Intelligence of the US First Army placed it between the Rivers Rhine and Roer. The US Ninth Army could find no location for it, whereas General Strong, Eisenhower's Scottish chief-of-Intelligence, could report on 10 December: 'There is no further news of the Sixth SS Panzer Army beyond vague rumours.'

In fact, the Sixth SS Panzer Army was sitting right under the Americans' noses, directly opposite the boundary between the US First Army's Vth and VIIIth Corps in the dark, dripping firs of the Eifel forest on what the GIs, who had been stationed here in peace for the past three months, called 'the ghost front'. For weeks now, every precaution possible had been taken to prevent the Allies from finding out about the presence of Dietrich's force. Virtually all Enigma traffic had ceased. Divisions coming into the line did so at night, marching from the railheads to their new positions under the cover of darkness. They marched along roads covered with straw to deaden the noise of their boots and each road was 'commanded' by a special officer in charge of the security of 'his' road.

Patrolling ceased so that there would be no chance of the *Amis* taking prisoners who might reveal what was planned. Would-be deserters were informed by posters pinned up everywhere along the front that not only would they be sentenced to death if caught, but that their families would be arrested and placed in a concentration camp, as well.

Artillery fire from the German side was silenced. Nothing must reveal the true strength of the Germans opposite the four weak American divisions strung along a hundred kilometres of front. Indeed, when the green 99th Division went into the line that December, it was told by veterans of that quiet front that there was only one single horse-drawn German cannon in their section of the line. When, later, a thousand German guns opened fire on the unsuspecting Americans, a wag in the 99th exclaimed: 'Hell, they must be flogging that poor old nag to death!'

Sepp Dietrich, the Sixth SS Panzer Army's commander, learned the reason for his new army's move to the 'ghost front' in the first week of November. That week he appeared at the Fuehrer's HQ, brandishing a folder marked in red *Geheimkommandosache* (roughly, 'top secret'). 'Do you know what this is?' he bellowed when he was admitted to the presence of Colonel General Jodl. 'I came to find out whether it's all a joke.'

Jodl, who knew that Dietrich had just been let into the great secret that Germany was going to counter-attack on the ghost front, assured the angry SS General that it wasn't a joke. 'It's a plan established by the Fuehrer in person,' he said.

'Then I'll protest to the Fuehrer himself about it,' Dietrich cried, face flushed with anger. 'He must have based it on highly inaccurate information. Do you know what this plan means to me and my army? It means reaching the River Meuse within two days, crossing it, capturing Brussels and then Antwerp. *That's all!* As if my armour would just be cutting through butter. And this pretty programme is to be carried out in the dead of winter, when the chances are nine out of ten that we'll be up to our waists in snow. Do you call that serious?'

Jodl, who secretly despised this noisy tough ex-NCO, assured Dietrich that the plan had been well thought out.

Dietrich flushed an even deeper red. 'Nobody can teach me anything about an offensive,' he snorted. 'There are only thirty men left of my original division, *die Leibstandarte*. Now I've set up a whole new armoured army.

I'm a general *not* an undertaker! I tell you that no one can carry out those orders. I insist on seeing the Fuehrer and telling him so myself.'

But Hitler refused to see his old Party comrade. He said he had better things to do than discuss the plan with Dietrich. Dietrich had his orders and it was his duty to carry them out just like any other commander. Wasn't his SS army being given the honour of leading the attack? Disgruntled, Dietrich went back to his headquarters on the ghost front and set about planning the execution of an attack that he simply did not believe had a chance of succeeding.

On Thursday 14 December 1944, General Mohnke, the new commander of the re-formed *Leibstandarte*, received his regimental colonels at eleven o'clock on a frosty snowy morning. Outside the remote, hidden-away forester's hut that served as the divisional HQ the brand-new Tigers and Panthers with which the *Leibstandarte* was now equipped were securely hidden among the snow-heavy firs. The *Amis* were only eight kilometres away on the other side of the Belgian-German frontier and Mohnke did not want their presence revealed to any prying reconnaissance plane.

Everything seemed controlled haste, and the regimental Colonels were pleased with what they saw. This was not the pre-war *Leibstandarte*, the one they had joined in the thirties, of course, but the division was up to full strength again and its equipment was top quality and brand new. Now they guessed that they had been summoned to HQ to hear to what use all this new equipment was going to be put.

The Colonels, Skorzeny, Hansen, Sandig, etc., were similar types – big, thickset officers, their chests heavy with decorations, their uniforms immaculate, riding boots highly polished, caps neatly squared and set at a correct regulation angle. There was, however, one exception – the commander of the division's 1st SS Panzer Regiment, who had arrived late, due to the traffic clogging the camouflaged narrow country roads.

The youngest of the Colonels – he was at least five years younger than the others – he was dressed in a black leather jacket and white polo-necked pullover, his sole decoration the Knight's Cross. His cap was battered, the insignia tarnished, and set at a decidedly non-regulation, rakish angle. As always, *Obersturmbannfuhrer* Jochen Peiper liked to be different.

Hurriedly Mohnke and his chief-of-staff Colonel Ziemssen filled the latecomer in on what he had missed, while Colonel Otto Skorzeny, the scar-faced giant who had rescued Mussolini from his mountain-top prison the year before, watched his young comrade. Years later he recalled the slight, tense *Obersturmbannfuhrer* as 'knowing something big was going on. Just how big I already knew, for the Fuehrer himself had told me and sworn me to secrecy… He was like a highly trained, nervous hound begging to be let off the lead.'

Now Mohnke got down to business. Their old commander, Sepp Dietrich, had given them the honour of leading the Sixth SS Panzer Army's attack on the American positions on the other side of the border in the Belgian Ardennes. Once again the *Wehrmacht* was going over to the attack and, just as they had done back in 1940, they would break through right to the English Channel.

Mohnke's announcement did not come as a total surprise to Peiper. Although, as we have seen, the Sixth SS Panzer had taken extraordinary measures to conceal its assembly area and the reason for its being there, Peiper's suspicions that there was something in the wind had already been roused. It was a question that General Kraemer, Dietrich's chief-of-staff, had posed five days before. He had asked Peiper if he thought an armoured attack in the local terrain was feasible. When Peiper had replied in the affirmative, Kraemer had then asked how long it would take an armoured column to travel eighty kilometres under winter conditions.

Peiper hadn't answered. Instead, he had driven one of his own Panthers eighty kilometres over the narrow roads of the area at night. Next morning, he had reported to a slightly amused Kraemer that the local roads 'were big enough only for a bike'. Now Peiper knew the reason for those questions.

Swiftly, Mohnke ran through the plan, which envisaged an attack by three German armies, the Sixth SS Panzer, the Fifth Panzer and the Seventh Army. The aim was to split the Anglo-American front, put Britain out of the war for a time (that country was already scraping the barrel after five years of war) and knock Russia out thereafter, while the British and Americans temporarily no longer posed a threat. If everything worked out well, Germany would negotiate with the Western Allies and undoubtedly obtain a better deal than was currently possible.

None of those present that day at the *Leibstandarte*'s forest HQ knew that Field Marshal von Rundstedt, after whom the great surprise attack would be named, had already passed judgement on the grandiose plan. When he heard the final objective, he had snorted with scorn, '*Antwerp!* If we reach the Meuse, we should go down on our bended knees and thank God… let alone trying to reach Antwerp!' Still, the regimental Colonels, old hares to a man, knew then what Peiper would say long afterwards: 'The Battle of the Bulge would be an advertisement for either side.'

The objectives set by the Fuehrer did seem highly unrealistic. Mohnke must have read their looks for he said, 'It is, I agree, an operation of the most extreme daring… Anyway, *meine Herren*, there can be no argument. It's the Fuehrer's orders.' And that was that.

Now' Mohnke started to detail Peiper's orders. He was to be given the 'decisive role in the offensive': a powerful force of 4,000 men, with seventy-two Panthers, plus a battalion of twenty-five assault guns and self-propelled tank destroyers. All his infantry would be carried in eighty half-tracks. Further, he would have attached to him thirty 68-ton King Tigers of the 501st Heavy SS Panzer Battalion. As Peiper calculated it in his quick mind at that moment, his column would trail out *twenty-four* kilometres in the slow, curvy narrow roads of the Eifel-Ardennes. Unless the weather was on the German side, he would be a sitting duck for enemy *jabos*, just as they had been back at Mortain.

Peiper, Mohnke told him, would be allotted Route D, one of the four road networks leading to the River Meuse picked personally by the Fuehrer. It started at the German border village of Losheimgraben and ran to the Belgian village of Honsfeld. From there it crossed the first of the many rivers and streams that 'Battle Group Peiper' would have to traverse until it reached the hamlet of Ligneuville. There Peiper would cross country, taking a winding track through the hills until he finally came to the small town of Trois-Ponts. Here he would take a first-class road, *Route Nationale N-23*, which ran directly to the River Meuse.

The Meuse was the only real natural barrier in the path of the German invaders once they had descended from the Ardennes hills to the plain of northern Belgium and France. Here Peiper would take the bridge across the river and hold it against all odds until the rest of the Sixth SS Panzer Army linked up with him. As General Kraemer, Dietrich's chief-of-staff, would implore him one day later: 'Jochen, get me that bridge at Huy, *even with only one tank*, and you have done more than enough!'

Peiper was not impressed by Route D, which he now viewed on the map. It had only one advantage: there was a relative paucity of bridges that might be blown up by the enemy. Otherwise, it was too narrow, too winding and too hilly for tanks to advance at speed – and speed, he knew, was of the essence if he were going to take advantage of the initial shock of the surprise counter-offensive. He told Mohnke what he had told Kraemer the previous Sunday. The roads of Route D were meant 'not for tanks but for bicycles'.

The divisional commander ignored the comment. He knew Peiper's arrogance of old. Hadn't Sepp Dietrich himself once called Peiper '*ein arroganter Hund*'? Instead, he appeased him by referring to the fact that Battle Group Peiper was going to be a totally independent command. It would be up to Peiper to make his own decisions once the offensive had started. Peiper liked that. He had always hated authority and had never really listened to the advice of his superiors. As the Germans phrased it, he was one of those individuals who liked to 'butt their head through the wall' in all his actions. However, there was a fly in the ointment. His battle group would lack sufficient fuel to enable it to reach that bridge over the Meuse at Huy. Again, Mohnke appeased Peiper by telling him that there was a large US fuel supply depot at the Belgian village of Buellingen, twelve kilometres from the border.

Peiper objected that Buellingen was on Route C, which had been allotted to the *Leibstandarte's* running mate, the Hitler Youth Division. In reply, Mohnke quoted the order of their corps commander:

> *'The Corps and, under the Corps' command, the division have freedom of movement within this area. Thus march routes do not have to be rigidly adhered to. Each division has expressed permission to deviate from prescribed routes whenever the situation arises.'*

This apparently satisfied Peiper and he listened in silence while Mohnke detailed how two infantry divisions – the 3rd Para and the 12th People's Grenadier – would open up the front for the corps' armour. Then once the *Amis'* line was breached, the armour would roll into Belgium.

Now the conference was virtually over and Mohnke concluded it by reading part of the speech that Hitler had given to his divisional commanders when he briefed them two days before: 'The battle will decide whether Germany is to live or die,' he had said. 'Your soldiers must fight hard and ruthlessly. There must be no pity. The battle must be fought with brutality and all resistance must be broken in a wave of terror. The enemy must be beaten, now or never. Thus will live our Germany! *Forward to and over the Meuse!*' Old hares as they all were, men who as young officers had been in daily contact with the Fuehrer before the war, they were not impressed by what Skorzeny called later 'the usual rhetoric'; their minds were already full of the task to come. Yet that command '*all resistance must be broken in a wave of terror*' would hang over the whole offensive like a sword of Damocles. In the years to come it would be quoted to those who survived by the victors until they were heartily sick of the phrase. But those fateful words, which they ignored this Thursday, would invariably shape and alter each one of their individual destinies in the bitter years of defeat…

For the next forty hours, Peiper and his officers worked flat out, co-ordinating the efforts of the new battle group, hastily arranging for petrol, ammunition, food and the hundred and one things that a self-contained command would need over the day or so when it would be cut off from the main division. Most of Peiper's men were new recruits and he knew there was little he could do to prepare them for combat in the few hours allotted them. Instead, he ordered them to avoid trouble wherever possible and demonstrated a few elementary tricks of the trade such as firing a blinding-white flare at an enemy tank and blinding its gunner before opening fire oneself; or eradicating enemy infantry by running across their foxholes and gunning the motor, thus flooding the holes with lethal gas. 'It's one way of saving ammo,' he told them with that air of callous indifference to human life and suffering that all of the old hares had acquired in those long harsh years in Russia.

Then it was Friday night and there was no more he could do. By now, Peiper knew he should have fallen into a heavy sleep. But sleep was impossible. It was always the same before combat, he told himself. One never got used to it; the nervous tension was too great. As he lay

there in his cot at the headquarters of General Engel's
12th People's Grenadier Division, the noise outside told
him others could not sleep either. Somewhere a little
group of young soldiers were singing. Their tunes were
not the bold marching songs they were taught by number
in their recruit depots, but those of an older, gentler
Germany, strangely haunting and emotive. Then they
sang the popular little ditty of that year, one which in
the bitter years to come Jochen Peiper, alone in his cell,
would always associate with that long night:

   'Es geht alles voruber,
   Es geht alles vorbei.
   Nach jedem Dezember,
   Kommt wieder ein Mai…"[6]

For a moment, Peiper's hard face relaxed. They were each
some mother's son, young men of half a dozen national-
ities remembering a woman's face, warm and loving. Now
they were far from home and about to go into battle. How
many of them, he wondered, would survive what was to
come? Then he closed his eyes again and fell into a dead
sleep, the silly, sad song forgotten…

PART TWO

THE COUNTER-ATTACK

'Drive hard, Peiper, and hold the reins loose.'

General Kraemer,
Chief-of-Staff 6th SS Panzer Army

1. 'THE HOUR OF DESTINY HAS STRUCK'

At one minute after midnight on Saturday, 16 December 1944, the Bletchley night shift was alerted. For weeks, with no messages coming through from Germany, the staff of the crypt-analytic and processing huts had begun to believe that the war had passed them by. They were jaded, too, with the months of highly concentrated effort that had followed D-Day. Now, abruptly, the German High Command was transmitting once again after long weeks of total silence. What was going on? Why had the long silent front in Western Europe suddenly burst into activity once more?

Tensely, the men and women of the night shift stood by. Some of them already realised that there was going to be another flap and dreaded what was to come. It wouldn't be the first time that some of them had been unable to stand the strain when the balloon went up and had collapsed with nervous tension. The minutes went by with leaden feet while they waited anxiously for the first decode.

Then they had it at last. Hastily, they grouped round the boffin in charge as he started to read it out by the poor light of the naked bulbs of their Nissen hut. It was from no less a person than Field Marshal Gerd von Rundstedt and it was addressed to all his commanders in the field to be passed on to subordinate units. It read: 'The hour of destiny has struck. Mighty offensive armies face the Allies. Everything is at stake. More than mortal deeds are required as a holy duty to the Fatherland.'

The men and women of the night shift looked at each other in bewilderment. Outside all was silent. The hutted encampment in the grounds of that Victorian Gothic red-brick house was shrouded in fog, dampening all sound. What did the midnight message mean? What were these 'mighty offensive armies'? *What* was at stake? What 'more than mortal deeds' were required at a time when everyone knew Germany was virtually defeated? Why, everyone in his right senses regarded the coming Christmas festival to be the last one of the war!

Some six hundred kilometres away in the Eifel-Ardennes area of the German-Belgian border, also shrouded in fog, the young soldiers of the first wave waited, crouched in the frozen shrubs in their white camouflaged suits. In the fields on both sides of the lithe country roads, the artillerymen waited expectantly around their cannon. On the roads themselves the tanks and half-tracks, the self-propelled guns and the trucks stood nose to nose, their commanders looking at the glowing dials of their wristwatches time and time again. All was tense, nerve-racking expectancy. From Monschau in the north to Echternach in the south, a hundred long kilometres of front, the artillery commanders phoned back their reports: 'All batteries ready to fire.'

Here and there the infantrymen and the tankers exchanged the usual nervous quips: '*See you in America… Don't drink all the cognac before I get there… Watch out for those French m'selles…*' Others urinated. A few of the bolder ones took a few hasty last puffs at forbidden cigarettes cupped in the shelter of their frozen hands. Then it came. From the gun commanders, as they brought their right hands down sharply, '*Feuer frei!*'

It was exactly five-thirty on the morning of 16 December. Suddenly, startlingly, frighteningly, the complete length of the ghost front erupted into fire and flame. The whole weight of the artillery of three armies, ranging from 3-inch mortars to 16-inch railway guns, descended upon the unsuspecting men of the four US divisions holding that long line. The morning stillness was ripped apart by that obscene, man-made storm, as the infantry, some of them cheering wildly, burst from the snow-heavy forests, followed by tanks, hundreds of them, cannon swinging back and forth like the snouts of primeval monsters scenting out their prey. The offensive had commenced!

An anxious Peiper was already up and waiting at General Engel's 12th People's Grenadiers' HQ by now. But as the messages came flooding in to the farmhouse HQ, with dispatch-riders skidding to a stop in the mud outside, the telephone ringing and self-important staff officers holding papers striding back and forth, it was clear that Engel's leading elements were not making the progress expected. All morning Peiper, growing angrier by the minute, waited for the expected breakthrough. But it didn't come. At two that afternoon, with Engel's grenadiers still apparently held up at the frontier, he left the HQ.

In the meantime, his battle group had left its base and was collecting immediately behind the infantry. When Peiper arrived on the scene, he found to his horror that his command was mixed up in a huge traffic jam made up of his own vehicles, others of the *Leibstandarte*, and those of the 3rd Para and the 12th People's Grenadiers. Meanwhile, enemy artillery was dropping shells on the jam.

As one of Peiper's young recruits described it afterwards: 'Nobody knew what to do till finally somebody had enough sense to give the order to dig in. When we had finished digging in, the order came through to mount up again… We advanced 500 metres and then we stopped again.'

Peiper, his temper mounting all the time, knowing just how important the element of surprise was, raced to the front of his stalled column. He found out that now they had bumped into a section of destroyed road.

Swiftly, he solved the problem by ordering his column to push ruthlessly ahead, shouldering any vehicle in its path off the road. A little while later, his column ran into a minefield, which should have been cleared by the *Leibstandarte's* engineers. It hadn't been. So again, Peiper took ruthless measures. He ordered a group of half-tracks to lead the way over the mines. Two of them were blown up but in the end the column was through without further losses, and as darkness fell the battle group was finally across into Belgium, the thin American line of main resistance broken, and heading for the dark wooded ridges beyond. *Kampfgruppe Peiper* was heading for the Meuse…

–

By midnight, Peiper's column was rolling into the first village on the ridge-line, Lanzerath. It had cost him three tanks and five halftracks to get so far, and his mood was not of the best. The village had been captured by the men of the 3rd Para's 9th Regiment, but there was no sign of the paras. No guides, no sentries, no nothing. One of his own men appeared out of the freezing darkness in the village's single street and a fuming Peiper told him he thought it looked as if the Ninth had gone to bed instead of waging war. 'They've got their CP [Command Post] over here, sir,' the man replied.

Peiper dropped to the ground and followed the man to the village's only *Gasthaus*, Cafe Palm, a two-storey structure with a slate roof and grey wooden shingles nailed to its walls. He flung open the door and was disgusted by what he saw. Dirty, unshaven paras were asleep everywhere. One of them was snoring on top of the zinc-covered bar and in the corner huddled wounded *Ami* prisoners. One of them, twenty-one-year-old Lieutenant Bouck, described what happened: 'About twelve, a group of officers came into the room. They were busy and excited about the situation. A map kept falling off the table at the far side of the room. One of the officers stuck the map against the wall with two bayonets.'[7]

Peiper treated Colonel Hoffmann, who had spent the war in the German Air Ministry up to now, with contempt, even though the para was senior to him. He demanded to know what lay in front of him. Colonel Hoffmann, the commander of the 9th Para, was decidedly vague about his men's dispositions. Without asking the older man's permission, Peiper grabbed the phone and called the major in charge of the paras dug in outside the village. What did he know of the *Amis* facing him, Peiper snapped.

The para major admitted he had his information from a captain, one of his company commanders. Peiper ordered the captain brought to the phone and repeated his question. The embarrassed captain said he hadn't seen the

American positions personally; he had his information from one of his noncoms.

Peiper gave up. He slammed down the phone in rage and told Hoffmann he wanted one of his three battalions. He wasn't going to risk his own precious *panzergrenadiers* at this stage of the offensive. Let the paras take the casualties if there really were *Amis* out there, which he doubted.

Hoffmann blustered and argued, but, in the end, he agreed to give Peiper his 1st Battalion. Hurriedly, Peiper gave out his orders. The 1st Battalion would attack the next objective, the little low railway station at the hamlet of Buchholz, at zero four hundred hours. Till then the men could get whatever sleep they could.

For his part, Peiper could not rest. There were more important things to do than waste the next three hours in sleep. He had to plan. Thus, while the others dozed once more, Peiper sat at the big scrubbed wooden table in the bar of the Cafe Palm (it is still there) brooding this new Sunday morning. It was 17 December. Little did he realise that this day would change his whole life. While the men all around him, German and American, would one day slip back into the decent obscurity of their civilian lives (if they survived), this Sunday forgotten with the years, the events of 17 December would haunt *him* till the day thirty-two years hence when finally he was murdered.

–

Just before dawn, *Kampfgruppe Peiper* caught up with the tail end of a large convoy of American vehicles 'bugging out'. As Peiper had suspected, there were no *Amis* at Buchholz, which had been taken by the paras without casualties (though unknown to Peiper there *was* an American radio operator concealed in a cellar there, broadcasting the first account of Peiper's force to the rear). Now with the American Army in the Ardennes in what seemed full retreat, Peiper was taking full advantage of the confusion. For he needed fuel badly and he thought by following this column into Buellingen he might obtain the precious '*Sprit*' before the *Amis* had a chance to blow up their depot.

Trailing the Americans, the German column stole into the village of Honsfeld, which was still shrouded in icy pre-dawn greyness. The paras he had taken from Colonel Hoffmann crept from house to house, guarding his tanks from any sudden *Ami* bazooka attack. Unprotected tanks in a built-up area were an easy target for enemy missile-launchers.

At the entrance to the village, Lieutenant Robert Reppa, of a cavalry reconnaissance squadron that was not fleeing with the rest, was trying to get some sleep sitting on a hard chair when he noticed a change in the sound of the retreating traffic. The Sherman doesn't sound like that, he told himself, and was immediately wide awake. He jumped from his chair and strode to the door. He flung it open. Before him was a huge tank, twice the size of the American Sherman. He slammed the door closed and whispered, 'My God, they're Germans!' What was he going do?

Meanwhile the paras were rounding up his men and having a merry time of it, too. As one of them recalled after the war: 'There were *Amis* everywhere. We disarmed them at once and broke up their weapons. Then we drove them on to the street and started to count our loot – in chocolate and cigarettes.' Not for long.

'Just as were about to mount up again all hell broke loose. Firing started from the windows to the far end of the village. An *Ami* mortar opened up on us, too. Our tank commander turned his cannon round on an enemy machine gun and scored a direct hit.'

Fierce house-to-house fighting broke out. Tracer zipped back and forth. Slugs howled off walls. Men screamed with sudden pain. Everywhere there rose the cries of the wounded, in English and German, '*Medic… Sanitater…*'

American dive-bombers appeared as if from nowhere, perhaps summoned by that brave lone radio operator. They fell screaming out of the sky. As Corporal Fruhbeisser, a para now attached to Peiper's command, recalled: 'Immediately our mobile flak took up the challenge… The air was full of flying 20 mm shells. *The Ami* planes broke off the attack and fled. But almost immediately *Ami* shells began falling on Honsfeld. All was confusion and sudden death.'

Peiper made a snap decision. He had been discovered, of course. But he was not going to be bogged down in this unimportant skirmish. Leaving a few tanks behind to support the paras, still hanging on to his own precious panzer grenadiers, he set off once more. He *had* to reach Buellingen and that vital fuel, or soon his tanks would run dry. Already he had used twice the amount of petrol he had calculated for this distance.

Buellingen proved easy. After destroying a couple of dozen light American observation planes on the ground, he rolled into the village against only slight opposition to find the *Ami* petrol dump still intact. Now he had the precious *Sprit* he needed for the next stage of his attack.

Two hours later, the tanks of his vehicles full to the brim, he was on his way again. The River Meuse and that vital bridge at Huy were a mere eighty kilometres away…

-

As we shall see, Peiper's bold drive behind the American lines for the Meuse would not succeed. But because it took place in conjunction with two other operations to the rear of the US front, it was exaggerated in the Allied camp out of all proportion to its real worth.

Attached to Peiper's battle group, there were several of those special teams recruited that autumn by Peiper's old comrade-in-arms, Colonel Skorzeny. Now in captured American Jeeps, these four-men teams were ranging far and wide ahead of Peiper's leading panzers, carrying out missions that they knew could result in their death in front of an enemy firing squad.

Back in 1942, the big, scar-faced Viennese whom Eisenhower would soon call 'the most dangerous man in Europe' had been invalided out of the *Leibstandarte* in Russia. Almost immediately, he had been recruited by Himmler to set up the *SS Jagdkommando*, the German equivalent of the SAS. Throughout 1943, the *Jagdkommando* had carried out long-range penetration missions in Russia, rescued Mussolini from imprisonment and, in 1944, kept Hungary in the war on Germany's side by kidnapping the son of the Hungarian dictator, Admiral Horthy, in Budapest.

One month later, Skorzeny had been empowered by Hitler personally to set up a special brigade, Brigade 150, to be composed of men who spoke American-English, would wear American uniform and drive American vehicles. It would be the mission of the brigade to spearhead the drive through the Ardennes, committing acts of sabotage, carrying out long-range reconnaissance and generally causing as much confusion and chaos behind the US lines as possible.

In the event, Skorzeny had found it difficult to find enough English-speaking volunteers to form a whole brigade, and it was the same with American equipment; the German Army had not captured enough of it for 3,000-odd soldiers. Still, Skorzeny had improvised, using disguised German tanks etc., and now two hundred of his best American-English speakers, broken down into four-man Jeep teams, were risking their lives far behind the US front.

One team had already successfully cut the land line between General Bradley's HQ in Luxembourg and General Hodges', whose army was currently under attack, at Spa. Another had penetrated the biggest town to Peiper's front, Malmedy, and had reported that the *Amis* were fleeing through it in panic. Another team had boldly posed as American MPs and had succeeded in directing a whole American regiment down the wrong road. And another had already reached that bridge at Huy and radioed back that it was totally unguarded, wide open for the taking.

Then, for one of the teams, luck ran out. At the little frontier township of Poteau, a sergeant watched as an American self-propelled gun approached, fleeing from Peiper's attack. He frowned. As the metal monster started to roll past, he thought the boots of the 'American soldiers' riding it looked strange. Before he could challenge them, one of the men on the deck cried cheerfully: 'We're from E Company!' Now the sergeant knew there was something wrong. In the cavalry, to which these men supposedly belonged, you spoke of 'squadrons' or 'troops', not 'companies'.

He rapped out a quick order. He and his men opened fire. The 'Americans' died instantly. Moments later their killers, worried that they might well have shot their own comrades by mistake after all, were examining the bodies to find that the dead men were wearing German uniforms under the American ones. The first of Skorzeny's teams had been discovered.

One day later, the second Skorzeny team would be captured alive and, before they were shot by firing squad, interrogated. They confessed everything about the long-range operation, including something that Skorzeny had not planned. It was based on a rumour that had circulated in the Brigade 150's training camp and which the scar-faced giant had not denied at the time, that fifty of these German-Americans were to rendezvous at the Cafe de la Paix in Paris and then were to launch an assassination attempt on no less a person than the Supreme Commander!

If that was not sufficient cause for alarm in the Allied camp, there was another long-range operation taking place to support Peiper's right flank. It was the last German parachute mission of the war. Here some 1,200 German paras were to drop on and round the highest point in Belgium, Mont Rigi, to cut the road network there and prevent reinforcements coming from the north to help stop the SS's drive for the Meuse. The operation went badly wrong. The pilots of the transports were poorly trained and there was a high wind blowing at the time of the night drop. As a result, the 1,200 paras were scattered widely over all the part of Belgium, as were the dummies in uniform that had been tossed out of the transports with them. As a result, German paras were reported throughout the Low Countries and France, setting off a German para-spy scare like the one that had demoralised the Belgian and French armies back in 1940. Again, civilians everywhere began reporting 'nuns who need a shave', ie disguised Germans, and again the order went out officially that any suspect nun should be stripped to the waist (preferably by another woman wherever possible). If she/he had angry red marks over the shoulders and chest, this would indicate a German spy had been caught; for the red marks meant the suspect had been recently wearing a parachute harness.

But not only were the civilians caught in what now turned into an unprecedented spy scare, the military were too. Both the para drop and Skorzeny's long-range opera-tion would turn out to be failures, militarily speaking, but they were tremendous victories in what we would today call psychological warfare.

Just like the civilians, the Allied top brass 'spied nuns doing up their garters behind every bush', as Jean Cocteau phrased it cynically. Eisenhower became practically a pris-oner in his own HQ. Whenever he moved, even to cross from his office to the mess, he was accompanied by a squad of MPs armed with sub-machine guns and preceded by a tank. For ten long days he would be cut off from his commanders and when finally he did decide to see Montgomery about the battle, he left his double behind in Paris to attract the 'Skorzeny killers' and set off by train, accompanied by a whole company of MP guards.

Montgomery later told his crony General Simpson: 'It was most impressive. The train drew into the station and immediately teams of machine-gunners leapt out, placed their machine guns on both platforms at each end of the train and guards leapt out and took up every possible vantage point. No question of letting any German assassination troops get at the Supreme Commander.' Montgomery, who had twice been warned by the War Office while in Normandy not to expose himself unnecessarily to enemy fire, commented, tongue in cheek, that he 'felt rather naked just arriving with a solitary armoured car' behind him.

Bradley suffered a similar term of voluntary imprisonment. He lost all contact with his field commanders save Patton, who moved to his HQ in Luxembourg to be with him. He was ordered to remove the three stars from his helmet and vehicle, and when he left his office, now by the back door, he was driven to his billet in an armoured car followed by squads of heavily armed MPs. Everywhere, thousands of soldiers were wasted setting up roadblocks to catch the para spies and fake Americans. Hundreds of GIs were wrongly arrested by their own people because they didn't know who 'dem bums' were or the name of Betty Grable's husband. It became so bad that Montgomery, travelling around in his battered old Rolls Royce adorned with the biggest Union Jack he could find so everyone knew who *he* was, asked Eisenhower for an American ID card. He was being stopped too often by zealous American MPs. One American general, hurrying to take over the defence of a threatened Belgian town, was actually arrested and imprisoned for twelve hours because he didn't know the answer to those 'damnfool questions'. Then, when his identity was finally established, his captors had the gall to ask for his autograph!

Now a third element would be added to the growing spy scare and panic this Sunday, 17 December 1944, and it would be Peiper's own men who would instigate it. Up to now, it had all been something of a joke, with, as

General Bradley commented after the war, 'a half million GIs play[ing] cat and mouse with each other each time they met on the road.' Now the farce was to turn into tragedy.

—

Just after Peiper's column left Buellingen, Peiper, himself just behind the point, came across a surprised American lieutenant-colonel. The officer had been heading for the front with a small convoy when he bumped into the SS. But the American recovered quickly and was astonishingly talkative for a senior officer. He told Peiper, who spoke excellent English as well as French, that at their next objective, Ligneuville, there was an American general billeted at the Hotel du Moulin.

He was General Timberlake, head of the 49th Anti-Aircraft Brigade, whose guns were ranged along the front in order to knock down the V-I missiles aimed at Liege and London. The prospect of capturing an *Ami* general intrigued Peiper. He suddenly wanted to add the unknown *Ami* to his collection of Yugoslav, Greek, Italian and Russian generals whom he had captured in the past. A sudden, bold strike and he might well capture the American sitting down to his Sunday lunch with his staff at the Hotel du Moulin, which surprisingly enough was German-owned and renowned for its cuisine. Why, before the war, the King of Belgium and his ill-fated Queen, Astrid, had eaten there before she suffered her tragic fatal accident while climbing in the nearby Ardennes!

It was just then, when Peiper was making his decision, that he heard the sound of shell fire to his immediate front. He flushed with anger. It was German fire all right, and it damn well might just alert the *Ami* general to the impending danger! He sprang into his vehicle and yelled a command to his driver. They moved off at speed.

Eight kilometres beyond, *Obersturmfuhrer* Sternebek, commander of the point, which consisted of two Panthers, was observing the crossroads at the little hamlet of Baugnez. It was just after midday and the military policeman who had been directing the traffic at the crossroads – which the GIs with a total lack of originality called 'Five Points', because five roads ran into it – had gone over to the nearby Cafe Bodarwe for a cup of coffee. Now Private Homer Ford, carbine slung over his shoulder, was stamping his frozen feet there and waiting for a slow-moving convoy to climb the long incline that led to the crossroads from the town of Malmedy.

Sternebek waited too. The convoy was completely soft-skinned: a tempting target for his gunners. In a whisper, he ordered them to load high explosive. They wouldn't need armour-piercing shells for this little lot. 'Immediately we opened fire,' he recalled after the war, 'several vehicles of the US convoy began to burn. But as we started to move to the crossroads at Baugnez, we were shot at with rifle and machine-gun fire. We returned the fire with our turret machine guns. Then as the lead tank was about sixty or seventy metres away from them, the Americans started to raise their hands in surrender.'

This then was the first encounter of Battle Group Peiper with an obscure American field observation battery, Battery B of the 285 Field Observation Battalion. It was a green outfit, as yet unattached to a corps or division, but in the manner of its death it would achieve greater fame than it would ever have done in combat. In the years to come, American presidents, senators, secretaries of state for defence, German chancellors and bishops, the Pope himself, would involve themselves in the fate of that particular American artillery battalion. For most of the men now shivering at the crossroads with their hands in the air, as behind them their vehicles burned fiercely, had less than an hour to live...

A little while later Peiper himself appeared at the crossroads. He rapped out an order that there would be no more firing. He didn't want the *Ami* general at his HQ only five kilometres away to be alarmed and alerted. Slowly, he started to drive by the new prisoners. Later he would report: 'Apart from a number of dead and wounded, injured and killed in that initial outburst, the prisoners could be divided into three groups. The first was those whose hands were tucked behind their helmets and had surrendered. The next group lay near the edge of the road and pretended to be dead. I remember well how some of my soldiers fired warning shots above them indicating they shouldn't play any games. Then there was a third group doing the same, but close to the edge of a wood, to which they were attempting to crawl when we weren't looking. Again our soldiers fired at them whenever they saw them moving.' And that was that as far as Jochen Peiper personally was concerned. He would have nothing further to do with the survivors of Battery B, whether they had surrendered or were pretending to be dead. His aim was now Ligneuville and General Timberlake of the 49th Anti-Aircraft Brigade.

2. 'THE FIRST SS WELCOMES YOU TO BELGIUM, GENTLEMEN'

Artillery Second-Lieutenant Lary's Jeep was hit almost immediately; the battery had been surprised by the German shell fire. He and Captain Keele, in charge of the convoy, dropped in the ditch at the side of the road together with their driver, Corporal Lester.

'Do you think it's a patrol which has broken through… or is it too heavy for a patrol?' Lary gasped to Keele.

The Captain shook his head. 'No, the fire is too intense,' he replied.

'Let's crawl up this ditch,' Lary suggested, 'and try to make a stand for it beside that house we've just passed.'

Keele agreed. The three of them, keeping as low as possible, began to crawl back to the Cafe Bodarwe.

They didn't get far. Abruptly, they were startled by the rattle of tank tracks on the road. Lary took a chance. He peeped over the edge of the ditch. Almost opposite was a huge black monster with the black-and-white cross on its metal side all too obvious. It was a German Panther. He dropped back into the ditch and pretended to be dead. The tank passed. But it was already too late to make a stand. Next to the cafe some twenty-odd GIs of the battery were raising their hands in surrender.

Lary attempted to rally them, but was dissuaded by Corporal Daub. The latter pointed up the road and said:

'Look up that road.' The officer did so. A whole column of German tanks and half-tracks was rattling down it. Hurriedly, Lary turned and sprinted back to where he had left Captain Keele.

The Captain was squatting in a crouched position, making no movement. 'Are you hit, Captain?' Lary asked anxiously. He was only twenty-one; he didn't want the responsibility of taking over the battery in this critical situation. Keele didn't reply.

Desperately Lary tried again.

Finally, Keele hissed: '*No...* Go away or they will come back and kill me!' Lary persisted, saying that it was no use feigning death. The Krauts would examine the 'bodies' anyway. Finally, Keele was persuaded. He joined the rest, hands raised in surrender.

Now the survivors of the artillery attack waited for the enemy. Lary pulled off his gold second-lieutenant's bars, hoping he would be taken for an enlisted man. Why, he was never able to explain later. Green as he was, he must have known officers received more favourable treatment in POW camps than did enlisted men. Perhaps Lary simply did not want to be singled out as an officer who would be forced to make decisions.

From his hiding place in the cafe, to which he had fled as soon as the firing had broken out the traffic, MP Homer Ford watched as the panzer grenadiers of Major Josef Diefenthal's 2nd Panzer Grenadier Battalion started to round up the prisoners. Later, Ford would identify Diefenthal personally because the Major wore a light tan US combat jacket over his own tunic. The Germans herded their prisoners to a field at the side of the cafe, robbing them of their warm winter gloves and other odds and ends as they did so.

Madame Bodarwe, the owner of the cafe, whose husband was fighting with the German Army in Russia, now felt it safe to come out and watch the proceedings. With her she had the farmer who lived opposite, Henri Le Joly. His brother was also in the German Army and his father had been a German soldier. He was frankly pro-German.[8] Some time later they were joined by a fifteen-year-old boy named Pfeiffer from one of the border villages. So there were now three civilian witnesses for what was going to happen.

Ford, for his part, had time just to watch Diefenthal and his men move off after Peiper in the direction of Ligneuville, when his hiding place was surrounded by the SS, and he and the rest of the men hiding there were rounded up. Now apart from one lone American, Sergeant Warren Schmidt, feigning dead, his 'body' immersed in a foot of water, the only living Americans at the Five Points crossroads were prisoners. The time was now about one-thirty in the afternoon.

–

While the tragic events at the Five Points crossroads started to take their course, Peiper, at the point of the battle group, was rattling down the steep hill that led to Ligneuville, intent on taking that *Ami* general. A Sherman tank of the US 9th Armored Division, which had broken down in the village, attempted to stop the Panthers. But the American tank was immobile and outgunned. Although it managed to cover the retreat of a convoy of US trucks fleeing from Ligneuville, it could not escape itself. Finally, a German armour-piercing shell slammed into its side, and that was the end of all resistance at Ligneuville.

Obersturmführer Sternebek in the lead tank rolled to a stop outside the Hotel du Moulin. As he reported later: 'The hotel owner seemed to be expecting us. I was ready to ask him if there were any enemy soldiers in the place when he said, "Good day, Mr Officer, the General and his staff have just departed a few minutes ago. He expects to return by Christmas."'

Sternebek was so surprised by this reply from Monsieur Rupp, the hotel proprietor, that he forgot to ask about enemy soldiers. Instead: 'I dropped from the tank, ran inside the hotel and found the table was still set for dinner. There were cigarettes still smoking in the ashtrays and half-consumed drinks everywhere. This proved just how hurriedly the General and his staff had fled.'

As Peiper summed it up, 'We got there too late and only captured their lunch', to which his men now helped themselves greedily. In the meantime, Peiper prepared his command for the next stage of the drive towards the Meuse. It was to be cross-country, taking a narrow winding steep road through the hills behind the hotel, which had marked the border between Imperial Germany and Belgium up to 1914. But before he could start, he would have to wait for the arrival of the divisional commander, General Mohnke, who would set up his forward command post in the Hotel du Moulin.

Thus it was, while his men enjoyed the General's lunch and the free cigarettes and drinks, Peiper was slightly disturbed by the sound of renewed firing to his rear. He frowned. Had there been an *Ami* counter-attack? But after a few moments the firing died away again and he dismissed the matter from his mind. He had other and more important things to do. The firing must just have been some minor rearguard skirmish. In fact, it was the start of World War Two's most infamous *cause celebre*.

–

'*The Malmedy Massacre!*' Jochen Peiper would snort in anger a quarter of a century later. 'Who knows and who cares any more? No one – *no one* – will ever sort out the mess now! Too many lies have been told these last twenty-five years'.[9]

Indeed, although there have been a good dozen books written about the events that took place at that crossroads on Sunday, 17 December 1944, what really happened is still in dispute. Naturally, in the climate of opinion that prevailed after the war, no one in the Allied camp was prepared to believe the statements of the Germans present. Those statements, made by members of Peiper's command in 1945-6, are generally regarded as suspect, forced out of them by illegal means. As for the three Belgian witnesses, Madame Bodarwe, M. Henri Le Joly and the boy Pfeiffer, no member of the American war crimes team attempted to approach them and try to find out what they knew. So what became known as the 'Malmedy Massacre', because the nearest large town to the hamlet of Baugnez was Malmedy, is based strictly and exclusively on the statements of the American survivors.

This is the picture that emerged. The survivors of Battery B were joined by some twenty other American prisoners taken by Battle Group Peiper, including engineers, MPs and two medical corps men, Samuel Dobyns and Roy Anderson, both of the US 99th Division. According to their testimony there were 150 prisoners at the crossroads before the trouble started. Henri Le Joly estimated there were thirty-odd, while *Obersturmfuhrer* Flacke, who was with Diefenthal's panzer grenadiers, thought there were about twenty of them.

The prisoners knew from their observations that their captors were SS because they bore the SS runes on their collars and helmets, and one of them had said mockingly in English: 'The First SS welcomes you to Belgium, gentlemen.'

By now most of Peiper's advance force had passed through on the way to Ligneuville. But there were his engineers and the heavy tank company, Number 501, still to come, and a self-propelled gun was causing a minor traffic jam because it was having trouble getting round the sharp corner at Five Points. Finally, it managed it and two Mark IV tanks appeared and were manoeuvred into position so that they could bring their turret machine guns to bear on the prisoners if necessary. Their numbers were 731 and 732.

This meant they belonged to the third platoon of the 7th Company. The last digit of the three identified the tanks even further. Number 731 was crewed by Sergeant Hans Siptrott as tank commander, Corporal Gerhard Schaeffer as driver, Private Arnhold as radioman and Corporal Wetengel as gunner, with Private Georg Fleps as his assistant. The latter, a Rumanian-German, one of those many 'booty Germans' now recruited into the SS, was in the turret of his tank with his pistol pointed at the prisoners. Number 732 was commanded by a Sergeant Clotten, but only two of his crew were ever identified. They were Corporal Koewitz and Private Vogt. The identification of the self-propelled gun, which belonged to Diefenthal's panzer grenadiers, who had already left the scene, made it clear that the two tanks were under the command of Major Poetschke, now the most senior officer still in the area. Unfortunately for the clarification of what happened at Baugnez, Poetschke (born, incidentally, in Brussels in 1914, making him a Belgian by birth) was killed in action in Hungary in March 1945.

As the SS prisoners told their American interrogators under great pressure after the war, Poetschke strode over to Siptrott in 731 and said: 'The prisoners are to be killed and it must be done quickly. Everybody is needed up ahead and there is no time to waste.'

Siptrott replied: 'But I don't have much ammunition, sir.'

The Major told him he was to do as he was ordered. Reluctantly Siptrott looked at Fleps, the booty German.

Raising his pistol, Fleps took aim. He fired. His bullet hit Lieutenant Lary's driver, who was standing immediately beside him (or so Lieutenant Lary said two years later when he was able to point out Fleps unerringly in the dock after only seeing him for a few seconds in 1944). The driver went down, falling backwards, carrying with him several other GIs in the next row.

Panic broke out. GIs shouted in alarm. Private James Massara from Battery B and a medic, Samuel Dobyns, pushed their way to the rear rank. They seemed to sense what was coming. Fearing that the terrified soldiers would make a run for it and bring down more fire on themselves, Lary cried out: '*Stand fast!*'

Fleps fired again. Why he used his pistol instead of the turret machine gun, which he should have used if he were really intent on massacring the American prisoners, was never explained. A doctor next to Sergeant Ken Ahrens went down. Someone cried in German (according to the American survivors) '*Schlag sie tot, die Hunde*' – 'kill them, the dogs'. On both tanks the machine guns opened up. The prisoners fell in heaps. Some were genuine casualties. Others were men who reacted quickly and pretended to be hit.

Methodically, the gunners worked their way up and down the ranks of the prisoners until, according to Fleps, there was only one American left standing. At that moment Corporal Schaeffer started the engine and he overbalanced, hurting his leg.

Within five minutes it was all over. By about ten past two, when 731 began to move off down the road that led to Ligneuville, silence had returned and the field was littered with the bodies of the dead and the dying.

But there were some there on the bloody field who weren't dead – yet. Among them there was Lary, wounded in the foot and legs; Ahrens, shot in the back; Dobyns, who had been commended in Normandy, ironically enough for having rescued Germans under fire and who was now wounded four times; and Privates Massara and Reem, who had not been wounded at all. Now they planned to escape.

But before they could do so, a new horror was inflicted upon them. An SS engineer battalion passed and some of its members began walking among the fallen, administering the *coup de grace*. If a body moved, a pistol was placed to the base of the man's skull and the back of his head was blown off. After the war, one of the SS, Jakob Weiss, testified at his trial that the engineers checked whether *the Amis* were dead or alive by kicking them in the testicles. He also testified that one of the engineers pulling the boots off a still alive American said: 'You can go back to sleep now.' Whereupon he shot him in the head. Weiss then added for good measure that he spotted

Private Gustav Sprenger, aged eighteen, kill five mortally wounded *Amis* with his pistol, laughing 'hysterically' all the while.

To Ahrens, all the SS killers seemed to be laughing. 'Maniacal', was Lary's description of it. Ahrens, feigning death, watched as a medic from Battery B, unable to stand the moans of a man lying wounded next to him, rose and gave first aid. A German engineer waited until he was finished, then cold-bloodedly shot both men. He, too, walked away, 'laughing'.

Lary heard a German approaching him. A pistol barked. The bullet shattered the head of the man next to him. Lary tensed for the inevitable. Nothing happened. The German muttered, '*Tod*' (dead) and, obviously thinking the young officer was already finished, walked away.

Finally, the firing died away altogether. The survivors – officially they were listed as numbering forty-four – listened as vehicle after vehicle rumbled away. Now they began to whisper: 'Anyone else alive…? Any of you guys still alive?'

Whispered responses came from all sides. Men started to plan a breakout. In the end there seemed to have been some twenty men unhurt or lightly wounded who were prepared to take the risk. Lary urged them to wait for darkness. It could be only a matter of an hour or so before it became dark at this time of the year, and there were German soldiers at the crossroads a few metres away.

But the survivors had had enough. Besides, it was freezing cold lying in the grass. Finally Private Massara, who was unwounded, jumped to his feet and *yelled* – surprisingly enough – '*Let's go!*'

They sprang to their feet and started pelting across the fields that led down the slope towards Malmedy. For a moment the handful of Germans at the Five Points crossroads were too surprised to move. Then they opened in a wild burst of fire. Lary, arms working like pistons, going all out, saw one man go down. But the rest kept on running.

Massara, Reem, Smith, Profanchik, Ford, Ahrens and three unidentified men reached the woods two hundred metres beyond Cafe Bodarwe. Twelve others swerved towards the cafe itself. Lary yelled a warning. They paid no heed to him. So he ducked into the shed at the back of the cafe, in which Ford had first hidden.

According to Lary, the SS men took a machine gun and set it up outside the cafe. They called upon the Americans to come out. The Americans refused. Thereupon the SS men set fire to the place (with what, Lary never stated). As the panic-stricken GIs tried to scramble out, they were mown down mercilessly.

–

Colonel David Pergrin, the dark-haired, bespectacled twenty-nine-year-old commander of 291st US Engineer Battalion, stationed at Malmedy below the crossroads, heard the angry snap-and-crackle of small-arms fire above the roar of the traffic passing below his office in the town. Instinctively, he guessed Battery B, which he had seen leave Malmedy, had run into trouble. For a while he concerned himself with his own affairs. Malmedy was full of fleeing GIs, panic-stricken Belgian refugees from the frontier villages and some 3,000 German nationals who had been evacuated there when the US Army had first moved into Germany. Now all he had to defend the place, if the Krauts were really up on the heights at Baugnez, was a company of engineers with no combat experience. It was a daunting task. Should he run, too, like the rest?

Already trouble had commenced in Malmedy. There had been some looting, and none of the troops passing through would stay and fight. At quarter past one that afternoon, an artillery unit had been passing through the town. Pergrin had personally appealed to its commander, a major, to stay and help him. The major had refused. After that he had gone to the local barracks just outside Malmedy and asked the commanding officer there if he could have the four hundred replacement infantry waiting to go up to the front from there. The officer had turned him down flat, saying his replacements were urgently needed in Liege, eighty kilometres to the rear, which was a patent lie.

Uncertain and unhappy, Pergrin finally decided to make a personal reconnaissance of the ridge-line to his front to see what was going on. Then he'd make a decision. At half past two then, he set off in his Jeep together with Sergeant Bill Crickenberger, both men being armed with Tommy guns. As their Jeep ground up the long steep incline that led from Malmedy to Baugnez for at least five kilometres, a brooding silence seemed to settle over the Belgian countryside. Pergrin, not an imaginative man, an engineer by training, felt that there was something seriously wrong somewhere. Beyond the bend, the two men left their Jeep. On foot, their weapons at the ready, they climbed to a vantage point in order to get a better view of the crossroads. Pergrin swept the area with his binoculars. But there was nothing, neither enemy nor friendly troops. Battery B seemed to have vanished.

Perhaps five or ten minutes later, four men came running out of the woods to their right, screaming. Pergrin, the ex-college football player, doubled across to them. They were the MP Homer Ford and three comrades. All were mud-stained, bloody and panic-stricken.

Almost incoherent with shock and fear, trembling badly, they stammered something about the Germans having killed *everybody*!

About this time, Lieutenant Tom Stack, one of Pergrin's officers, and another lieutenant were probing the area in front of the engineers' roadblock on the Malmedy-Baugnez road when abruptly three figures rose from a ditch right in front of them.

The other officer hit the Jeep's brakes, while Stack whipped up his Tommy gun. But he didn't fire, for he could see the men were GIs. Again, these survivors were incoherent with shock and fear. Stack loaded the trembling men into the Jeep, whipped round, and off they raced back to the Engineer Battalion aid station in Malmedy itself.

There the collected survivors were fed and dried, and had their wounds attended to, while Pergrin interrogated them once they had calmed down. In essence they all told the same story.

They had surrendered to the SS, had been lined up in three ranks in a field next to the Cafe Bodarwe, where after a while they had been shot down by their captors in cold blood. They had been unarmed and had made no attempt at resistance. For no reason apparent to them, the Germans had opened fire and mown them down.

As he listened, it began to dawn on the Colonel that up there at the crossroads, now obviously in Kraut hands, there had been something akin to a massacre this afternoon; and it was something that ought to be reported to higher headquarters. So, despite his own parlous state in Malmedy, he wrote out a quick report outlining the basic facts and sent it up through 'channels'. Some hours later, the same message, amplified a little and put into 'officialese', was forwarded from First Army HQ to that of General Bradley in Luxembourg. It read: 'SS Troops vicinity L 8199 captured US soldier, traffic MP [this would be Homer Ford] with about two hundred other US soldiers. American prisoners searched. When finished, Germans lined up Americans and shot them with machine pistols and machine guns. Wounded informant who escaped and more details follow later.'

By that evening, Eisenhower himself had the startling news. By midnight the information was on its way to Washington.

The world, however, was going to learn about the Malmedy Massacre not from US official channels, but through the press. Hal Boyle and Jack Belden, both veteran correspondents of *Time* magazine, had celebrated the usual Saturday night wing-ding at base the night before. As a result, they had each risen late with a hangover, eaten a leisurely breakfast and then discovered all the other correspondents had taken off for the new front in the Ardennes. That had not worried the veterans. Belden had reported wars and disasters from all over the world. Boyle, for his part, had reported on the disastrous American rout at Kasserine Pass in Africa back in February 1943. Both fancied they knew just where the Krauts might well be in the Ardennes by now on this early Sunday afternoon. So they headed for Malmedy, the second largest town of the area.

Their hunch paid off. They came across the survivors and, as Hal Boyle said later, he knew they had 'the best story of the war'. They listened while the escapees – 'half frozen, dazed and weeping with rage' – told what had happened at Baugnez.

Lary appeared on the scene, helped down to Malmedy by a friendly Belgian farmer. He shook a bullet out of his foot and with it the bloody remains of some of his toes. 'We didn't have a chance… we didn't have a chance,' he kept repeating through his tears.

After Lary, the last survivor, came in and told his story, the two veteran newspapermen raced back to Spa, the headquarters of General Hodges' First Army, to file their story. It would be one that went round the world. Now the matter started to escalate. By six o'clock Major General William Kean, First Army's chief-of-staff, knew of the incident from Pergrin's report and the two newspapermen's dispatches. He wrote in his diary: 'There is absolutely no question. General Vanderbilt [the attached Air Force Commander] has told every one of his pilots about it during their briefing.' Later that night in Paris, Hemingway, struggling into his clothes in the Hotel Ritz, getting ready to go to the front in Luxembourg, told his younger brother Leicester to burn all his papers. 'This is the real thing. The SS are massacring our boys up there!'

Some units began to issue orders that no SS or paras would be taken prisoner. A fragment of an order given out by 26th US Infantry Division's 328th Regiment survives: 'No SS troops or paratroopers will be taken prisoner but will be shot on sight.' South of Bastogne, men of the green

US 11th Armored Division would take half a company of captured German soldiers into some woods and shoot them in cold blood. Charles MacDonald, future US Army official historian, then a captain in the 2nd Infantry Division, recounts that two of his men, ordered to take a prisoner to the rear, returned almost immediately. They had shot him in cold blood… And so it went on and on. The horror escalated.

But in a way the incident came as a godsend to the hard-pressed American High Command. By the fifth day of the surprise German attack, more than 25,000 American soldiers would have surrendered to the enemy. Indeed, a mere twenty-four kilometres away from where the survivors were now being interrogated, 10,000 American infantrymen of the ill-fated US 106th Infantry Division were considering surrender. They were trapped in the forest and, green as they were (they had been in the line only five days before the German attack commenced), they were not prepared to fight to the end. In the event, they would lay down their arms, making their surrender the biggest by US troops since the Civil War.

Now the US High Command could stress that it was no use surrendering to the Krauts. If you did, the enemy might shoot you anyway. So it was better to keep your weapon and make a fight for it. That way you had at least a chance of surviving. You ought to hate the Germans, just like those SS killers at Baugnez obviously hated the Americans.

President Roosevelt in far-off Washington made the point quite clear when he was informed of the shocking massacre by his elderly Secretary of State for War, Stimson. 'Well, *now*,' he said cynically and in no way shocked, 'the average GI will hate the Germans just as much as do the Jews.'

—

Who could have know that Sunday what ramifications those events at Baugnez would bring with them? Could anyone, even in his wildest dreams, ever have imagined that they would be the deep concern of a President of the United States; aid the career of that monster who would give his name of one of the ugliest periods of recent American history, McCarthyism; shake US military justice to its foundations long before the My Lai massacre of the Vietnam era; and result thirty-odd years later in the brutal murder of a broken old man in a remote French village? I doubt it strongly.

But that was all in the future. Now as Sunday, 17 December 1944 came finally to a close, the first soft flakes of the new snow had begun to drift down sadly at Baugnez. By midnight the seventy-odd bodies sprawled out in the field near the still smouldering ruins of the burned-out Cafe Bodarwe would be covered by the first mantle of the new snow. More, much more, was to come. It would be another two months before they were seen again – at least by American eyes. By then the US authorities would know who their murderers had been – the men of the *Leibstandarte Adolf Hitler.*

3. 'OH, MY POOR CHILDREN WITHOUT A MOTHER!'

Just after breakfast on the morning of Monday, 18 December, General Hodges, the commander of the US First Army, learned that Peiper's armoured column had broken through and appeared to be heading for Spa, where he had his HQ. Now if the wind was in the right direction, he and his staff officers in the Hotel Britannique – where the German Kaiser had first realised there was no hope for Germany and he would have to surrender to the Western Allies in 1918 – could hear the thunder of the guns coming closer.

The fact that there had been reports of paras dropping everywhere, disguised as Allied soldiers, together with the report of the Malmedy Massacre from Pergrin, and now this, made the staff officers decidedly jumpy. By mid-morning, the civilians were beginning to leave, and those who decided not to had begun to pull down the Allied flags and pictures of Churchill and Roosevelt that had adorned the fronts of their houses. This sense of impending panic transferred itself to the lobby of the grand hotel. 'The canteen commandos', as the frontline soldiers called the rear echelon clerks and typists, started to throw anxious glances through the tall French windows of the Britannique. It was as if they half-expected at any moment to see the first of the enemy panzers barrelling down the steep hill that led into the spa town from the east.

Hodges himself was becoming increasingly jittery. His ADC noted: 'the situation is rapidly deteriorating. It is not yet known whether 12th Army Group full appreciates the seriousness of the situation, though both General Hodges and General Kean [chief of staff] talked with General Bradley half a dozen times during the day.'

Some time that morning one of the US Army's most dashing corps commanders, General 'Lightning Joe' Collins, appeared at the HQ. 'Nice to see you, Joe,' Hodges greeted him. 'Big Simp [General Simpson, commanding the US Ninth Army] is letting me borrow you until we straighten out this mess down here. The Germans have broken through all along the front.'

Just as that moment there was a knock at the door. Colonel Monk Dickson, Hodges' Chief-of-Intelligence, popped his head round and said: 'General, if you don't want to get captured you'd better get out of town. The Germans are only a mile away.'

'Later, later,' Hodges said, forcing a smile, though he could hear both the rumble of artillery and the snap-and-crackle of what might be small-arms fire.

Dickson tried again. 'But General, there is no time to lose.' Hodges waved him away. 'Hm, Joe,' he said to the dashing young corps commander, who looked ten years younger than his forty-eight years, 'you're going to be my strategic reserve.'

By mid-afternoon, though, there was no more time for little jokes. Kean told Hodges then that he ought to be prepared to leave at once and that a Cub plane was waiting to take him away. Hodges agreed.

Now the staff of an army numbering half a million men started to flee in near panic, frightened into frantic haste by a mere 4,000-strong SS battle group. Communications broke down and suddenly Supreme Headquarters had lost touch with one of its major HQs. At the Hotel Britannique, the terrified canteen commandos began tossing their kits out of the windows to vehicles waiting below, their drivers impatiently gunning their engines. In the town itself, as the American convoys streamed westwards, with as yet not a German in sight, all evidence of the three-month American presence there had been removed. The mayor himself went over to the local prison and hurriedly released twenty Belgians suspected of having collaborated with the Germans during the Occupation.

Two hours later, when two officers of the US 7th Armored Division drove through Spa, they found it deserted. There was not an American flag in sight and in the gutters they spotted torn-up photos of President Roosevelt. They ventured into the Hotel Britannique. It was completely deserted. On the walls of the abandoned headquarters, they discovered top-secret maps of front-line troop locations. It was obvious to the two combat-experienced officers that the canteen commandos had fled in such a panic that they had left behind information for which a German Intelligence officer would have given a fortune. Sadly, shaking their heads in mock wonder, they went on their way to the battle awaiting them. Even the top brass was 'bugging out' now...

–

Peiper was unaware of his great success. All he knew was that he had failed to capture General Timberlake. He did not know that, this long Sunday, he had achieved a triumph beyond his wildest dreams: he had forced the headquarters of a whole *Ami* army to flee in panic! And for a while, at least, he had disrupted the communications of the First Army.

Now, after a day of minor skirmishes, which had hampered his progress and forced him to change directions a couple of times, he changed his route somewhat. As Sunday gave way to Monday, his long column of tanks and half-tracks was crawling up the serpentine that led to the hilltop village of La Gleize: a circle of small white-painted houses on the crown of the hill, grouped round the small church and a two-storey-high schoolhouse. Here he would send out a detachment to capture a bridge a couple of kilometres away. Once that was in his hands, he could take the main highway to the town of Werbomont and from thence, with luck, he would roll to the Meuse.

So far, his losses had been light and his food, water and fuel were adequate. If everything went well now, he might well be at Huy on the Meuse within twenty-four hours. Once he had captured the bridge at Huy, his job was over – and he would be glad. He had been without any real sleep for seventy-two hours now. So the slow convoy ground its way to the heights, the huge Tigers bringing up the rear at fifteen kilometres an hour, with Peiper's units in between scattered over thirty kilometres of winding, hilly road. It was a situation fraught with danger, Peiper knew. He had experienced the merciless power of the enemy *jabos* back in Normandy and he both feared and respected it. If the *jabos* caught him in the open, strung out as he was all over the place now, there would be all hell to pay. Peiper felt his nerves begin to tingle electrically with apprehension once again...

The attack came in immediately the overcast lifted that Tuesday. Sergeant Karl Wortmann, who found himself in the middle of the column, remembered many years afterwards what it was like. 'We were stretched out some two kilometres, with a solid wall of rock to our right falling to the valley below. Suddenly sixteen Thunderbolts came hurtling in breast-to-breast from the valley. For us there was absolutely no room to manoeuvre. The tank crews and the panzer grenadiers baled out and crawled under the vehicles, which were laid out for the enemy as if they were presented on silver tablets.

'We did have two flak panzers in the column, both armed with quadruple, quick-firing 20 mm cannon. They opened fire at once. A wall of steel broke in front of the attackers. But the "vultures from the sky", as we called them, came zooming down, attacking us mercilessly, dropping bombs and shooting us up with their machine guns. It was just too much for our two flak panzers.

'Still the gunners kept up their fire, the sweat pouring down their faces, as the enemy planes attacked again and again. Now some of the tank gunners, angered beyond measure, took up the challenge. They grabbed the turret machine guns, set them up on the road, and joined in. But the *jabos* simply couldn't be driven off.

'And all the time we were taking casualties. The medics kept running from one wounded man to another.

'A Thunderbolt was hit. It staggered as if it had run into an invisible wall. Then it came hurtling down in flames to explode in a ball of fire on a hillside nearby. Still the attack continued. Finally, after half an hour, they flew away. Just after that *Obersturmbannfuhrer* Peiper made his appearance and thanked us for our effort in withstanding the attack.'

The attack had cost Peiper three precious hours, plus the loss of several tanks and about a hundred men. But now, at five, it was already dark and the fog was creeping in from the firs once more. Peiper knew he would be safe from the air till morning. He ordered his leading group forward to capture the vital bridge to their front. They needed no urging. Even the youngest soldier among them knew just how important it was to get out of these winding steep hills before the morrow. They set off in a rush…

Ahead of them in the gloom and darkness, a handful of Colonel Pergrin's engineers from the 291st Combat Engineer Battalion, which had been the bane of Peiper's life these past two days as they had blown up bridge after bridge in his line of advance, were squatting in a roadside cafe sorting out explosives. It was too dark to do the job outside.

Meanwhile, one of their sergeants guarding the bridge they were hoping to destroy could hear the rattle of tanks on the other side of the hill. He waded into the stream's icy water and began to set up the leads. Inside the cafe his comrades were similarly alerted by the noise. With fingers that felt like thick, clumsy sausages, they fixed the explosive charges as the noise of the approaching tanks grew ever closer.

Just as the first vehicle topped the rise that led to the bridge, its central span disintegrated in a spectacular flash, followed by a thick mushroom of smoke. Peiper's way forward had been blocked once more. Angry and frustrated, his men turned back the way they had come. Their CO would have to find a new way out of La Gleize.

–

While Peiper fumed in the little hilltop village, wondering what he was going to do on the morrow, unknown to him his rear had already been cut off by the Americans. Now some twenty kilometres or so separated him from the mass of the *Leibstandarte*, and as Mohnke was setting all his hopes on Peiper's spearhead, Peiper ordered an immediate attack to re-establish the link.

The task was given to *Obersturmbannfuhrer* Hansen, an old comrade of Peiper's, one of those blond, hard-faced giants who might well have stepped from an SS recruiting poster.

At the same time, the *Leibstandarte*'s reconnaissance battalion, under the command of another veteran *Sturmbannfuhrer*, Knittel, was also ordered to help re-establish the link with Peiper at La Gleize. In particular, Knittel's team was to regain control of the largest town to Peiper's rear, Stavelot. Knittel's command, which consisted of a few light tanks, light armoured vehicles and some mobile artillery, advanced more quickly than Hansen's panzer grenadiers. Swiftly, Knittel reached the outskirts of Stavelot and set up his command post in a burnt-out farm. There he divided his command into two groups under the orders of Captains Goltz and Koblenz, who would continue the advance to La Gleize on two separate roads.

But already Knittel was able to note a new threat. As he radioed to Mohnke: 'Have reached the outskirts of Stavelot – *under the fire of partisans*' (author's italics). The Malmedy Massacre was already achieving world-wide coverage in the Allied press. Now it seemed that another massacre was in the making as Knittel prepared to deal with those Belgian 'partisans'.

But it was the American forward artillery observers who presented the most immediate danger. They soon spotted Knittel's vehicles, in particular those of Koblenz's command. Hemmed in by a stream on one side of the road and a steep hillside on the other, there was no place for Koblenz to go as a tremendous hail of shells descended. Within minutes, his advance came to an abrupt halt. Then the American gunners turned their attention upon Goltz, who had succeeded in advancing to the next village, where the Belgian villagers ran out to meet them, thinking they were Americans, 'with smiles on their faces'. Those smiles didn't last long.

Two hours later, Knittel, in the basement of the burnt-out farm, had learned that both his commands had suffered serious casualties and that both were pinned down, unable to move forward to help Peiper. In fact, Knittel had lost one third of his strength. Understandably, his mood and that of his men was bitter, more especially as they now knew that Hansen was making no progress towards La Gleize either. *Die Leibstandarte*, the elite of the elite, the Fuehrer's own Praetorian Guard, upon which he had set such high hopes, had come to a complete halt everywhere!

–

According to the Belgian investigators into the events of that third week of December 1944, the killings by the *Leibstandarte* started without warning or any provocation on the part of the local Belgian civilians.

Tony Lambert-Bock, for instance, despite the battle raging all around him, suddenly decided he needed a shave. All morning, while Knittel's men had attempted to move forward, he had hidden with the rest of his family in a cellar. Now he was going to get washed and shaved.

His family told him not to go upstairs. But he ignored their warnings. A moment later they heard him ascend the stairs. A few minutes after that the civilians cowering in the cellar heard a single shot. For a while no one dared to go and see what had happened. In the end Lambert-Bock's son ventured cautiously upstairs. He found his father lying dead on the floor, shaving-soap lather still wet on his unshaven face. Frantically he clattered down the stairs back into the cellar, crying, '*Ils ont tue mon papa!*'

One hour later, five German soldiers of Knittel's outfit forced their way into the house occupied by a Monsieur and Madame Georgin, Madame Counet and the Nicolay family. While two of the Germans checked the upper rooms, the remaining three herded the civilians into the kitchen. One of the SS men yelled threateningly: 'You have been hiding bandits here!'

The terrified Belgians knew well what the SS man meant. The German '*Banditen*' always referred to partisans. 'Bandits – no!' they responded. 'We've had none of them here. No Americans either. Not one.'

The SS didn't believe them. For some reason known only to themselves, the Germans picked out Louis Nicolay and ordered him to go outside. Obediently, he complied.

A few moments later the heavy silence was broken by a single shot. Madame Nicolay started to cry. She knew what that single shot meant.

Now Marcel Georgin was ordered outside. He obeyed tamely enough. But he was *not* going to allow himself to be slaughtered like a dumb animal. The single SS man indicated that the Belgian should walk by him. As he did so, he heard the click of a safety catch being released. He hesitated no longer.

Summoning up all his strength, he bolted. The German shouted. Next moment he fired. The Belgian dropped to the *pave*, feigning death just as the Americans had done at Baugnez.

For five long minutes he lay there, his heart thumping crazily. Then, unable to stand the tension any longer and hoping that the coast was clear, he started to crawl to the bank of the nearby river. He made it. He eased himself carefully into the icy water. He must have made some noise, perhaps a gasp, for now his luck ran out. Just as he thought he was getting away with it, a machine gun began to chatter. (Later, Georgin said it was a German machine gun.)

He felt a tremendous blow in his right arm. It was like the kick of a mule. He dropped heavily on the opposite bank of the river, his arm nearly severed by a vicious salvo of slugs.

Much later, when he was able to return home, he learned from neighbours that his wife and the rest of the civilians who had sheltered in the house that day were dead. Presumably the SS had shot them after he had escaped.

–

That evening and far into the next day, the trapped SS men of Knittel's command shot civilians all along the road that led to La Gleize. The Belgian post-war inquiry found that four civilians were shot at the hamlet of Ster and fifteen outside the place. At the village of Renardmont, nineteen were shot and, again, according to the inquiry, 'their houses set on fire to hide the crimes'. In the village of Parfondray, twenty-six civilians were slaughtered and at the Hurlet Farm just outside the village a dozen civilians were mown down by a German armed with a machine gun. When the SS had departed, the frightened survivors crept out of their hiding places to find the dead ranged from nine-month-old Bruno Klein-Terf to seventy-eight-year-old Josefine Grosjean-Hourrand. There was only one survivor of the massacre, two-year-old Monique Thonon, covered in the blood of her dead mother but still alive.

According to the Belgian sources, the only ones available, Knittel's SS men seemed to have had only one objective that terrible day – the slaughter of as many harmless civilians as possible.

There was one eye-witness: Madame Regine Gregoire. Born a German at the border village of Manderfeld, she spoke German as her native tongue. Now she was a refugee in a house owned by a Belgian family named Legaye, together with her two children.

During the fighting, American soldiers had taken over the top floor of the Legaye house and started sniping at the trapped SS. Towards evening, one of the GIs had come running into the cellar where the civilians cowered in fear and told them that the *Boche* were attacking in force; they, the Americans, were clearing out.

Shortly afterwards, there was a brief fire-fight up above. Then the cellar door was flung open and a grenade tossed in. This was standard operating procedure in house-to-house fighting. The stick grenade exploded with an ear-splitting roar in the confines of the cellar and Madame Gregoire yelped with pain as something struck her leg with the force of a red-hot poker being plunged into her flesh. She had been hit by shrapnel.

But there was no time to concern herself with her wound. For from up above a harsh voice commanded: '*Heraus... raus hier!*'

The Belgians were terrified. They urged Madame Gregoire, whom they knew spoke German, to tell the SS that they were only harmless civilians. Hastily, she did as they commanded. All she got for her pains was that '*raus!*' in an angry, impatient voice.

Madame Gregoire did not dare refuse that harsh command any longer. She led out the file of scared civilians. The rest were ordered into the garden and told to lie near a hedge, while Madame Gregoire was given instructions to tend to one of the SS men who had been wounded. Another soldier handed her a shell dressing to cover the man's wound with, as he lay moaning on a couch, snapping angrily, 'One of you civilians shot at us here.'

'That's not true,' she reported later she had replied. 'It's you who wounded one of us with your grenade.'

For her pains she received a kick and the SS men bellowed at her: 'Don't shout at me like that!'

Soon after that, Madame Gregoire was startled by a fresh outburst of firing. She rushed to the window and saw, according to her own testimony, two soldiers armed respectively with a pistol and a rifle systematically slaughtering the men, women and children crouched terrified near the hedge. Later, this first group of murdered civilians was discovered to be Prosper Legaye, aged sixty-six, his wife Marie, sixty-three, their two daughters Jeanne, forty, and Alice, thirty-nine, and their granddaughter Marie-Jeanne, nine. There were also O. Lecoq, sixty-eight, and Henri Daisomont, aged fifty-two, who had fled the village in 1940 before the advancing

Germans and had sworn he would never do such a thing again.

A few minutes, later another group was cruelly shot, including Madame Prince, who, according to Madame Gregoire, cried just before she was shot: 'Oh, my poor children without a mother!' When the horror was finally over, there remained only Madame Gregoire and her two children alive of the civilians who had taken shelter in the Legaye house. Angrily, she told the SS men standing next to her: 'There was nobody here but innocent civilians!'

The soldier answered: 'The innocent must pay for those who are guilty. The people of Stavelot have been harbouring American soldiers.'

With that she was led away to another cellar. Forty-eight hours later she was rescued by the returning Americans. Surprisingly enough, as the only eye-witness of a brutal atrocity she had survived. No one could ever explain why the SS had not shot her there and then...

–

In the end, according to the immediate post-war inquiry of the Belgian Prince Regent's war crimes commission, the *Leibstandarte* had massacred 130 civilians in the valley of the River Ambleve. There was not a single family in the whole valley who had not lost a relative, as is evidenced by their gravestones to this very day.

In the climate of opinion that reigned at the end of the war, after the release of those terrible details from the Nazi death camps, everyone was prepared to believe the worst of Hitler's own elite guard. The Prince Regent's investigating committee does not seem to have taken into account the fact that the Ambleve valley was the scene of an American barrage of such intensity that it stopped Knittel's two columns in their tracks – and an artillery shell makes no distinction between a soldier and a civilian. Indeed, one day after the Gregoire incident, US machine-gunners killed eight members of the Chalon family as they tried to leave their home at the hamlet of Houmont; the Americans had mistaken them for Germans.

But even if the *Leibstandarte* were not responsible for *all* the deaths, frustrated young SS men must have gone on a rampage. Ever since the fall of Western Europe to German arms in 1940, German security forces had waged a bitter war in the shadows against various resistance and partisan movements. During their retreat to the Reich after the slaughter of Falaise, they had been plagued by French and Belgian partisans all the way until they reached the safety of the *Westwall*.

Panzermeyer, that dashing former member of the *Leibstandarte*, was captured, wounded by the Belgian partisans of the White Army, as it was called, and summarily sentenced to death. He was only saved by the US forces. One of his company commanders, *Sturmbannfuhrer* Hans Waldmueller, was not so fortunate. He was killed on the spot by his captors, again the White Army. This whole remote, well-wooded, hilly area had been known as a '*Terroristennest*' by the Germans ever since 1940. In the summer of 1944, German forces fought a pitched battle with a group of them under their commander, Emile Wolwertz, who was killed. But as soon as the Americans started to push into the area, the White Army joined them and fought a series of skirmishes with them until they reached the German border.

Indeed, a little maliciously, Ernest Hemingway noted in a letter to General Lanham after the war: 'Maybe they ought to send us both back to Houffalize [a Belgian town near the German border] where I saw the members of the *Armee Blanche* take off their arm-bands when the little fire fight [with the SS] started.'

Not only did the White Army fight back in September to aid the Americans, but there is evidence that they donned their uniforms again in December to battle against Peiper. *SS Obersturmfuhrer* Frank Hasse, a company commander, was killed by the partisans on 24 December. A wounded SS man left behind by Peiper in Stavelot was beaten to death. Partisans helped artillery spotting of targets for the Americans at several places. And at the post-war trial of the *Leibstandarte* criminals, one Belgian witness, Jean Elias of Trois Ponts, after testifying that he personally had discovered the bodies of fifteen Belgian civilians murdered by the SS, claimed proudly that he had later helped the Americans to capture the nearby hamlet of Aisemont.

He was asked: 'Were you wearing American uniform at the time?'

When he answered in the affirmative, the defence counsel asked: 'Where did you get the American uniform?'

'I got it from the Maquis.'

'What is the Maquis?' was the next question.

'It is the Army of the Resistance.'

'It is composed of Belgian civilians, is it not?' the defence counsel stated.

'Yes,' was the answer.

Today, long after the heat and anger of that battle, one might conclude that what happened in the Ambleve valley was a mixture of deliberate murder, armed civilian guerrilla activity and the tremendous battering the whole area took from the American artillery and air in the confused fighting of that rugged countryside dotted with hamlets on all sides. But whatever the explanation, at the time, those fighting on the Allied side were firmly convinced that the SS were guilty of all the deaths. Indeed, the massacre of the Belgian civilians in the Ambleve valley was deliberately used to bolster up the morale of the attacking troops.

After the war, combat engineer Corporal Eliot recalled: 'Before starting the job [an assault on an SS position on the other side of the River Ambleve], we were shown what happened in the cellar of one of the houses. Apparently, the Germans had gathered all the people left in the town into the cellar of one of the houses and there they proceeded to punish them for befriending the Americans. Men were dismembered and shot. One pregnant woman had been cut open and left to die. This scene was viewed by hundreds of GIs.'

As Eliot recalled: 'The tanks drove right over the enemy positions and literally buried them alive. Prisoners were then rounded up and brought to the bridge. Here they were stripped of all American clothing and marched, some practically naked, most without shoes, to that partic- ular cellar and forced to view the awful scene in it. From there they were marched through the town into a wooded section from whence shortly came the sounds of much shooting.'

Eliot commented afterwards: 'I have always read Amer- icans treated prisoners justly... I have always been glad that the 291st [Engineer Battalion, his own outfit] had no part in the executions.' The reprisals had begun. That night, Dietrich reported to the High Command of the *Wehrmacht*: 'From the point of the 1st SS Panzer Division, no new reports.' Peiper was cut off irrevocably. Now he and his men, those monsters in SS uniforms who had perpetrated the massacres at Baugnez and now in the Ambleve valley, would suffer the full weight and bitterness of the American counter-attack.

4. 'WE MUST BE ALLOWED TO BREAK OUT IMMEDIATELY'

By the morning of Thursday, 21 December, *Obersturmbannfuhrer* Peiper's hard-pressed battle group was definitely surrounded at the hilltop village of La Gleize. Down below in the valley, General 'Slim Jim' Gavin's paratroopers of the US 82nd Airborne Division held the line of the River Ambleve. On the heights itself, two old opponents of Peiper's pinned him down to the village and the immediate perimeter. There were the men of General Hobb's 30th Infantry Division, 'Roosevelt's Butchers', and those of General Rose's 3rd Armored, who had stopped him at Mortain in the summer.

Peiper's position was not very good. There was no question of continuing the advance to the Meuse now. He was low on food, ammunition and, above all, fuel. Now he was no longer on the offensive but the defensive, warding off American counter-attacks constantly.

It was a 'fight to the death', as one of Peiper's men, *Untersturmfuhrer* Reiser, recalled long afterwards, 'and then they would be attacking yet once again, with the CO crying, "Everyone out for the defence!" Out we'd tumble from the Command Post, tankmen, runners, radiomen, armed with *panzerfausts* [the German missile launcher] and rifles and take up our positions in the ruins, with the snipers already knocking off the first of the *Amis* as they came up both sides of the village street…

'Then it would be over again and we'd carry away our – and their – wounded into the packed cellars. Till the next time.'

Indeed, by now Peiper had so many wounded that he decided to chance using the little grey stone village church as a makeshift hospital, decorating the already shell-damaged steeple with a huge Red Cross flag.

On that same Thursday, *Rottenführer* Eugen Zimmermann was wounded in the arm and hip by grenade splinters and carried into the church. But it was already so packed with wounded and frightened local civilians that he could only find a place next to the church door. 'This probably saved me,' he recalled after the war. 'Hardly had I been carried in, when enemy tanks and artillery began to shoot the church apart.

'Next to me, a badly wounded comrade had just been moaning and begging for water, crying "*Durst… Durst* [thirst]", when the wall disintegrated and a huge stone fell and crushed him.

'A terrible panic broke out, especially among the civilians. I had only one thought – get out! The best I could, I crawled through the door and headed for the churchyard. There I hid myself among the tombstones, while the terrible bombardment continued. Finally, it ceased and I was spotted by two American stretcher-bearers, whom we had taken prisoner a few days before. They carried me, half-conscious, into one of the cellars, where I fainted.'

Now as midday brought a little peace, although there was a terrible 155 mm American cannon only two hundred metres away from the village, steadily pounding it to rubble all the time, Peiper tried to contact HQ and report his parlous state, while his radio batteries still functioned. For they, too, were running out.

'We're in a very bad condition,' he said to the unknown radioman at the other end. 'Very urgently need *Otto*. Without *Otto* can't do anything.'

At the other end, the listener at divisional HQ indicated that he understood Peiper's urgent request for '*Otto*', the code word for fuel. But he explained it was difficult to supply Peiper. Hansen had suffered a lot of casualties trying to break through Gavin's paras to reach Peiper. Perhaps Division could arrange an airdrop by the *Luftwaffe*. 'We will do what we can,' he assured Peiper, who signed off. Unshaven, his already thin face now emaciated to a death's head, from which the red-rimmed eyes blazed like those of a man demented, Peiper handed the headset back to the radio operator and considered his position for a few minutes. He was not totally out of fuel. Hansen had floated a few jerries down the River Ambleve, where his men had picked them up. A daring halftrack driver from Hansen's command had also found a little wooden bridge, unguarded by the *Amis*, at the river, and had managed to smuggle a load of jerricans to him that way. But latest reports were that American Shermans had now moved into position near the bridge.

He shook his head and went into the other room, where his subordinate commanders were waiting for him, as ordered. They were all old hares, veterans of the fighting in Russia – Diefenthal, Gruble, Sickel and the rest – and he gave them the bad news first, as had been the custom on the Eastern front.

They were virtually surrounded. Their supplies were dreadfully low, especially petrol, and their casualties were mounting rapidly. However, Peiper continued, offering the worried-looking officers some hope, the battle group had managed to throw back all *Amis'* efforts to attack La Gleize from the east and west, and so far no threat had developed from the south.

Peiper allowed himself the ghost of a smile. 'But, gentlemen,' he added carefully, 'the divisional commander *has* assured me that we will be relieved.' Hansen had been ordered to launch a new attack across the river below and link up with them.

His officers' relief was obvious. Eagerly they began to discuss what they would do when Hansen linked up with them. If they cleared away the wounded and their hundred-odd *Ami* prisoners, refuelled, etc, there was still hope for that great drive to the Meuse.

As they talked excitedly among themselves, while that damned great *Ami* cannon two hundred metres away thumped and thumped and thumped, Peiper, strangely silent, realised that he had made them believe in something in which he no longer believed himself…

-

By early afternoon, General Mohnke, commander of the *Leibstandarte Adolf Hitler*, had made his dispositions. He had succeeded in moving Hansen's men across the Ambleve between Trois Ponts and Stavelot. Hansen himself had established his command post some three hundred metres away from the bridge they had used to cross, while his men groped their way through the fog towards the positions held by General 'Slim Jim' Gavin's paras.

All that morning the paras had been hearing alarming reports from fleeing civilians that the Germans were building up their strength for an attack in the area. Now Gavin's men could hear the rattle of tracks, muted by the thick fog. Suddenly, the first of the German tanks appeared out of the mist, rumbling along a little road running parallel to the paras' foxholes. It was too tempting. The nearest US bazooka team couldn't resist. They blasted a rocket into the leading German self-propelled gun. It disappeared in a burst of angry yellow flame. The bazooka team yelled with joy and engaged the next tank. They hit it, too. But then their luck was out. Angry SS panzer grenadiers rushed their positions, firing from the hip as they did so. Within minutes, all the brave little team were dead or taken prisoner.

But the para howitzer crews further to the rear had heard the sound of firing and guessed what was happening. Firing blind through the fog, they plastered the Germans advancing along the road. The attack there came to a halt.

But the American paras on the *other* bank of the River Ambleve were in a desperate position. Now they found themselves seemingly trapped with the SS already on the other side of the river. Colonel Vandervoort, who commanded the paras, had been in situations like this before. He had jumped into enemy territory in France and then later in Holland. Now he decided he would attempt a manoeuvre that was frowned upon in every staff college – he would make a withdrawal across the river in daylight.

At first, everything went well. Then Hansen sensed the *Amis* were pulling back. He started to exert more pressure on them. The Americans' pace quickened. The paras became jumpy. Men started to throw themselves over the cliff-like bank into the freezing water and scramble across the Ambleve the best way they could.

Within minutes everything was confusion and panic. Abruptly the SS were in among the fleeing paras. A group of Hansen's men followed the paras over to the other side. They discovered a bridge. It would bear the weight of armour. They seized it. Another group joined them. The paras' 2nd Battalion was now in full retreat. Mohnke grabbed his chance. Immediately, he rushed tanks to the bridge. It looked as if the *Leibstandarte* were moving again!

Then his hopes of reaching La Gleize were dashed to the ground once more. Just after the fourth tank had passed over, there was a miserable rending and groaning. Next instant the central span collapsed into the Ambleve in an angry flurry of wild white water.

A frantic Mohnke called up his combat engineers. The youngsters did their best. They plunged waist-deep into the freezing water and started to play out their lines. But the American artillery had spotted them and they had already zeroed in on the bridge the day before. A deadly hail of accurate fire descended upon the engineers, plastering both sides of the river and throwing up huge spouts of water.

For a while the combat engineers stuck it out grimly. Men screamed as they were hit and disappeared beneath the water, which suddenly flushed pink. Others let go of their holds and were carried away. But after a score of their comrades had been killed or wounded, the rest gave up. They scrambled out of the water and ran for their lives, telling their CO they would go back when the fog thickened again and gave them cover once more...

That wasn't to be. Without armoured support, the two platoons of Hansen's men who had followed the fleeing paras across the river hadn't much of a chance. Soon afterwards they ran into the line that the American commanders had managed to re-establish on the far bank and were mown down mercilessly. The four armoured vehicles that had managed to get across before the bridge collapsed were easy meat for the paras, now that the tanks were no longer protected by their own infantry. In rapid succession they were destroyed one by one by paratroopers armed with grenades.

By late afternoon Hansen's attack had run out of steam for that day. Admittedly, they had weakened the front of the 82nd Airborne Division considerably, and now there were gaps in it here and there. On the morrow Hansen would attack again. But again, the attackers would run out of luck. In the end Hansen would call off the attack for good and order the two SS battalions to go over to the defensive on the line of the River Ambleve...

That night Peiper received one of his last messages from divisional HQ. It told him that there was no hope of breaking through to him in La Gleize. Hansen had failed.

Unterstumfuhrer Reiser, who was present at Peiper's command post when the message was received, remembers well the reaction: 'Immediately the CO [Peiper] assembled his commanders, Poetschke, Diefenthal, etc, etc, and began discussing a breakout. With almost the last of the juice [for the radio batteries] Peiper *demanded* from divisional HQ permission to break out. He said: "Our position in La Gleize is absolutely hopeless."'

–

By that night, Peiper had withdrawn his command from the perimeter to what was left of central La Gleize: the upper street, on which there were the ruins of a handful of houses and two modest hotels; and the lower one around the church, the village square with its school, bistro and priest's house. There, in the cellar of the village school, Peiper took up his own command post and waited for Mohnke's reply, not realising that already his request to withdraw was occupying no less a person than Dietrich himself.

In the meantime, Peiper sent for his senior American prisoner, a West Pointer, Major Hal McCown, the executive officer of one of the 30th Division's infantry battalions, who had been captured the day before. He was escorted into the cellar by *Oberscharfuhrer* Max Bergmann. Bending his head − McCown was very tall − at the entrance to the cellar, McCown saluted and Peiper stretched out his hand to welcome him. Now, as that terrible 155 mm cannon continued to pound outside, the two of them, the SS Colonel and the West Pointer, sat down at the table and began talking far into the night.

Later McCown, who finally became a general, reasoned that Peiper didn't want information from him. He simply wanted to unburden his soul to this apparently sympathetic American. All the same, McCown was struck by the *Leibstandarte* officer's fanaticism. Peiper was all he had been taught to expect from an SS officer.

After observing that 'We can't lose. Himmler's new reserve army has so many new divisions your G-2 will wonder where they come from,' he went on to talk in general about his devotion to the National Socialist cause. 'Oh, I admit that many wrongs have been done,' Peiper said, as the candles flickered wildly under the impact of yet another shell exploding. 'But we think of the great good Hitler is accomplishing. We're eliminating the Communist menace, fighting *your* fight. And the Fuehrer's concept of a unified, more productive Europe!

Can't you see what good that will bring? We will keep what is best in Europe and eliminate the bad!'

It was obvious to the American that Peiper had swallowed the latest propaganda line of the 'New Europe', united in a common cause to fight the Soviet menace, hardly aware of just how close the man in the street in Western Europe and America felt to the Red Army, their ally.

All the same, McCown felt his antipathy turning to sympathy as the night hours sped by towards a new dawn. Peiper seemed to him to be a man with a sense of humour, highly intelligent, and possessing a greater degree of culture than comparable officers in the US Army.

McCown was prompted to ask about the safety of the other 150 US prisoners in the hands of the SS. By now he was almost certain that it was Peiper's outfit that had recently shot a large number of US prisoners after they had surrendered near Malmedy. Many of Peiper's teenage soldiers didn't strike him as particularly stable. Keeping his own counsel, he asked casually about the treatment of Russians captured by the SS on the Eastern Front.

Peiper smiled in reply. 'I'd like to take you to the Eastern Front,' he said. 'Then you'd see why we've had to violate the rules of warfare. The Russians have no idea what the Geneva Convention means. Some day, perhaps, you Americans will find out for yourselves. And you have to admit our behaviour on the Western Front has been very correct.'

Feeling more confident now, McCown, who had observed only one breach of the rules during his time in German captivity (the Germans had made American POWs carry ammunition), asked: 'Colonel Peiper, will you give me your personal assurance that you'll abide by the Rules of Land Warfare?' Solemnly Peiper looked at his captive. 'You have my word,' he replied.

As the new dawn came creeping up in the east, McCown thought he had the measure of Colonel Peiper, whom he had begun to like, as did all Americans who got to know him (even the US public prosecutor who demanded the death penalty).

If Peiper no longer had much heart for the battle and had resigned himself to defeat, despite his brave words, then there was little hope left for the whole rotten National Socialist system. After all, the *Leibstandarte* was Hitler's own Praetorian Guard. Now one of its leading representatives seemed about ready to throw in the towel. One thing McCown knew for certain: Peiper would honour his promise. Nothing would happen to the American prisoners in his hands.

As the horizon to the east started to grow lighter, Peiper got wearily to his feet and nodded to Bergmann to take the Major back to his cellar. Thus, they parted, in a strange kind of way, friends in spite of being foes, and another day of battle commenced...

–

While Peiper waited impatiently, taking casualties all the time, his request to withdraw from La Gleize had been considered at the highest level. Dietrich was inclined to give him permission to do so, but first he had consulted Hitler's HQ. But Hitler turned him down. Obviously, the High Command still believed that a link-up with Battle Group Peiper could be achieved and the drive to the Meuse could continue.

Peiper knew this was totally unrealistic. He was burdened with several hundred casualties, and the fuel that the *Luftwaffe* had promised to drop him by parachute had floated instead into the American lines. That morning he received a call from divisional HQ. His hopes rose. Now that HQ realised the para drop had been a failure, would he be allowed to withdraw? He was disappointed. At the other end the strange impersonal voice, distorted by static, said: 'If *Kampfgruppe Peiper* does not report its supply position accurately, it cannot reckon on receiving a supply of fuel and ammunition. Six Royal Tigers ready for action east of Stavelot. Where do you want us to send them?'

Peiper flushed angrily. Divisional HQ simply had no idea of his true situation, he told himself. 'Send them *via airlift* to La Gleize!' he snapped, as outside that damned 155 mm cannon blasted away again. Then, with a note of pleading in his strained voice, he said: 'We *must* be allowed to break out immediately!'

There was a moment's silence at the other end. Then General Mohnke came on the radio. 'Can you break out with all vehicles and wounded?' he asked. Peiper's hopes soared. For the first time, HQ was actually considering the possibility of withdrawal. 'Last chance to break out tonight,' he said hastily. 'Without wounded and vehicles – please give permission?'

Mohnke, who knew he was risking Hitler's displeasure, even punishment, by what he was going to attempt, did give a direct reply. He said he would take it up with the corps commander once again.

Peiper was satisfied. He decided he would go ahead and plan the breakout while he waited for the final permission to do so. Hurriedly, he summoned his surviving senior officers and sketched in his plan. He informed them that Hansen's nearest troops were on the other side of the Ambleve. They would make their way to reach them by a steep track, which led down from the heights to the rear of La Gleize. At the hamlet of La Venne, there was apparently a gap in the lines of the 82nd Airborne Division. With a bit of luck, they would be able to feed the surviving thousand men of the battle group through it and reach Hansen's command.

During the course of the briefing (there would be another later that evening) permission finally came through for Peiper's breakout. It would take place at two o'clock on the morning of Christmas Eve. The password would be '*Frohe Weihnacht*' – Happy Christmas...

–

Now, as his officers began their preparations, Peiper concerned himself with his own wounded and the American prisoners. He had Major McCown brought to his cellar command post once again and told him: 'We have been called back.'

McCown forced a smile, though he was not particularly overjoyed by the prospect of spending several months in a German POW camp. Still, now he would not be killed. Remembering how Peiper had promised him during the night to give him a ride on a Tiger tank, he quipped: 'Well, I've always wanted a ride on a Royal Tiger.'

Peiper said nothing. He didn't tell McCown they wouldn't be *riding* out of La Gleize this coming Christmas Eve; they would be *marching*! Instead, he continued with: 'My immediate concern is what to do with the prisoners and my own wounded.' Then he suggested a solution. If he agreed to release all the prisoners, once the battle group had left, would McCown, who would be kept as a hostage, guarantee that the American commander who took La Gleize would release all German wounded when they were fit again? He said his wounded would be left behind under the care of the surgeon of his third battalion, Dr Dittmann. Once his wounded had been released, Peiper would in his turn send McCown back to his own people.

The return of the SS wounded was an important point of principle for Peiper. The *Leibstandarte* prided itself on never abandoning its wounded. On the Russian front they had seen what the Ivans had done to wounded prisoners who bore the hated name of 'Adolf Hitler' on their sleeve.

McCown replied: 'Colonel, that proposal is a farce. For one thing, I have no power to bind the American command regarding German POWs. After all, you are not in a very good bargaining position.'

'I know,' Peiper agreed. 'But I'd like to go ahead with the plan in the hope that your commander will agree.'

McCown considered for a moment. 'All I can do,' he announced finally, 'is to sign a statement that I heard you make this offer. I can't do anything more.'

Peiper nodded his approval. That would suffice. He ordered another captured US officer, Captain Bruce Crisinger, to be brought in. Thereupon, McCown drew up a statement in English, which both officers signed. Then the statement was handed to Crisinger, who would stay behind. He would give it to the senior American officer in the force that finally took La Gleize. That done, both officers were led away and Peiper continued his planning.

Thus it was that 150 healthy American prisoners were soon going to be freed so that they could take up arms once more against their erstwhile captors.

With what was known of the *Leibstandarte*'s infamous record, this third week of December 1944, when there were massacres and general mayhem on all sides, one wonders why Peiper had not simply ordered them shot. That would have been a much easier solution. Was he really so concerned about the fate of his own wounded, many of whom, he knew, would have to spend long periods in hospital before they were set free by the *Amis* – if they ever were?

So many questions without answers. But they were questions that Peiper's post-war prosecutors would not even pose. The fact that he was, as senior officer of *Kampfgruppe Peiper*, responsible for the Malmedy Massacre was sufficient. No one on the Allied side was interested in the least in the fact that the 'La Gleize Massacre' had *not* taken place...

–

Now the hours passed till Christmas Eve, 1944, the last of the war. The last time Peiper had celebrated Christmas Eve in the West was at Metz in France, back in that year of tremendous German victories in 1940. Dietrich had still commanded the *Leibstandarte* then, and the Fuehrer himself had attended their Christmas Eve celebration at the newly named '*Sepp Dietrich Kaserne*' in the French barracks they had taken over. They had sung '*Stille Nacht, Heilige Nacht*', toasts had been drunk and Adolf Hitler had personally handed over Christmas presents to his brave SS men that afternoon in front of the Christmas tree, as was the German custom.

Thereafter had come Russia, with Christmas Eve after Christmas Eve being celebrated in the line. They had still sung 'Stille Nacht, Heilige Nacht', but that had been about it. There might have been a few more pieces of 'old man' in the 'green fart soup',[10] and perhaps a bottle of firewater to share with a comrade or two. But otherwise it had been the same grim unrelenting misery of the Eastern Front.

Russia had left its mark on Peiper, both physically and psychologically, as it had done on all the surviving old hares. He had seen more than his share of violent death over the past four years. Perhaps he realised that violent death would be his own fate (the fact that that violent death would come thirty-two years later was, of course, beyond his ken). That knowledge and the experiences he had undergone in the artificial life of the front had cut him off from all the desires and emotions of the normal father and family man, which he now was. He had three small children, one boy and two girls. But his real family was the Leibstandarte, the company of his old comrades, the old hares, who had survived time and time again, and those fresh-faced innocents, those eighteen-year-old lads who filled the gaps, eager for some desperate glory – and an early death.

By this fifth Christmas of the war, Peiper, who knew well enough that Hitler's vaunted 'Thousand-Year Reich' was falling apart all around him, probably wanted death. His personality had been tempered and hardened into that particularly German combination of naive, almost boyish, idealism, linked to the savage spirit of a brutal soldier of fortune who knows only one loyalty. Not to God, not to his country, not even to his own family, but to his own unit, which was all these things in one – die Leibstandarte SS Adolf Hitler.

Now, if the *Leibstandarte* was to go under, this coming dawn, then he, Jochen Peiper, was prepared to go under with it. There was no alternative, was there?

It was midnight. The firing had ceased now. Even that infernal 155 mm cannon had ceased pounding the ruins. An icy silence had fallen over La Gleize. The frost sparkled on the *pave*. The sentries tucked their heads deeper into the protection of their coat collars, and began looking more frequently at the green-glowing dials of their wrist-watches, as the wrecking parties crept from vehicle to vehicle fixing the explosive charges. It would not be long now…

5. 'FROHE WEIHNACHT'

Two o'clock!

During the night it had snowed. Now the messengers' nailed boots crunched on the fresh snow as they sped from tank to tank, giving the password – *'Frohe Weihnacht'*.

Karl Wortmann and his crew had fallen into an exhausted sleep in the steel coffin of their icy tank when the whispered password woke them. 'Happy Christmas?' Wortmann asked as he was awakened from a drugged sleep. But Christmas was tomorrow. 'Christmas is tomorrow,' he grunted to the messenger. 'No it isn't,' the other man whispered. *'It's right away!'*

Wortmann realised that it was the password for the great breakout. 'Immediately I got my crew moving. Quickly I put a couple of egg-grenades in my pockets, grabbed my pistol and machine pistol and got out. Hurriedly we fixed the sticky grenades, as ordered, to the engine and cannon and prayed they'd go off in due course, and then we were off.'

Now strung out in a long line, the surviving eight hundred men of Peiper's command still capable of move-ment were trekking down the hillside from La Gleize across country. 'The once so arrogant *SS-Kampfgruppe Peiper*... was a sad-looking bunch,' one of them, an NCO named Laun, recalled long afterwards. 'In a single file we set off over the road bridge south of the village. The

Tigers, Panthers, numerous vehicles, SP [self-propelled] guns and weapons of all kinds were left to the Americans – that is, those not already knocked out by the American artillery.

'The route led up and down through swampy ground that was often as not as frozen as it looked. Our Panzer-fausts loaded us down – none of us knew why we bothered to take them. One by one, slyly and cautiously, they were discarded. A few machine guns and carbines followed.'

Peiper, doubling up and down the column all the time, encouraging, cajoling, threatening his weary men, forced a cracking pace.

He knew that they had to be well away from La Gleize before the noise of their exploding vehicles alerted the Americans that something untoward was going on in the surrounded Belgian village.

Marching just behind Peiper, covered by his guard – a young soldier named Paul Froehlich, who kept his pistol levelled all the time – Major McCown felt the pace was murderous. After the first hour, Peiper gave his gasping, weary men a five-minute break. But he himself took no time off. Instead, he checked men solicitously, encouraging them to keep up and laughing at any sign of weakness. In spite of the fact that Peiper represented everything that McCown had been taught to hate, he could not but admire the man. He was a damn good soldier and a born leader whose men obviously admired him totally.

After the second five-minute break, the first charge up above them exploded. In their cellars the American prisoners were shocked into consciousness, their faces suddenly taut and alarmed. Another explosion rocked La Gleize. Outside, tank after tank left behind by the battle group went up in flames. The last defenders of La Gleize, a handful of volunteers, were destroying their equipment so that it would not fall into the hands of the *Amis* on the morrow. *Kampfgruppe Peiper* was not going to offer the American victors any presents this particular Christmas.

By half-past four that wintry snowy morning, La Gleize was encircled by flames, and everywhere dazed Americans were standing wondering what new tricks the SS were trying to play on them…

Dawn came, and still they marched. The men were out on their feet. Wortmann did not know how he continued to march. 'All of us were at the end of our strength as we now proceeded through a tight valley towards the Ambleve River. We were weak, too, from hunger. But we kept going, I think, because we just wanted to get out of this mess. That was to be the best present anyone could give on this day – Christmas Eve, 1944.'

McCown, who was not burdened down with equip-ment like the others, wondered what was happening to the rest of the prisoners from his old outfit, the 30th Infantry Division, left in La Gleize. Despite his aching leg muscles and snow-blinded eyes, he smiled a little to himself. *They* would be celebrating Christmas tomorrow with their own buddies. With luck, they would even have turkey, cranberry sauce and all the trimmings. After what they had been through, the authorities would probably make some special provision for them, such as forty-eight hours in Gay Paree with all the delights of 'Pig Alley'[11]. However, what would Christmas Day 1944 bring for him? Barbed wire – and a hunk of black bread, washed down with ersatz coffee.

McCown's face must have revealed his gloomy thoughts, for Peiper, again marching at the head of the column, suddenly turned and pointed to a snow-covered fir tree brilliantly lit by the first light of the sun. 'I promised the other night,' he said cheerfully, 'I would get you a tree for Christmas. Well, there it is.' He laughed, and then turned and concentrated on the route ahead once more.

Sometime later, McCown caught up with Peiper again and, pointing to the ever-present Froehlich with his pistol, said: 'Can't you tell this guy to stop calling me "boy". I am a major, after all.'

Peiper smiled. 'It's the only English he knows,' he explained. Then he turned to the young soldier and told him what McCown had just said. The latter nodded his understanding and said, 'Colonel, can't you get the Major to give you his word of honour that he won't escape? I'm sick of holding the pistol up like this.'

Peiper translated Froehlich's words and McCown said: 'All right. I'll give you my word.'

With a grin, Froehlich put his pistol back in its holster…

Just after eight that morning, Peiper gave his men a fifteen-minute break. They flopped exhausted into the snow, without even bothering to take cover, while Peiper tried to join the column up again; it had been split in two. Behind them on the heights, shells were falling on La Gleize again. They could see tiny figures, silhouetted black against the mantle of snow, advancing on the village, from which the birds had flown.

McCown, who had tied his white handkerchief around his helmet so that, to Peiper, he looked like 'an umpire at a tactical exercise', said somewhat sadly of his divisional commander: 'Poor General, they'll fire him for sure for this one.' Then the firing stopped as the advancing Americans discovered the SS had gone.

Peiper's smile vanished. Now the *Amis* knew they were making a break for it.

–

But Roosevelt's Butchers were not the only ones to realise that the birds had flown the coop this Christmas Eve morning. On the day before, Field Marshal Montgomery, who had by now taken over control of Hodges' battered First Army, had decreed that certain elements of his new command would make a strategic withdrawal; 'tidy up the front', he phrased it, as if he were some kind of military housewife. Included in this withdrawal would be the US 82nd Airborne holding the Ambleve River line.

General 'Slim Jim' Gavin, commanding the 82nd Airborne, was not pleased with Montgomery's decision. He was 'greatly concerned' about the attitude of his soldiers, for 'the division had not made withdrawal in its combat history'. There was another problem, too. Just as his men had commenced withdrawing that dawn, one of the division's Jeep drivers reported he had encountered troops wearing full field equipment walking in the woods toward the east. They hit the ground and took cover and acted very evasively as his Jeep neared them.

A little later, another trooper, a telephone lineman who was out checking his lines, reported his Jeep had been shot up by what he assumed were Germans in the rear.

Now the regimental commander in the area asked Gavin whether he should stop his withdrawal and deploy his regiment to search and destroy these wandering Germans (for the moment, the American paras did not know these were Peiper's men) or should he continue?

Gavin made a decision that morning, which, unknown to him, saved Peiper and his survivors. As he wrote after the war: 'It seemed to me that the most important thing was for the regiment to be in position on the new fine … and be prepared for a very heavy fight. We had identified at least four divisions that we could expect to move against us and we could not afford to have an entire regimental sector involved in scattered small-unit fighting … I therefore ordered him to move on with his withdrawal without delay.'

Thus it was that the two opposing forces, Gavin's 505th Regiment and what was left of Peiper's battle group, would now be involved in a highly unusual and novel manoeuvre – both of them withdrawing through each other. Gavin had insisted to the 505th'st commander that he did want any chaos in the regimental sector. Now Slim Jim was going to find that this was exactly what happened. *Total chaos!*

It was noon now. Peiper's survivors had been marching through the rugged wooded terrain of the Ardennes forest for ten hours. As Sergeant Laun recalled after the war: 'Midday found us exhausted with empty stomachs. No one had any food with him. Orders had been to take small arms, nothing else. A burning thirst caused by the dry cold bothered us most. The men tore ice from the trees to suck… others threw themselves over each puddle to drink the mucky water…' And all the time the enemy was searching for them. 'Overhead *Jabos* circled trying to spot us. Despite the cold we perspired profusely in our heavy clothing. The forest seemed without end.'

McCown, too, was finding the going increasingly tough. They had already covered, in his estimate, twenty miles (thirty kilometres) and food had been limited to a handful of hard biscuits, washed down with a shot of cognac. Peiper's surgeon had handed him a piece of candy, and for a time the sugar had given him renewed energy. But only for a time. By noon his legs were feeling like jelly and he had little control over his limbs.

But Peiper would not relax the pressure. '*Tempo... tempo...!*' he cried angrily when the men's pace seemed to flag, and the young captain in charge of McCown's part of the column threatened any man who dropped out with his pistol, yelling: 'If you fall behind, you'll be shot!'

About two, Peiper allowed his exhausted men to take a longer rest. They threw themselves in the cover of some tall pines and sprawled out full length, some of them falling asleep immediately. Laun was so hungry now that he ate his last chocolate bar, his iron ration kept for emergencies, and, forgetting his earlier horror of the puddles of muddy water: 'I threw myself on to such a puddle, my lips cracked and chapping.' But soon he found that the dirty water was beginning to make him feel sick. He felt that 'morale was like the thermometer – *at zero!*'

Max Bergmann thought differently. Where he lay sprawled in the pines with his group, someone started to hum the tune of '*Stille Nacht, Heilige Nacht*' to himself. 'The melody,' he recorded long afterwards, 'went from man to man in a matter of seconds, as if there was an invisible conductor present directing the humming... At that moment, we all realised that it was really Christmas. A wartime Christmas in 1944, my sixth Christmas at the front...'

But Peiper had no time for that typical *gemutlich* German sentimentality, which affected even these battle-hardened and brutalised SS troopers. Christmas Eve or not, he knew his first duty to his soldiers was to get them out of the mess in which they found themselves. They had already spotted one group of Americans, which indicated to him the *Amis* were searching for the survivors of his battle group (Peiper did not know these were Gavin's paras busily engaged in withdrawing to the new line of defence). That time, luck had been on their side and the Americans had not spotted the survivors. But now the light was beginning to fade and they might well just blunder into the enemy in the darkness. It was time to be off once more.

Now the officers and NCOs went from man to man, waking those who were asleep, urging the others to their feet. Men rose like punch-drunk boxers, swaying groggily as if they had just got up after a count of ten. Others simply could not be roused or were overlooked. As Laun said: 'They were never seen again. So we started off once more, some of us almost asleep on our feet.'

Now Peiper proceeded more cautiously. He knew he was somewhere near the main road that ran between the town of Trois Ponts and the village of Basse-Bodeux, and he reasoned that the *Amis* would have patrols somewhere on that road looking for him. Therefore, he sent out small recce parties, made up of the fitter men, to find, if possible, a safe crossing point.

Sometime later, one of the reconnaissance patrols reported they had reached the road, and there wasn't an *Ami* in sight. Gleefully they maintained the Americans were celebrating Christmas instead of patrolling the road. Peiper had to take their word for it. He was growing very tired himself. So he ordered his men to cross in bunches, moving at double-quick time.

Max Bergmann was just about to cross with his group, 'when suddenly American soldiers popped up from the bushes and grabbed some of us, pulling us into a wood. Our comrades reacted immediately. They started firing into the trees. That shook the Americans and they let us loose. Now a wild small arms battle broke out. The column disintegrated. Men started to run in all directions, as our commanders yelled, "*Stay together… don't split… up…!*"

McCown, at the end of his strength and as surprised as his captors by this wild outburst of firing, dropped gratefully to the snow, heart pounding. Slugs sliced the air above his head. Someone yelled at him in German. It might have been his guard, Froehlich. If it was, he thought, the German youth had better start coming to look for him.

Now McCown realised that this was his chance, although he had given his word of honour to Peiper. He began to crawl forward to the trees, where he rose to his feet and headed towards the sound of American fire. He pursed his cracked lips and began to whistle. Afterwards he forgot what the tune was, but he knew it was something American, which the ambushers would recognise; at least, he hoped they would.

After what seemed an age, he heard a harsh voice shout, 'Halt, goddammit!' McCown breathed a sigh of heartfelt relief. He knew he had been saved. Minutes later he was being led to Colonel Ekman, the commander of the 505th Parachute Infantry, to whom he would tell his tale. There would be turkey and all the trimmings for Christmas, after all.

-

Twenty minutes after McCown escaped, the fire-fight with the withdrawing American paras ended and the group of escapers dashed across the road and plunged into the thick undergrowth on the other side, where they collapsed, hearts beating like triphammers, while the doctors did their best for the wounded.

Once again they formed up, this time in single file, and set off. But not for long. As Max Bergmann recalled afterwards: 'Hardly had we got over the shock of bumping into the Americans when we heard the sound of motors. We froze.' A vehicle was heading in their direction!

'We stayed as quiet as mice. An American armoured car was heading towards us, crawling along at a snail's pace. It was obviously looking for us. After all, over twenty hours had passed since we had left La Gleize, and eight hundred men simply did not vanish from the face of the earth.'

But luck was on their side. The enemy crew did not spot them, and as the armoured car vanished into the darkness, they set off on their weary march yet once again. They came to the bank of the River Salm, the last natural obstacle. Somewhere on the other side was the rest of the *Leibstandarte*.

But as dawn started to break slowly, as if God on high was reluctant to throw light on the war-torn world below, they discovered that there were American tanks everywhere along the bank, guarding the fords and bridges. How were they going to cross with their wounded?

Peiper knew he couldn't stay where he was much longer. Already some of his patrols had brushed with the Americans in wild skirmishes. The main body would be discovered soon. But the River Salm was in flood, rushing through the two high banks, flecked with white foam and freezing. 'Even to look at it,' Max Bergmann remembered, 'made a shiver run down your spine.'

Then Peiper remembered how, in Russia, the partisans behind German lines had made secret bridges by building stone causeways just below the surface of the water, which could not be spotted from above. He rapped out a series of orders. All the fit men formed a human chain and began tugging stones from the bank on their side and handing them along the line of soldiers to the volunteers who were balancing in the icy rushing water, attempting to make a rough-and-ready bridge.

Peiper waited impatiently as the day grew lighter, flashing anxious glances up and down the river, half-expecting the *Amis* to appear and begin shooting at any moment. And this time there would be no escape for them. They were sitting ducks on the river bank and in the River Salm itself. It would mean either surrender or wholesale slaughter. But luck still remained on their side. Now the first of the escapers began to cross the make-shift bridge, hanging on to the belt of the man in front, desperately trying not to slip on the wet stones beneath their hob-nailed boots.

'Those thirty-forty metres of the water seemed endless,' Max Bergmann remembered after the war. 'A couple of times, the human chain broke when comrades slipped on the stones and fell into the river. But somehow we made it to the other side.'

They did so just in time, for now they had been spotted. Frantically breaking into smaller groups, they scrambled up a steep hill east of the village of La Venne under enemy fire and finally disappeared into the cover of the thick woods at the top. Beyond lay their own comrades.

Peiper had done it! A week before, he had rolled into battle with about 3,000 men. Of these, some eight hundred had finally attempted the breakout from La Gleize. Out of that number he had brought 770 to safety this Christmas Day morning. Although the great drive to the Meuse had ended in defeat, Peiper's performance during the week-long battle so impressed the Fuehrer that he would, on 11 January 1945, award him Nazi Germany's highest decoration for bravery in combat: the Swords to the Knight's Cross he had already won in battle. Peiper of the *Leibstandarte* would be the only soldier in the 600,000-strong German force involved in the six-week Battle of the Bulge to be given that award...

But on that Christmas morning, awards for bravery – 'tin', as the old hares of the *Leibstandarte* called such baubles contemptuously – were far from Peiper's mind. He was exhausted and at the end of his tether. For the first time in his long combat career, he had been slightly wounded in the last skirmish. Now he could go on no longer. He collapsed and had to be carried the last few metres to the command post at La Venne by his surgeon, Dr Sickl. There, like most of his men, he fell into an exhausted sleep (some of the survivors slept a solid forty-eight hours).

History does not record Peiper's thoughts on that day. But he could hardly have realised that 25 December 1944 marked the zenith of his career with the *Leibstandarte*, indeed of his whole life.

For some people it is a dramatic event, which signals that life had changed irrevocably. The wounded soldier staring for the first time at the shattered stump of his leg knows that from now onwards he is fated to be a cripple. The father who yells too late to stop his child running in front of the speeding car that will kill it is well aware already of the sense of loss to come.

But for most people the change does not come so dramatically. It is usually a simple process of ageing – being passed over for promotion in favour of a younger man; the first discovery of a sagging chinline; the discouraging realisation that one's sexual power has vanished. It is only when we look back later on that we recognise that a particular day was a turning point in our lives.

Such was to be the case with *Obersturmbannführer* Jochen Peiper. That Christmas Day, the last of the Second World War, he was only twenty-eight, but at the height of his military career. After his brilliant performance during the drive for the River Meuse, he stood every chance of becoming the Armed SS's youngest general. Indeed, in a month's time he would be promoted and become the assistant divisional commander of the *Leibstandarte*.

At the moment he was exhausted and slightly wounded, admittedly, but otherwise he was fit, virile and supremely resourceful. Yet that day – unknown to him, as he slept that exhausted sleep – marked the watershed in his career, and his life. In far-off Brussels and Paris, the accountants were already beginning to assess the debt owed to them by a certain J. Peiper. On the other side of the Channel, at a remote Yorkshire military hospital in Harrogate, the survivors of the events at the Baugnez crossroads were being interrogated by the War Crimes team. Soon now these accountants of death would present the reckoning…

6. 'NUTS'

On Christmas Day, Adolf Hitler rose late, as was his custom. Like his greatest enemy, Churchill, he seldom went to bed before two in the morning. Instead, he sat up late, talking and talking, and sometimes watching movies. Though, unlike Churchill, who preferred historical epics such as *Lady Hamilton*, Hitler liked musicals, with plenty of leggy blondes: the kind of Hollywood product that he had forbidden his own subjects to see.

That afternoon he joined his staff in the underground chambers of his command bunker in southern Germany, from which he was directing the battle in the Ardennes. There he sat with them around the candle-lit Christmas tree and even accepted a glass of wine, which he appeared to enjoy. Yet his physical appearance continued to disturb his intimates, as it had done ever since the abortive assassination attempt back in July. His face was haggard and his voice quavered.

After a while the discussion between Hitler and his senior officers turned to the situation in the Ardennes. Jodl mentioned the report he had received from Model, who was in charge of the German forces there. The Field Marshal, 'Hitler's Fire Brigade', was still confident that he could reach the River Meuse, explaining that both his flanks were up in the air.

Colonel-General Jodl finished reviewing the Model report and then said: '*Mein Fuehrer*, we must face the facts squarely and openly. We cannot force the Meuse River.'

Hitler shook his head. He refused to accept Jodl's thesis. 'We have had unexpected setbacks,' he conceded. But they took place 'because my plan was not followed to the letter.' He felt that 'all is not yet lost'. Jodl listened carefully as Hitler proceeded to ramble on in his usual manner, talking at great length about something that could have been summed up in a few words. To Jodl it was clear that, despite the rhetoric, Hitler was accepting a modification of the original plan. This was to clear up all American resistance east of the River Meuse before attempting to cross the great waterway. Here he gave the priority to the capture of the Belgian city of Bastogne, which was already surrounded by the German troops. Once Bastogne was taken, there would be no threat to his flank from the south and they could concentrate on the assault on the Meuse riverline.

Jodl suggested, instead of the continued attack on Bastogne, which had been holding out against everything the *Wehrmacht* could throw at it since 17 December, a plan to seize Luxembourg City – Bradley's HQ. With a bit of luck, they could capture the city, which would be an important boost to the fragile morale of the German soldier in the Ardennes.

Hitler rejected the idea out of hand. He still believed that the Army was capable of crossing the Meuse and capturing Antwerp, his original objective. So Jodl gave up, and enjoyed his last free Christmas. One year from now he would be a prisoner of the Allies, soon to be sentenced to death at Nuremberg.

Three days later, however, Hitler admitted to Jodl that the situation in the Ardennes was really serious, even desperate. But, he added: 'As much as I may be tormented by worries and even physically shaken by them, nothing will make the slightest change in my decision to fight on until at last the scales tip in our favour.'

By continuing the attack in the Ardennes, he said, he had forced the Americans to withdraw fifty per cent of their troop strength from other sectors of the front. This meant those sectors had been left 'extraordinarily thin'. He led Jodl to the map and pointed out Alsace in eastern France, with its long border along the Rhine. There, on New Year's Eve in three days' time, he would launch a new surprise offensive at the weakened US front. The result would be that Patton's Third Army attacking in the Ardennes from the south would be forced to pull back and help their own people in Alsace. Then the German offensive in the Ardennes could 'be resumed with fresh promise of success'.

Hitler now ordered that Model was 'to consolidate his holdings and reorganise for a new attempt on the Meuse'. Model was also to 'make another powerful assault on Bastogne. Above all, *we must have Bastogne!*'

–

Six days before, while Peiper had been planning his breakout from La Gleize, Sergeant Oswald Butler of the US 101st Airborne Division, defending Bastogne, was on duty in a lonely farmhouse overlooking a road. Shortly before midday on that 22 December, he spotted four figures plodding towards him, one of them carrying what looked like a bedspread on a pole. He recognised the uniform. It was German. He picked up the phone that linked him with his company commander and snapped hastily, 'There's four Krauts coming up the road. They're carrying a white flag. It looks like they want to surrender.'

Butler was wrong. The boot was on the other front. The Germans had come to demand that *the Americans* surrender!

Half an hour later, Colonel Harper of the 101st Airborne informed the division's chief-of-staff, Lieutenant Colonel Moore, what was going on. 'I have some Germans,' said Harper. 'They have a request for surrender. I'll bring them up to the command post.' 'Good,' Moore said, and then opened the door to the next room, where General McAuliffe, commander of the 101st, was taking a nap. Swiftly he woke his chief and filled him in on what was happening. A few minutes later Harper came in and handed Moore two typewritten sheets – one in German and one in English. Moore scanned the latter hurriedly. It read:

> 'To the USA Commander of the encircled town of Bastogne.
>
> 'The fortune of war is changing. This time the USA forces in and near Bastogne have been encircled by strong German armoured units… There is only one possibility to save the encircled USA troops from total annihilation: that is the honourable surrender of the encircled town…
>
> 'If this proposal should be rejected one German Artillery Corps and six heavy AA Battalions are ready to annihilate the USA troops in and near Bastogne…

*'All serious civilian losses caused by this artil-
lery fire would not correspond with the well-known
American humanity.'*

The German Commander

McAuliffe asked, stifling a yawn, 'What's on the paper?'

'They want us to surrender.'

McAuliffe glanced carelessly at the two sheets, laughed
and then said, *'Aw, nuts!'*[12] With that he dropped the
sheets to the floor and drove off to congratulate some of
his paras who had just wiped out an enemy roadblock.
When he came back, Colonel Harper, who was still there,
told him that the German emissaries were still waiting for
an answer.

'What the hell should I tell them?' McAuliffe said,
taking up a pencil.

'That first remark of yours would be hard to beat,
General,' someone suggested.

'What did I say?' the General asked.

'You said "nuts".'

Everyone in the HQ liked the one-word answer, so
McAuliffe sat down and wrote:

> *'To the German Commander.*
>
> *'Nuts!'*

The American Commander

Sometime later Harper met the Germans and gave them
McAuliffe's answer. 'But what does it mean?' one of them
who spoke English asked.

183

Harper lost his temper. 'If you don't understand what "Nuts" means,' he snorted, 'I'll tell you. In plain English it is the same as "Go to Hell!" And I'll tell you something else. If you continue to attack, we'll kill every goddam German that tries to break into this city!'[13]

Thus, the legend was born, one that has found its place in every American high school history; and the men of the 101st Airborne – 'the battered bastards of Bastogne', as their hard-working PR man entitled them – continued to do just what Harper had threatened, kill every goddam German that tried to break into this city.

Four days later, Patton's Third Army, which had started its drive on 22 December, finally broke through to the beleaguered paras in Bastogne. Almost immediately the supply situation there began to improve. The Third Army had a corridor two kilometres wide leading into Bastogne, and as the December weather picked up, gliderborne supplies were flown in, braving the ring of German flak guns around the place.

Still there were elements of seven German divisions besieging Bastogne, and the green American divisions that Patton was being forced to use to broaden the corridor were finding the going very tough; their casualties were high. Worse still for the 'battered bastards', Model, on receipt of Hitler's order to capture Bastogne, was already beginning to switch his armour from Dietrich's Sixth SS Panzer Army front to the area. Soon the Second Battle of Bastogne was about to commence...

–

Colonel Peiper was in the process of playing a little trick on a fellow officer when the orders came in. Peiper was given to malicious little tricks. Once, the year before in Italy, he had saved a handful of Jews from Germany from being arrested by the local Fascist police. Their spokesman, a Berliner like himself, asked how they, the rescued Jews, might express their thanks. Peiper replied they should go to the house of one of his 'friends' that night and serenade him with Yiddish songs. The 'friend' was a National Socialist official, 'a golden pheasant', as they were called on account of their splendid uniforms, who was rabidly anti-Semitic.

Now Peiper, who was temporarily 'unemployed' (for his command had virtually vanished), was passing the time of day with Dr Sickl at his aid post, where officers came to be deloused and have their hair cut by one of Sickl's orderlies, when a company commander from the 501st SS Heavy Tank Battalion came in.

The company commander, a somewhat pompous man who had been a rich dentist in civilian life, asked if this was the place where he might get his hair cut.

Sickl was about to explain that his orderly was employed in the other room cutting another officer's hair, but Peiper, who had taken an instant dislike to the company commander, was quicker off the mark. He pointed to Sickl, who wore a white apron just like all his orderlies and said: 'That fellow there cuts the hair around here. Sit down!'

Dutifully the man from the 501st sat and Sickl, who had never cut anybody's hair in his life, went to work with a pair of surgical scissors. Finally, after a quarter of an hour, a grinning Peiper personally brought in a mirror so that the company commander could admire himself in it.

The officer gasped with horror when he saw himself in the mirror, shot a poisonous look at the 'hairdresser' and stormed out of the aid post without even as much as a thank you.

Half an hour later, Peiper's mood had changed. He was very serious again. What was left of his *Kampfgruppe* had been divided up among the division, and as he was wounded and had only ten 'runners' – tanks capable of moving – there was no place for him in the coming operation on the new front. But as one of the most experienced officers in the *Leibstandarte*, he had been asked by General Mohnke to go as an advance party.

Together with another officer, he was to make contact with Colonel Ludwig Heilmann's 5th German Parachute Division, which had held up Patton's drive to relieve Bastogne for four long days.

Now, Heilmann's 'Green Devils', as they called themselves, were about finished and it would be Peiper's job to discover what aid – and information – they could give him for the planned attack on the Bastogne Corridor. In the end, from his observations of the American lines at Heilmann's CP, which was located in a railway tunnel, Peiper concurred with the swift plan drawn up by Mohnke that the best means to attack was in the form of a pincer. The division would be broken into two battle groups, the one in the north to be commanded by *Obersturmbannführer* Poetschke; the one in the south under the orders of *Obersturmbannführer* Hansen. The rest of the *Leibstandarte*, grouped in the centre, would support the attack to left and right with covering fire.

Now luck was on the side of the Germans once more. The excellent weather of the Christmas period, which had allowed the resupply from the air of Bastogne and enabled Allied planes to range far and wide, had gone. It had been replaced by overcast, snowy conditions. Using these, the

Leibstandarte hastened to the division's start line without difficulties. Allied reconnaissance planes did not even spot their move from the old Sixth SS Panzer Army front to the new one. It looked as if they were going to spring a complete surprise on the *Amis* holding the Bastogne Corridor.

–

At twenty-five past six on the foggy morning of New Year's Eve 1944, the *Leibstandarte*'s last attack in the West in World War Two commenced. In the van of *Obersturmbannführer* Poetschke's pincer attack was the notorious 7th Panzer Company, which had played the main role in the events at the crossroads of Baugnez on that fateful day.

There were eight Panthers in all. Somehow or other, their crews had all survived the drive on La Gleize. Siptrott commanded one, Clotten another – NCOs who would be under sentence of death by hanging within the year. But, of course, they did not know that, this foggy December morning. The first Panther raced forward, going all across the road. Nothing happened! Then Siptrott tried barrelling across the snow field and ran straight into the Americans who had been waiting for him and the rest. Once again Ultra had not let the Allies down.

There was that old familiar booming, rending sound as metal struck metal. Siptrott's tank reared back on its rear sprockets like a horse being reined in at full gallop. White smoke started to pour from the ruptured engine. Hurriedly, Siptrott baled out.

Clotten was next. After the war, his gunner, Reinhold Kyriss, recorded: 'His [Clotten's] mood was not good. He was nervous and hesitant. At all events, Clotten ordered the tank to stop between two little woods and the engine turned off. He thought we could hear what was going on better that way. Everywhere there was the sound of battle.

'We started up again but soon stopped. One of our tracks broke as we were rolling over a tree stump. Hurriedly we tried to repair the thing, while over our radio we could hear the commander yell "*Achtung, Panzerfeind!*" ['Attention, enemy tanks!']. That's the last we heard of our comrades.'

Clotten was lucky – that day. He was the only survivor of the first attack. Every other Panther was shot up crossing the field. For the point of the *Leibstandarte* had run into a battle-hardened veteran division, the US 35th, in whose ranks the future president of the United States, Harry Truman, had once served. Patton had hurriedly thrown it into the Corridor to bolster up his green troops.

Now, as it grew ever lighter, Mohnke, a shawl over his head to fight off the biting cold, raged. What was happening? Why had not the two pincers – Hansen's and Poetschke's – linked up? Soon the morning mist would clear and then those damned *jabos* would come zooming in, machine guns and cannon singing that old song of death.

–

General Mohnke was not the only senior officer wondering what in three devils' name was going on that morning. Lieutenant Eberhard Kosch of the *Leibstandarte* was waiting in his tank to direct the fire of thirty-four artillery batteries whenever he was given a target. But so far no one had offered him one. The front seemed to have gone to sleep.

Suddenly an impatient voice came on the line. 'What's the situation?' it demanded.

'I'm trying to find out,' Kosch snapped irritably. 'Anyway, *who* is that?'

The answer nearly made him fall out of his turret. '*Model*,' came the answer. It was the commander of Army Group B personally. 'Now, I want to know what's going on.'

Hurriedly, the young Lieutenant gulped: 'I'm going to see for myself, sir.' Swiftly, he gave the orders to move. The tank lurched, dodging shell-shattered tree trunks, swung round the edge of a wood and came to an abrupt stop. Seven Panthers were burning to his front, tiny figures, uniforms already afire, springing from the hatches, twisting and turning in the snow in an attempt to put out those cruel blue flames.

A young tank officer staggered up to Kosch's tank. His face was smeared with oil, his tunic scorched. He was obviously suffering from shock. Pointing a trembling finger at Kosch in an accusing manner, he quavered: 'Seven cannon fired at me.'

Kosch did not know what to do. Suddenly the radio squawked once more. Again it was Model. 'Well, what's going on?' he demanded.

Kosch said: 'The whole situation is confused, sir. You just can't tell friend from foe.'

Just then one of his operators nudged the Lieutenant. 'Seven of our tanks have reached Bastogne, sir. But they're catching hell from artillery and infantry. The commander says his own infantry jumped off the tanks and ran to the rear.'

The operator held up an earphone so that Kosch could hear. Someone was screaming, 'God damn it, send me some infantry! My damned infantry – the scum – ran off!'

Kosch grabbed the radio phone. 'We'll do what we can,' he said hastily. 'I'll forward your report.'

'Forward my ass!' the other man yelled.

One minute later, the phone rang again. It was the same tank commander somewhere over at Bastogne. 'I can't stay here any more!' he yelled wildly. 'I have only five vehicles. They'll be knocked out in a few minutes. I've got to move out... I'd rather have our own fire on top of me than the goddam *Amis* crawling up my ass. Everything here is fouled up!'

For the first time that day, Kosch called up his artillery support and began plastering the *Ami* positions to the front, though he was deadly scared that he might be directing the fire upon his own tanks. A moment later the phone call confirmed he was not. The unknown tank commander in Bastogne cried over the line, 'We're getting out... Keep pouring it on!'

–

By midday it was clear that the *Leibstandarte* had reached the road that led to Bastogne from Martelange, but had failed to close the pincers and thus cut off the corridor. Still, the attack had Patton worried. Soon he would write, '*We can still lose this war!* The Germans are colder, hungrier and weaker than we, to be sure. But they're still doing a great piece of fighting.'

But if Patton was despondent, the Germans were even more so. The 7th Tank Company had been wiped out – and the *Leibstandarte* had gone into the attack with about twenty tanks, so that was a serious loss – and the infantry had run away. Now the mist was clearing and the *jabos* were coming in looking for 'kills'. Not only that, but the *Amis* seemed to be counter-attacking already, though at first General Mohnke's staff did not believe that the notoriously slow Americans could recover that quickly.

It was Kosch, well forward still, looking for targets for his artillery, who discovered them. He had just swung round a wood, with the mist clearing rapidly, when he spotted them: dozens of Shermans with the white star of the Allies on their sides, followed by hundreds of infantry plodding stolidly through the snow like weary farm labourers returning home after a hard day's work in the fields.

Kosch didn't hesitate. '*Amis!*' he yelled, and commanded the artillery co-ordinates down the speaker to the waiting batteries at the rear.

Within minutes there was a tremendous roar. A man-made hurricane of whirling steel flew over his head. *Crash!* The shells of more than thirty batteries slammed into the ground. Men reeled back on all sides. Shermans shuddered and came to an abrupt halt. Some broke into flame at once. The Sherman tank was notoriously flammable. Their crews nicknamed them 'ronsons' after the famous lighter. Here and there, as the surviving infantry began to dig in frantically, damaged Shermans started to fire thick white smoke in order to cover their retreat. But there were plenty more of them lurking in the area.

Kosch was pulling back to his own HQ, located at Bras, seven kilometres east of Bastogne, when one of his phones rang. It was the commandant of one of the *Leibstandarte*'s few surviving tanks.

'Kosch,' he gasped. 'Twelve Shermans with infantry have just come through my position. They're driving towards Bras.'

'Are you sure?'

'Take my word as a good friend. I think they're from that damned 4th Armored Division.' This was Patton's crack armoured division, which had relieved Bastogne first four days before.

'But what the hell are they doing that far east?' Kosch asked, but he received no answer.

Hurriedly, he turned and rolled towards the spot where the supposed breakthrough had taken place. Just under two kilometres east of Bras, he saw ten Shermans coming from Bastogne. He told himself it was impossible – a mirage. One of the German infantry divisions supporting the *Leibstandarte* was supposed to have that road under control!

But it was no mirage. These really were the Fourth's tanks. Excitedly, he called for fire. A minute or two later there was a tremendous screeching sound like the wail of giant banshees. To his rear, at several spots dark-brown fingers of smoke thrust their way into the grey sky. Two whole batteries of multiple mortars had opened up. Next instant their 105 mm electrically powered rockets fell out of the heavens.

One tank shuddered to a stop, burning fiercely, its infantry swatted from the steel deck as if by an invisible hand, but the rest came on.

'What in the devil's name do you think you are doing?' the divisional chief-of-staff, Colonel Ziemssen, yelled over the phone. 'You're firing at your own tanks!'

'They're Shermans,' Kosch retorted.

'How could Shermans be that far east? Cease fire and report to the commander's HQ at once!'

A few minutes later Kosch was doing exactly that.

'Just who do you think you are, Kosch?' Ziemssen bellowed, red in the face. 'The Field Marshal [he meant Model] gave us permission to fire on Bastogne. But that didn't mean you could waste shells as you like. And on your own tanks, too. You'd better keep your damned tired eyes open after this!'

Suddenly the roof disintegrated above them and plaster rained down in a grey shower. A beam came rumbling down at an angle. Mohnke, the chief-of-staff and the rest darted for cover under a heavy table.

'*Tank fire!*' an NCO at the door yelled in alarm.

Kosch flashed a glance out of the window. The Shermans he had spotted earlier on were just outside. Despite the imminent danger, Kosch could not avoid being sarcastic at the expense of the elegant staff officers – 'rear echelon stallions', as they were called maliciously by the frontline troops – cowering under the table. 'General,' he said, 'don't be afraid. They are *our own* tanks!' Laughing uproariously at his own humour, Kosch watched as the staff scrambled madly to get away. Then he flashed a last look out of the shattered window. Suddenly – and strangely – he sensed a strong feeling of comradeship for the *Amis* out there in the snow. For a fleeting moment they were closer to him than these elegant panicked staff officers who wore the same uniform as he did...

–

All that afternoon and into the next day, the *Leibstandarte* battled to close the pincers. That day the Americans flew

3,500 sorties against the *Luftwaffe*'s 550. But despite the strength of the American air attack, the points of both Poetschke's and Hansen's battle groups managed to reach the Martelange-Bastogne road once more.

For the green 11th US Armored Division, the thirty-first was 'a day of horror', as the divisional history recorded it. It was completely stalled and Patton was furious with it. The Eleventh simply did not know how to fight. From top to bottom, as Patton saw it, it appeared to lack the most elementary tactical and combat knowledge. On that New Year's Eve he drove personally to the Eleventh's divisional headquarters to deliver a stinging attack on its commander, for the Eleventh now seemed totally stalled in its attack against the *Leibstandarte* and its supporting infantry of the 5th German Parachute Division. Later he put a brave face on the fiasco in the 'Bastogne Corridor' when he was asked at a press conference, 'What about the [enemy] concentration of armour?' The correspondent meant that of the *Leibstandarte.* Patton grinned, showing his dingy, sawn-off teeth and answered, 'They've got damn little armour left – unless they have reproductive tanks? As always, Patton was good for a laugh and decent copy.

Meanwhile, the 11th Armored, smarting under Patton's attack, gave vent to its frustration at the village of Chenogne. It had been their objective on the thirtieth but they had failed to take it. Now, after severe house-to-house fighting with half the village in flames, they had managed to do so and the Germans were prepared to surrender.

The first to emerge from one of the houses was a medic, a large red cross painted on a white cloth on his chest. He came out waving a Red Cross flag and pleading for mercy. Half a dozen rifles cracked and he staggered and dropped to the snow. Behind him, other Germans emerged from the burning house – only to be shot down one by one as they did, so that a heap of bodies piled up outside the doorway.

Now Germans were surrendering everywhere in the burning village. In the end there were sixty of them lined up on the village street. A sergeant appeared and snapped, '*Not here!* The others hiding in the woods will see. Take them over that hill.'

Pfc John Fague, an eye-witness who recorded the incident, knew what the NCO meant. The prisoners were going to be shot, for the word had been passed down through the ranks that no Germans were to be taken prisoner this day, especially if they were from the SS; and the sergeant did not want the other Germans still holding out in the woods above the village to see what was happening.

So a group of volunteers marched them away over the hill to be shot. Later, as the attack continued, a Jeep came racing up to the infantry. An officer shouted something at the column. The man in front of Fague turned and said: 'Did you hear that? Somebody fouled up. We're supposed to *take* prisoners.'

Fague did not reply. Instead, he turned and looked at the sixty-odd mounds in the snow that hid the bodies of the murdered Germans.

For his part, Patton noted in his diary: 'The 11th Armored is very green and took unnecessary losses to no effect. There were some unfortunate incidents in the shooting of prisoners (I hope we can conceal this).'[14]

–

For the whole of the first week of the New Year, the *Leibstandarte* fought bitterly to hold its positions. Division after division, both infantry and armoured, was thrown at them. Desperately, they clung to their line. On 4 January, the same day that Patton said grimly, 'We can still lose this war', one of the SS surgeons, Dr Knoll, noted in his diary: '15 hours of sleep in the last 120. For over one hundred hours solidly we have patched up and treated 500 Germans and Americans.' And that was in only one battalion.

That same day, General Robert Grow, who had commanded the veteran US Sixth Armored Division ever since it burst into Brittany with Patton's Third Army back in August 1944, noted in his diary, after his Sixth had been beaten back by the *Leibstandarte:* 'This is the first time in combat that my boys have fled. And the 1st SS Panzer Division bursts right into the retreat.'

But the battle for the Bastogne Corridor was almost over now, despite Hitler's urgent warnings that attempts to cut it must still be made. The British and American troops under Montgomery's command in the north were now thrusting into the 'Bulge', which the Germans had pushed into the American line in the Ardennes. The attempt was to link up with Patton's army attacking from the south. It was going to be another Falaise, with the two armies linking up to the rear of the main German battle line at the Belgian township of Houffalize, where, in the previous September, Hemingway had seen the 'White Army' run away from the SS.

If something was not done *soon*, disaster loomed ahead for the *Leibstandarte SS Adolf Hitler*…

PART THREE

THE DEFEAT

'It always looks like a muddle. It often is. But the actual business of fighting is easy enough. You go in, you come out, you go in again and you keep on going in until they break you or you are dead.'

British Hussar Officer, 1941

1. 'ALL YOU CAN EXPECT IS A PLATE OF HOT PAPRIKA GOULASH!'

On the day that Hitler finally gave the order that would allow the *Leibstandarte* to withdraw, Karl Wortmann, who commanded one of the division's flak panzers, was cowering shivering with cold in a foxhole. Long afterwards, he remembered how on that January day: 'We were under artillery fire all the time. During the daylight hours, enemy *jabos* circled and attacked our position at tree-top height. The very earth trembled when they dropped their bombs. Hour after hour the machine guns chattered on both sides and the mortar bombs howled. It was a man-made hurricane. And the echo of the guns and shells ran round the valleys and hills. One could almost imagine with all this noise and racket that the heavens above were about to burst and fall in on us!'

But it was not only the enemy with his planes and guns with whom the weary, haggard survivors of the great surprise counterattack had to contend. There was the cold, too, which wore down even the veterans of the Russian front.

It was the coldest winter in Western Europe within living memory. The dead froze hard as boards where they had fallen. There was no hope of burying them; the ground was rock-hard, but as it had begun to snow again, the heavy fat white flakes took care of that. For the living, their existence outdoors, without any source of warmth, even hot food, was one long, never-ending misery.

Tank engines had to be started up every ten minutes throughout the night or their engines seized up for good. All optics had to be smeared with grease constantly, or they would fog over and make accurate shooting impossible. Men's feet turned purple with cold, as did their ears if they were exposed; and if nothing was done about it, the purple colour would change to a dull, ugly white and then the men knew they had frostbite. Virtually everyone suffered from what the men called the 'thin shits', due to the icy dirty water that they were forced to drink. Ersatz coffee, whenever it did reach the frontline positions, was invariably cold or luke-warm. But it was useful for thawing out frozen feet or trying to wash away the mess that had by now accumulated around everyone's loins and lower body.

'Felt lice', as they were called, were rampant. Everyone, including Peiper and Mohnke, had them. They lived in the seams of their shirts, their dirty underwear, their hair, even their eyebrows. In this case, at least, being freezingly cold all the time had one advantage: the lice did not itch in these arctic temperatures. The *feld* lice preferred to keep nice and snug next to the warm skin of their 'host'.

And all the while, as they now retreated, leaving behind them the yellow stains of their watery faeces on the snow, they were expected to turn and fight. For what was left of the battered *Leibstandarte* was now being constantly harassed and pursued by elements of three whole US divisions.

Morale, even in the *Leibstandarte*, was beginning to fall rapidly. The heady enthusiasm of 16 December 1944, when the great counter-attack was launched, had long vanished. It had been replaced by a bitter, sullen war-weariness. Even before the offensive, Hitler, worried by the problem of morale, had ordered that command should be transferred to the next in rank whenever a troop commander faced with a difficult decision felt he should give up the fight. In such cases, the officer was to ask the officers and men under him, in order of rank, if one of them wanted to carry out the mission. The man who accepted automatically became the senior person, whatever his rank, while the officer reverted to the ranks. Now in early January the order was broadened. Whenever a group was surrounded or in a situation where its commander might be tempted to surrender, the next in rank was to take over automatically and continue the fight.

To ensure that this did take place and that all orders were obeyed without question, draconian measures were introduced. Relatives, even sweethearts, could be punished by being sent to the concentration camps for any 'crimes' committed by their menfolk at the front. All senior commanders knew, in addition, that their wives and children were, in fact, hostages, who could be used to make sure they fought to the last.

Men thought likely to desert or who were regarded as defeatists were arrested even though their intentions were only suspected. They were sent to the notorious SS military prison outside Danzig. From there, after a short sharp spell of punishment on bread and water, they were usually dispatched to a penal battalion. These penal battalions were made up of politically unreliable men and those who had committed military crimes.

The penal battalions were known as 'Ascension Day Commandos' for they were used on missions such as clearing mines, attacking enemy artillery positions, etc, from which there was no return. The only way out for a man posted to the dreaded penal battalions was – heavenwards!

Still, despite the terrible weather conditions, the lack of food and equipment, the slump in morale and the horrific casualties (most battalions of the *Leibstandarte* had now lost more than sixty per cent of their strengths), they fought on, steadily working their way eastwards. On 12 January, for example, in an attempt to stop the American encirclement of the retreating German troops, a composite force of the surviving two hundred SS men of the *Leibstandarte*'s two panzer grenadier regiments launched an attack, supported by seven armoured vehicles.

Hans Schmidt, who was there, recalled after the war: 'Our objective was to clear the road of the enemy and re-capture an important crossroads. We attacked in line without any support because we had lost our machine guns and I could not even fire my rifle because it had frozen up. As soon as we moved, the whole weight of the American artillery fell upon us. Men went down everywhere in their dozens. It was pure hell. I dropped quite close to the American positions. Most of my comrades were already dead. Still the Americans kept firing for a long time at anything that moved, even the wounded. After some time the Americans got out of their positions and started to search the dead and the badly wounded. Probably they were looking for weapons and souvenirs.

Suddenly our own artillery opened up. But the shells dropped short, right among the survivors.'

The shells made the Americans flee, but Hans Schmidt dared not moved. Instead, he lay freezing in the snow till darkness. When he finally did rise, he found three other comrades who had not been wounded and one man who had been badly hit. Together the four of them carried the wounded man back to the aid station. 'When the MO saw my feet, he ordered me sent to hospital immediately. Both were black with frostbite.'

Behind them, more than 120 men stiffened in the snow, some of them with one of their hands raised high as if in supplication to Heaven to have mercy on them. But an observer on the morrow would note that God had looked the other way on that Friday, 12 January 1945. For the American victors, who had searched the bodies before they had fled from the German shells, had merely raised the dead men's hands – *so that they could cut off the wedding rings from their fingers...*

–

On the morning of Tuesday, 16 January, an American Army photographer, Staff Sergeant Douglas Wood, was looking for some footage at the command post of Colonel Hugh O'Farrell, who belonged to the 2nd US Armored Division. As the guns thundered, Wood and O'Farrell could see, down below in the valley, German troops passing through Houffalize. It was obvious to both the Americans that the link-up between the two attacking US armies, the First and Third, had not taken place. The Germans were still escaping from the Ardennes through the town.

About this time, a lone figure came out of the nearby woods. O'Farrell's men waved for him to come to them. He didn't. Instead, he returned to the shelter of the trees, appearing some minutes afterwards with five other men. This time, however, they did approach the waiting GIs of O'Farrell's command, all of them with their weapons at the ready, prepared to shoot at the slightest sign of trouble.

But there was not going to be any firing this particular morning. Wood recognised the uniform first. 'Our people!' he cried, and raised his camera. This was going to be a historic shot. For these Americans, soaking wet and freezing after wading the River Ourthe, were from Patton's Third Army. As the two groups, representing great armies nearly a million strong, began slapping each other on the back and shaking hands, Wood's camera whirred. This was the long-awaited link-up!

But in the end the 'historic link-up' ended on a low note. Sometime afterwards, Colonel Miles Foy of the 11th Armored Division of the Third Army appeared on the scene. He, too, was soaked and shivering. Wood led him to O'Farrell's tank and cried: 'There's a colonel here from the 11th Armored to see you, sir.'

O'Farrell stuck his head out of the Sherman's turret and looked startled. Foy did the same. Finally Foy blurted out, 'Well, Jesus Christ, if it isn't O'Farrell! I didn't recognise you in a tank... Haven't seen you since Fort Knox!'

The Bulge was closed and the last German counter-offensive in the West was over, although the battle was not considered officially ended until twelve days later, when the lines were restored to those that the Allies had held on Saturday, 16 December 1944.

British war correspondent R. W. Thompson of the *Sunday Times*, who went down into Houffalize later that day, when the last of the Germans had gone for ever, felt 'there was that kind of vacuum that seems to grip a place in the first moments; the enemy have gone; all that remains is dead; and there is this terrible silence that is as eerie a sensation as any I know...' Some time afterwards, he encountered 'the truckloads of prisoners going back over the roads now swirling with clouds of powdered snow in the fierce east wind'. These were 'a token of the achievement of the Americans, while the great guns with their huge white muzzles and white-painted carriages are a token of what still remains to be done as the enemy is harassed unceasingly in his retreat and the two armies drive relentlessly into his flanks'.

Yet again, just as at Falaise, the *Leibstandarte* had paid the bloody butcher's bill, but it *had* escaped the final reckoning. For already it was being withdrawn across the border into the Reich. The Fuehrer could not bring himself completely to sacrifice those men who bore his name on their sleeves. The *Leibstandarte SS Adolf Hitler* had another four months to live, fight and die, before it vanished from the face of the earth for good...

–

Back in October 1944, *Obersturmbannfuhrer* Otto Skorzeny, who had left the *Leibstandarte* to form the SS's own version of the SAS, had done it once again. This was the man who had snatched Mussolini, the Italian dictator, from underneath the very noses of his captors; had planned a kamikaze bombing raid on the House of Commons to kill Churchill; had suggested an aerial bombardment of New York with V-2 missiles taken across the Atlantic by U-boat; had then kept Hungary in the war as Germany's ally with yet another of his bold, unconventional strokes.

At dawn on 16 October that year, the scar-faced SS giant had assembled his strike force beneath Castle Hill in Budapest. It was not very large. Four tanks, a troop of Goliaths, miniature remote-controlled tracked vehicles, each packing two hundred kilos of high explosive, and two companies of SS parachute infantry. But it was all that was available to Skorzeny to assault a fortified complex dating back to the Middle Ages and reputedly held by a whole Hungarian division. But Skorzeny was counting on surprise and boldness, for he knew they must capture the second traitor, who was about to betray the Fuehrer and take Hungary out of the war on Germany's side.

He knew the risk was high. Yet he knew, too, that he if he could take Admiral Horthy alive, now that his son was safely in German hands, Hungary could be blackmailed into continuing the war. That would mean the saving of countless German lives. For if the Horthys surrendered their country to the Russians, the whole German central front would collapse.

Skorzeny looked at his most prized possession, a gold watch given to him by Mussolini. On the back there was engraved the date of the Italian's rescue '12.9.43'. 'Do you want Mussolini time?' he would always joke whenever a comrade asked the time. It was exactly one minute to six, and above them on the hill nothing stirred. The Hungarians would still be in their beds, he hoped. He gave the signal and prayed he would be lucky for a second time.

Hurriedly, his SS commandos sprang into their vehicles. Motors burst into noisy life. Rudely the dawn stillness was shattered by impatient drivers gunning their engines. The air was abruptly filled with the stink of fumes.

Skorzeny touched the Knight's Cross at his throat, won for rescuing the Duce, as if to reassure himself, and then barked the order, '*Los... vorwaerts!*' Next to him his driver thrust home first gear. The little Volkswagen four-wheel-drive moved forward. Behind it the rest of the column followed. The daring coup had begun. Operation *Panzerfaust* (Missile-launcher) was under way...

Skorzeny had arrived in Budapest, the Hungarian capital, a few days earlier. His cover was a very unlikely one for such a tough-looking individual; it was that of *Herr Doktor* Wolf, a German tourist, armed with an ancient Baedeker guide. But the cover was sufficient for him to reconnoitre the layout of Castle Hill, the seat of the country's government, and observe the antics of the Hungarian dictator's son, 'Miki' Horthy.

Miki, or Miklos, his real name, was the *enfant terrible* of the Horthy family. He ran a stable of mistresses, threw wild expensive parties with plenty of champagne, Tokay and unlimited supplies of rationed food, and studiously avoided being sent to the Russian front. All the same, he was the apple of the Hungarian dictator's eye; for Admiral Horthy had already lost his other son, Istvan, in Russia.

Now, however, the Hungarian playboy had turned into a diplomat, albeit a covert one. As reported by the local Gestapo, Miki was secretly aiming to take Hungary out of the war, negotiating with the Russians through a third party, Tito's Yugoslav partisans. He had seen the writing on the wall. Germany was about to go under. He didn't want Hungary to go down with her.

In the end, Skorzeny, alias Dr Wolf, had decided the best way to keep Admiral Horthy loyal and toeing the line was to kidnap his darling son Miki. That would stop the talks with the Yugoslavs and Miki could be kept as a hostage for Admiral Horthy's good behaviour. Thus it was agreed with the local Gestapo, who had been covering these clandestine meetings between Miki and the Yugoslavs, that the next time they met, Miki would be kidnapped and immediately spirited away to the Reich and house arrest.

On a sparkling early Sunday morning, the plan, maliciously code-named Operation Mickey Mouse, was put into action. The plotters were meeting in a small house fringing one of the capital's tiny squares. When Skorzeny drove up, the square was virtually deserted. There were two empty Hungarian trucks outside the meeting place. A little further on, there was a canvas-backed Hungarian Army truck parked close to Miki's private car.

Skorzeny, dressed in civilian clothes in his guise as Dr Wolf, parked, then lifted the bonnet of his little car, pretending to fiddle with the engine. Across the way, the canvas back of the Army lorry was jerked open momentarily as someone took a peek at him. Skorzeny just managed to get a glimpse into the back. There was a heavy machine gun set up there, crewed by three Hungarian soldiers. The traitors had come prepared for trouble. Soon they were going to get it.

Time passed. Two German military policemen strolled into the square. They looked just like any other 'chain-dogs', as MPs were nicknamed from the silver plates that hung around their necks. Obviously, they were on a routine patrol this quiet Sunday morning.

Abruptly, they lost their casual air. Suddenly they were running, pelting towards the house where the secret meeting was being held, unslinging their machine pistols as they ran. The Hungarians in the truck ripped back the canvas. The machine gun chattered into angry life. One of the MPs was hit. He slammed to the cobbles. Skorzeny dashed forward. Slugs cut the air all around him. He grabbed the wounded MP by the collar. Grunting and swearing, he dragged him to safety.

Now all hell was let loose. Hungarian soldiers streamed into the square from all sides. Skorzeny's men rushed out of their cover to meet them. Wild firing broke out. Skorzeny yelled at his driver. Too late! The man yelped with pain as he was hit. Now his little group of men in civilian clothes began returning the Hungarian fire with their pistols. But that damned heavy machine gun was too much. They started to retreat. Skorzeny knew he had to do something. He tugged out his whistle and blew a shrill blast. It was the signal his second-in-command, Baron von Foelkersam, had been waiting for.

He came swiftly round the corner at the head of the SS paras. The paras fired from the hip as they ran, all of them big, tough and frightening-looking in their camouflage smocks. The sight took the heart out of the Hungarians. Hurriedly, they began to back off.

Skorzeny did not wait for them to recover. With his men tossing grenades to left and right, they made hastily for the house in which Miki was located. Above them, on the roof, Hungarian soldiers who did not possess grenades dropped bricks and chunks of marble on to their heads. But the unusual missiles didn't stop Skorzeny's paras. Within minutes they had forced the door of the house and were storming inside, only to find that a couple of Skorzeny's men previously planted in the house were already holding Miki Horthy captive at pistol point.

The playboy-turned-diplomat, who spoke fluent German, was flushed and angry. He was threatening terrible revenge on his kidnappers. But Skorzeny, gasping from the exertion, had no time to play games with the Hungarian. All the same, he did not want to use physical violence on his precious hostage. But how was he going to shut him up and get him out of the house?

Skorzeny's gaze swept round the apartment hurriedly. Outside, the angry snap-and-crackle of the fire fight continued. Then he spotted what he wanted: a large flowered carpet and a piece of thick curtain rope at the French window. He rapped out an order.

Without ceremony, the playboy was flung to the floor. While he struggled and kicked, the delighted paras wrapped him in the carpet and then trussed him with the cord like a reluctant beast being readied for the market.

'To the airfield!' Skorzeny yelled. 'I'll follow.' He turned to a grinning von Foelkersam. 'And no more shooting,' he ordered. '*Understood?*'

The Baron nodded. They left, together with their new hostage. The whole operation had taken exactly ten minutes...

That Sunday morning, Skorzeny waited nervously at his hotel, chain-smoking, wondering how Admiral Horthy would react to the news that his son had been kidnapped by his erstwhile allies, the Germans. During the time he waited, his spies came to report periodically on what was happening in Budapest. By ten o'clock the whole of Castle Hill had been sealed off. Troops were everywhere. All roads to Admiral Horthy's residence had been barricaded and Hungarian engineers were even laying hurried minefields in the general areas. Skorzeny's mood dropped to zero.

At noon, Radio Budapest interrupted its programmes. The speaker announced the nation should stand by for an important speech by the dictator at two o'clock that afternoon. Skorzeny groaned. It looked as if his whole plan had gone drastically wrong.

At two o'clock, Skorzeny, his officers and an interpreter listened to Admiral Horthy's speech. The ageing Admiral of the landlocked country, who had obtained his rank in the Austrian Navy in World War One, commenced with an angry tirade against his ally. Germany had lost the war. There was no hope for Hitler. Then he made his own position clear. Although he personally had suppressed Bela Kun's Communist government of 1919 in Budapest in a bloody counter-revolution, he now intended to make a separate peace with the 'red beast'. Already he had asked for an armistice with the Red Army. Hostilities between the Russians and the Hungarians would cease forthwith.

Skorzeny had gambled and failed, he realised. The fate of over one million Germans on the central front lay in his hands. There was no alternative open to him. He must take out Admiral Horthy himself. With a bit of luck, the fact that Miki, his son, was in German hands would help. In the last resort, he could threaten to have Miki killed…

–

Now their convoy rolled slowly up the hill towards the seat of the Hungarian government. Baron von Foelkersam, from one of the Russian-occupied Baltic states, had a macabre sense of humour. He said to Skorzeny: 'Bit unpleasant if we got hit from the flank, eh?'

Skorzeny, who had already considered that unpleasant possibility, didn't answer. He couldn't. His heart was thudding. Any minute, he expected the vehicle to roll over one of the mines his spies had reported the Hungarians had placed in the road.

They came level with the first sentries. Skorzeny waved to them as cheerfully as he could. The Hungarian clicked to attention. Behind him, his tank commanders raised their hands to their helmets to return the salute. Skorzeny let out a sigh of relief. They were through the first barrier!

At thirty kilometres an hour, they rolled towards Admiral Horthy's house. In the harsh light of the October dawn, they could see three Hungarian tanks parked in the drive. Would they fire on their former allies? Suddenly, the first Hungarian tank raised its cannon, but higher and higher: an indication it was *not* going to fire. Seconds later they rolled by the three tanks. A barricade loomed up. It was manned by troops. Skorzeny signalled to the Panther tank immediately behind his vehicle. It swung out of the column. Skorzeny's driver braked and it rolled to the front of the assault group. The tank driver revved his engine. At top speed the Panther crashed into the barricade and demolished it to reveal *six* anti-tank guns and their crews in position beyond!

Skorzeny did not see what happened next. He sprang out of his vehicle. His bodyguard of six NCOs and Baron von Foelkersam raced after him. Whistles shrilled. Officers bellowed orders. All was controlled confusion.

A bare-headed Hungarian colonel came rushing at the Germans, pistol in hand. Von Foelkersam knocked it from his hand. Another Hungarian tried to bar their way. Skorzeny grabbed him. 'Lead us to the commandant of Castle Hill – *at once!*' he snarled.

The Hungarian might not have understood German, but he understood the tone. Tamely, he ran on with the group of Germans, shouting instructions on how to find their way. Now from deep inside the fortress, the attackers could hear the sound of firing. But so far no one, save the lone colonel, had tried to bar their excited progress.

Skorzeny rushed into a room. A Hungarian was crouched at the window, firing a machine gun. An NCO pushed by Skorzeny, grabbed the machine gun and flung it into the courtyard below.

Skorzeny had to use force to prevent him doing the same with the surprised Hungarian gunner. They pushed on. A door was flung open to their front. A Hungarian stood there in the uniform of a major-general. Skorzeny guessed immediately this was the man they sought.

'Are you the commandant of Castle Hill?' he rapped.

Without waiting for the surprised general to answer, he added: 'I demand you surrender Castle Hill at once! You are responsible if any more blood is spilled. I ask you for an immediate decision.'

Tamely, the general gave in. 'I surrender Castle Hill to you,' he said, 'and will order immediate cessation of hostilities.' Thereupon the two men shook hands and it was all over.

At the cost of twenty German casualties, the senior Horthy was in German hands. Soon he would be sent to the Reich in a special train to become 'the guest of the Fuehrer' (as it was put politely). In his place, the pro-German Hungarian aristocrat Count Szalasi would take over immediately. He would order the Hungarian Army to take up arms against the Russians once more. In due course, the Hungarians would still be fighting loyally at Germany's side long after all her other Allies in Europe had deserted her. The one-time humble captain in the *Leibstandarte* had pulled off a tremendous success.

But Skorzeny's bold *coup d'etat* lasted a mere three months. On that same Christmas Eve when his one-time comrade Peiper was extricating his survivors from La Gleize, Christmas shoppers in the eastern part of the Hungarian capital[15] watched curiously as tanks began to rumble through the main streets.

In itself this was nothing new. Ever since the war against Russia commenced in 1941, tanks had been passing through the capital on their way to the front or returning from it. But these tanks were different from any the civilians had ever seen before. Suddenly, someone noticed the red star decorating their turrets. These were Russian T-34s. *The Red Army had broken through!*

The shoppers scattered in panic as the air-raid sirens began to sound their shrill warning. Everywhere German and Hungarian soldiers were roused from their barracks, offices, leave hotels, even their hospitals, and formed up into hasty battle groups. Tigers from two SS panzer divisions went into action, stopping the drive of the Russian T-34s outside the Hotel Gellert. All that day and the following one, all thoughts of Christmas forgotten now, the Germans and Hungarians under the command of SS General Pfeffer-Wildenbruch pushed the Russians back to their starting point and fought off all attempts to cross the Danube.

By the first week of January, however, the SS General was surrounded in Budapest with nine divisions, two of them SS, the 8th SS and the 22nd SS Cavalry. Now, as the *Leibstandarte*, worn, weakened and demoralised, straggled back over the frontier into the security of the Reich, Pfeffer-Wildenbruch's 70,000 men were holding back the attacks of two Soviet Armies. Soon, *very soon*, something drastic had to be done – or those Germans, including the two SS cavalry divisions, whose men were virtually condemned to death if they fell into Russian hands, would be overwhelmed. It was not surprising, therefore, as the survivors of the *Leibstandarte* gathered around Bonn in the last week of January to receive yet more new tanks and more bewildered teenage recruits or reluctant culls from the *Luftwaffe* and the Navy, that the rumours began to fly thick and fast about their next assignment.

It was clear that it would be left to the infantry to defend the frontiers of the Reich in the West. Armoured troops such as Dietrich's Sixth Panzer Army would be employed to fight an offensive battle. Some of these 'latrine-o-grams', as they were nicknamed, maintained the *Leibstandarte* would be sent to join *Reichsfuhrer SS* Himmler's Army of the Vistula. After all, Himmler was their supreme commander, wasn't he? Others suggested that the *Leibstandarte* would be ordered east, but not to the Russian front. Instead, Hitler's guard would be posted to their old garrison town – Berlin – where it would be their duty to protect the capital and, naturally, the Fuehrer, against the Russians.

But the newly promoted full-Colonel Peiper guessed right in that last week of January 1945, when he was approached by Sergeant Hans Caspary, one of the few surviving old hares from the division's pre-war Berlin days. Hans Caspary, a big, gruff man who came from the Moselle area, knew the new *Standartenfuhrer* Peiper from peacetime and thought he dared risk a direct question. '*Standartenfuhrer*,' he said, standing to attention, 'can I ask a question?'

Peiper grinned up at the big NCO. 'All right, Caspary, stop playing toy soldier. You've built your ape now' – he meant standing at attention – 'what's your question? Fire away.'

'Well, *Standartenführer*, where are we going? Some of the boys,' he said hopefully, 'think it's Berlin.'

'Yes, you'd like that, you old rogue,' Peiper replied. 'Whores and suds for breakfast each morning, no doubt. That's what you're after.' He shook his head in mock sorrow. 'But you're not having them. All you can expect from your new assignment is a plate of hot paprika goulash!'

Caspary's face fell. 'Great crap on the Christmas tree!' he exclaimed, forgetting that he was talking to the new assistant divisional commander. '*Hungary!*'

2. 'KISS MY ARSE'

On the morning of Sunday, 11 February 1945, while the *Leibstandarte*, as part of Dietrich's sixth SS Panzer Army, secretly took up its positions to the west, General Pfeffer-Wildenbruch ordered the breakout. Ever since early January, entrenched in the Buda hills, his German and Hungarian troops had held out bitterly, shelling any attempt by the Russians to cross the ice-covered Danube.

The breakout would take place in three groups, and although few of his weary soldiers thought they had a chance, the SS, in particular, felt it was better to die fighting than to be slaughtered in cold blood as prisoners of the Ivans. Little did they know that morning that the Russians already knew they were going to attempt to break out; they had spies within Pfeffer-Wildenbruch's forces. Before dawn that Sunday, the Red Army commander had covertly withdrawn his men from the nearest buildings surrounding the trapped enemy force.

At first light, the signal flares started to hiss into the grey winter sky above Pfeffer-Wildenbruch's positions. One after another the three groups sprang from the ruins and foxholes that they had defended so obstinately these last terrible weeks. Most of them were armed only with handguns – rifles, carbines, machine pistols, etc. – and they ran straight into a withering hail of Russian fire.

Artillery and rocket fire slammed down everywhere. Great gaps appeared almost immediately in their ranks. Panic broke out. Now it was every man for himself.

All that long, horrific Sunday, small groups of Germans and Hungarians attempted to break out, desperately trying to find an escape route through the shattered, burning streets of Buda, the ruined houses shaking like theatre sets every time a fresh barrage of Russian shells slammed down. A Hungarian divisional commander led out the survivors of his group, a handful of Hungarians and four SS men. They were a few of the fortunate ones.

The commander of the 8th SS Cavalry, General Rohr, died in the breakout. His comrade, General Zehender of the 22nd SS Cavalry, ran into a roadblock and knew he had no hope of escaping. He shot himself through the head on the open street.

Now, as the new day approached, the Russians butchered the survivors as they lay wounded or just help-lessly exhausted in the debris-littered streets. Sound trucks drove up to the wooded Buda hills and broadcast appeals for the survivors to come out. They would be 'treated decently'. If Germans emerged, especially if they were SS, they were stripped naked and shot there and then. If they were Hungarian, they were given the choice of the Gulag death camps or joining the Free Hungarian Army, now fighting on the Russian side. Those who did were given a piece of red cloth to attach to their Royal Hungarian Army uniforms and were immediately employed rounding up their fellow Hungarians still in hiding.

In the end it was a complete, appalling massacre. Pfeffer-Wildenbruch surrendered and survived. But of his 70,000 men, only seven hundred escaped to the German lines to the west. The rest were killed in battle or more likely murdered in cold blood. That Monday the Soviet commander claimed that his men had captured 30,000 prisoners. But that wasn't true. In fact, he had only a few thousand in his divisional cages and they were mostly Hungarian. So to make up the difference, he simply sent the dreaded 'Greencaps', the NKVD secret police, who wore a green cloth around their caps, on to the streets of the capital to round up 25,000 civilians, who became instant 'Hungarian soldiers'.

Now, as the stories of the butchery of the Russian prisoners, the widespread looting and rape, began to circulate in Budapest, the war-weary Hungarians, who had been longing for peace ever since Admiral Horthy's angry broadcast of the previous October, began to have second thoughts. Was 'liberation' by the Russian Bear such a good thing, after all? It would take nearly another half a century, right into our own time, before they really started to find an answer to that overwhelming question...

–

The disaster at Buda did not deter Hitler from his ambitious plans for Hungary, the source of most of the Third Reich's vital petroleum products. Ever since his defeat in the Ardennes, he had been toying with various plans to recapture Budapest, cut to pieces several Russian armies, throw the survivors over the Danube for good, and ensure that the oil fields at Nagykanizsa remained in German hands. It would be an operation on the scale of those he had proposed in those years of victory, 1940-42. It would be the *Blitzkrieg* all over again!

Ten days after the fall of Buda, General Woehler, the commander of the German army group responsible for Hungary, conferred with his two army commanders, General Black of the Sixth Army and Sepp Dietrich, posing as 'Chief of Engineers, South East', the newly arrived commander of the Sixth SS Panzer Army.

Together they came up with four plans, which Woehler thereupon submitted to the Fuehrer. Of these, Hitler selected one, which would have not only the positive results he desired, but also great propaganda value. It envisaged a strike southwards, covering and capturing a great deal of ground, which would look good in the press, with the offensive then turning north to recapture Budapest.

Woehler and his commanders now proceeded to play their parts in the coming offensive with somnambulistic unconcern. No one pointed out just how useless it was to conduct a major operation in order merely to gain ground. Due to the Sixth SS Panzer Army's lack of infantry, the army wouldn't be able to hold it once the tanks had captured the terrain, if the area came under serious Russian attack.

But if Hitler's senior Army generals, those Prussian *Monokelfritzen* whom he hated, obeyed without protest, his own SS generals were loud in their objections. General Gille, an old National Socialist and the commander of the 4th SS Panzer Corps, for instance, sent one of his junior officers, Lieutenant Kernmayr, to Woehler's headquarters. With him Kernmayr brought two newly captured Russian officers and some disturbing news. Under interrogation, the Russians had revealed the *Stavka*, the Russian High Command, knew the Germans were coming.

The *Stavka* had already cancelled an attack along the Danube towards Vienna. Now the Russian troops on the west bank of the Danube were digging in, creating an elaborate system of defences, well covered by extensive minefields and lavishly supported by antitank guns. In addition, according to the two Russian prisoners, the Red Army had massed 3,500 armoured vehicles to meet the impending challenge.

Colonel Count von Rittberg, Woehler's chief-of-Intelligence, pooh-poohed the young SS officer's fears. He said he wasn't alarmed by the Russian build-up, but he would tell Woehler about it over lunch.

So Kernmayr waited, fuming, while von Rittberg went riding, played a game of chess and drank a glass of champagne at a small birthday party. It was dark when he finally deigned to talk to the SS Lieutenant once more. 'The General was most interested in your tale,' he told Kernmayr cheerfully. 'Most interested. Please give my regards to General Gille.'

Kernmayr, although much junior in rank to this elegant staff officer, was a typical product of the SS officer corps, tough and arrogant and not easily fobbed off. He stood his ground and demanded: 'What's going to be done about it?'

The Count smiled winningly. '*Mein lieber Mann*,' he said in a soothing voice, 'don't worry.'

'But what am I to report?' Kernmayr persisted. 'After all, this is an extremely dangerous threat to our flank.'

The Count remained unmoved. Kernmayr reminded him that their Hungarian allies out on the 4th SS Corps' flank possessed only two machine guns per company and were in no position to stop a massive Russian armoured counter-attack.

Von Rittberg kept smiling. Everyone thought Intelligence officers were 'nervous Nellies', seeing bogeymen in the shadows all the time. He wasn't that kind of

Intelligence officer. He always tried to remain positive. 'Everything's under control, my dear fellow. Army Group will do all that's necessary.'

But nothing was done… Woehler was determined that Dietrich's Sixth SS Panzer Army would attack on time, whether the SS liked it or not. In these last few months, ever since the general's attempt on Hitler's life, the SS seemed to believe they were a law to themselves, especially the Fuehrer's favourite SS armoured divisions. Now, with the Fuehrer's power crumbling rapidly 'die Herren von der SS', parvenus and upstarts for the most part, would have to learn to take orders from those who had always controlled Germany's destiny, the Prussian military aristocracy.

–

As February started to give way to March, the weather began to play up. As the time came ever closer for the start of the great offensive, ironically named *Fruehling-serwachen* (the Rise of Spring), the heavy snows of late February yielded to a sudden rise in the temperature. Within twenty-four hours, the roads over which the heavy German tanks would travel thawed out and became a sea of black, thick goo. Everywhere the new 68-ton ponderously slow Royal Tigers, moving up to the front under cover of darkness, got stuck, miring down to their bogies in the clinging Hungarian mud.

Peiper, who would lead the *Leibstandarte's* armoured attack group, while Hansen commanded a similar battle group made up of panzer grenadiers, moved forward on 3 March to reconnoitre the division's jumping-off point. It was pouring with rain. Arriving at his destination, he stopped his vehicle and, sweeping his arm around dramatically, he exclaimed with that tough, cynical smile of his:

'Gentlemen, we are now at the start line.' His officers followed the direction of his gesture. As far as the eye could see, a vast morass of thick black mud stretched to the horizon.

They looked glum. Even the Tigers with their particularly broad tracks, designed specifically for the thick mud of a Russian winter, would have trouble with this stuff.

Back at divisional headquarters north of Lake Balaton, Peiper called 1st SS Panzer Corps HQ (the *Leibstandarte* belonged to 1st SS Corps). Angrily, he shouted over the bad line: 'I have tanks, *not* submarines. You can kiss my arse, but I won't do it.'

'Keep calm, Peiper,' the frustrated corps commander said appeasingly. 'We're doing something about it.'

At the *Leibstandarte*'s HQ, where everyone was disgusted with the apathy of the higher headquarters and apprehensive of the slaughter to come, a new slogan spread, as the Fuehrer's 56th birthday drew ever nearer: 'We're going to present the Rumanian oil fields to the Fuehrer for his birthday.' It was a slogan Hitler's Imperial Guard received with a muffled curse or a soft burst of cynical laughter. The *Leibstandarte* knew they'd never see the Rumanian oil fields again, and perhaps, in their heart of hearts, some of them secretly wished that their Fuehrer would never celebrate another birthday...

On Monday, 5 March 1945, the weather in Hungary grew even worse. That morning the thaw gave way to a raging blizzard. Even Woehler wondered if he could attack in this kind of terrible weather. That evening, however, as the snow turned to rain again, Sepp Dietrich reported his Sixth SS Panzer Army was 'substantially ready' for the assault. At ten o'clock that same night, Woehler decided that if Dietrich of the SS, who had constantly tried to delay the start of the attack, was about ready, then that was it. He ordered the offensive to commence just after midnight next day.

The actors were in place. The stage was set. The last act could begin…

–

Just after midnight, Peiper's battle group neared its jumping-off point. It was freezing and sleeting at the same time, but the mud was as bad as ever. Peiper's heavy tanks were up to their bellies in the black goo. To the left and right, the panzer grenadiers had left their half-tracks and were moving up on foot, each man clinging on to the belt of the man in front of him in the gloom. Their commanders thought the infantry would be able to advance better and more quickly on foot than in their tracked vehicles.

The dawn started to break at about six-thirty. Abruptly the first shells of the German barrage flew over the advancing men's heads. The German shelling was weak; ammunition was rationed. Russian counter-fire, on the other hand, was spectacular and terrifying: hundreds of guns and rocket-launchers pouring a furious, murderous hail of steel upon the advancing German infantry. The panzer grenadiers went to ground, trapped and awed by that tremendous barrage. But there was no place they could dig in. The ground was too water-logged. That dawn they either died where they crouched, shaking with fear, trembling violently like men suffering from a tropical fever, or they 'took their hind-legs in their hands', as the SS phrase had it, and rushed forward.

One who did so was *Panzergrenadier* Diether Kuhl-mann. He stormed a hill to the front, together with comrades, firing from the hip with their machine pistols, crazed and carried away by the atavistic, unreasoning blood-lust of combat. The Russian defenders were caught completely by surprise. They had relied on their artillery to deal with the Fritzes.

Now the young SS men were inside their trench system, hacking, slicing, kicking, firing, mowing down everything that looked 'Ivan', butchering the survivors in that fury of battle that comes from too much stress and strain, when a human being becomes a primeval animal again, heart full of murder and revenge.

It was only later, when not a single Russian remained alive and the gasping ashen-faced SS men, their every limb trembling with what they had just undergone, had time to explore the Russian position, that they found they had blundered into a Russian secret weapon: a whole row of automatic flame-throwers, which could be activated by a button from a remote control.

That day, Diether Kuhlmann, one of the old hares, survived to fight on. But his comrade, Herbert, did not.

Together with his friend and comrade, Diether Kuhlmann had run into a Russian ambush in a little Hungarian township, whose name they never learned. They had shot up the Russians and forced them to flee. But in the skirmish, Herbert had been hit. Now he lay in his blanket, alongside the rest of the wounded from Kuhlmann's company, moaning softly, waiting for the medics to come.

'I squatted next to Herbert in the straw,' Kuhlmann remembered long afterwards. 'The only light came from a flickering candle. Outside the barn the cold wind whistled. My breath came in quick gasps. Suddenly I found myself blubbing like a little child. Herbert moaned and moaned and moaned. I remember we had fought side by side together in Normandy, then Falaise, after that the Eifel and Ardennes, now here in Hungary. Herbert had been at my side all the time.

'The stretcher bearers came in and took him out, still moaning, though more softly now. Suddenly it shot through me: *I'd never see Herbert again!* And he was only eighteen years old, just like me…'

Yet another of the old hares, for that was what these eighteen-year-olds were now – veterans, had bought it. Later, Sepp Dietrich would comment cynically with a wry grin: 'The Sixth SS Panzer Army is aptly named, gentlemen. That it is. For it's only got *six* tanks left!' But it was not only Dietrich's panzers that were being eliminated; it was these young men from half a dozen countries who made up the backbone of his army…

Thus, that second week of March 1945 passed in a merciless, relentless slogging match, with the German armoured steamroller grinding slowly eastwards and pushing the reluctant Red Army in front of it, as it contested every metre of that killing ground. Casualties soared as the heavy tanks bogged down time and time again, and the panzer grenadiers had to assault the Russian positions without the aid and protection of armour.

Time and time again the SS generals protested to Dietrich. Stadler, the commander of the SS *Hohenstaufen* Division, told the Commanding-General, the man who had founded the Armed SS: 'A concentrated armoured attack is impossible. Telkamp [the leader of one of his tank regiments] is leading the point personally and he tells me his heavy vehicles are simply sinking up to their axles in mud… Two of his tanks have actually sunk into the damned stuff up to their turrets!'

Otto Kumm, the new divisional commander of the *Leibstandarte*, who back in 1942 fought so long with his 3,000-strong regiment that at the end he had exactly *thirty-five* men left, also protested to his old comrade Dietrich. Hansen's losses in infantry were terribly high, and the only kind of replacements he was receiving to fill the gaps were middle-aged NCOs from the *Luftwaffe* and frightened, callow booty Germans from Rumania. The Rumanians were, in addition, to being frightened, also badly demoralised as their homes had recently been captured by the Russians.

Kumm's plea was rejected, just as the others were. Dietrich knew that this offensive was the Fuehrer's pet project and his last hope, too. After all, the Red Army was already fighting on German soil to the north of Woehler's army group. Although he personally had warned on the second day of the attack not to expect a quick breakthrough, he knew that any officer who opposed Hitler in this matter would find himself in serious trouble. The attack *had* to go on!

So it did, with Berlin urging all the time: 'Tempo... tempo... tempo... speed is of inestimable value...'

Naturally, of all Dietrich's senior officers, Colonel Jochen Peiper of the *Leibstandarte*'s armoured battle group made the most progress. Peiper had got off to a bad start. Rainwater had seeped into the petrol tanks of some of his panthers and he had been forced not only to drain the tanks of precious, strictly rationed fuel, but also to steal gas from another unit. Thereafter he had pushed ahead, taking harebrained risks by sticking to the main roads without protection of infantry, and fighting off attack after attack.

While the rest of the *Leibstandarte* bled – by now the division had suffered 1,435 casualties – Peiper rolled on and on. At the point, his lead tank had had both its exhaust pipes shot off, and its armour was marred by the shining silver scars of Russian antitank shells, its camouflaged paint peeling and hanging loose like the symptoms of some loathsome skin disease. Still, it and the rest continued.

By now *Kampfgruppe Peiper* was way ahead of the rest of the division. In the four days it had covered forty-five miles and was some twenty miles away from Budapest itself. But even the legendary Peiper, who in 1943 effectively broke through a whole Soviet army, could not carry the offensive by himself. Besides, German Intelligence had discovered that the Russians were soon to go over from the defensive to the offensive.

As Woehler reported to Hitler: 'Today there is no longer any doubt that the Russians are preparing an offensive operation. The first definitive signs were detected yesterday… At least 3,000 vehicles are moving out from Budapest. The intention will be to strike toward Lake Balaton in the rear of the German force.'

Hitler refused to allow his SS panzer divisions to withdraw, and an unsuspecting Peiper continued his attack, edging his way ever closer to Budapest, while the Russians prepared to launch their great attack.

Then it happened. On the afternoon of 18 March, the Russians struck. In snow and fog, they launched the first attack without armour or air support. They caught the leading element of the German-Hungarian armies completely by surprise. The SS held, but the Hungarian Third Army further north collapsed. Next day the Russians began to push through the mountains against virtually no opposition. The Hungarian Third Army, war-weary and demoralised, had simply vanished.

Hastily, Woehler called off the whole offensive. On the nineteenth, he ordered Dietrich to start withdrawing and block the gap the fleeing Hungarians had left. If he were unable to do so, the Russians coming out of the narrow belt of the mountains would have nothing ahead of them but the main road to Vienna.

It was now that Peiper was contacted by his corps commander, General Priess, who asked him what the devil he was doing so far ahead of the rest of the 1st SS Panzer Corps. 'Don't you know,' the hard-faced Priess bellowed, 'that the Russians are attacking towards Vienna now?'

In disgust, Peiper turned about and began to fight his way back to his starting point, for the Russians had already cut off his rear. With his remaining twenty-five tanks he made it, after smashing into one of the Red Army's spearheads with such reckless abandon that his Panthers managed to knock out a staggering 125 of the big new Russian Stalin tanks.

Now the situation began to deteriorate rapidly. The SS panzer divisions started to retreat in earnest, with the advancing Russians hard at their heels. At Stuhlweissen-burg, the SS *Viking* Division soon found itself virtually surrounded. The divisional commander, General Ulrich, called his corps headquarters and asked what he was supposed to do. Corps HQ answered: 'Stuhlweissenburg is to be held at all costs!'

Ulrich realised that if he tried to hold the Hungarian town against the whole weight of a Soviet army heading his way, he would lose his division. His men would be slaughtered. Against orders and knowing he was risking his own head by doing so, he ordered the town evacuated. To his rear, an old comrade, General Stadler, commanding the SS *Hohenstaufen* Division, did not hesitate in helping; although he, too, realised the risk he was running. He ordered his troops to clear a corridor through which the *Viking* could retreat.

But with the Russians on their heels, the SS men of the two divisions grew jumpy, seeing enemy tanks everywhere, ready to panic at the drop of a hat. It was about now that General Balck, commanding the Sixth Army, paid his one and only visit to the *Hohenstaufen*. Balck, broad-faced and Prussian, and no friend of the SS, spotted on his way to the division what he thought was a company from the *Viking* fleeing westwards. When Balck reached Stadler's HQ, the two generals fell to quarrelling. Stadler and the rest of the SS were cowards, Balck bellowed. Why, he had just seen a company of them running away!

Stadler retorted that if the Commanding General were right, then they were men from another outfit – not his. He and his men had done more than their bit to hold their section of the front.

Balck grew red in the face. He accused Stadler of insubordination. If things went on like this, he would demand that Stadler be placed in front of a court martial. 'The Fuehrer has ordered you to hold your positions,' he cried, 'and that's that! *Understand?*'

Fuming with rage, Balck motored over to Woehler's HQ and told him what had happened. Accepting Stadler's word for it that it was not the *Hohenstaufen* that had run away and been unable to hold its positions, he said to Woehler, another general who was no friend of the SS, 'If the *Leibstandarte* can't hold their ground, what do you expect us to do?'

Now the fat was really in the fire. Immediately, Woehler radioed the startling news to Hitler's HQ that his very own Imperial Guard had abandoned its positions. The fact that the elite of the elite, the *Leibstandarte*, had run away, indicated the kind of pressure his army group was being subjected to.

Obersturmbannfuhrer Otto Guensche, formerly of the *Leibstandarte*, now Hitler's adjutant, was present when Woehler's message reached the Fuehrer's headquarters. Hitler flew into a tremendous rage. 'It was a terrible scene. Everyone was silent when Hitler ordered that the *Leibstandarte* should no longer have the privilege of bearing *his* name on their sleeve. All present fell silent, including Himmler, the head of the Armed SS.'

Suddenly, Marshal Goering, who was no longer in favour at the Fuehrer's court, spoke up. He said that the SS, especially the *Leibstandarte*, had fought bravely on all fronts since the beginning of the war. These SS divisions had had a complete turnover of personnel, due to casualties, several times. He thought it unfair that they were to be deprived of their armbands.

For a while everyone was silent after Goering's words, including Himmler, who had not spoken one word in defence of his SS divisions. Then Hitler broke the heavy silence. He said his order *would* be carried out. Dietrich had to be informed at once. *Obersturmbannfuhrer* Georg Maier was present at Dietrich's HQ when Hitler's telex message arrived. It was between five and six o'clock on the morning of 27 March 1945, he remembered long afterwards. The radioman handed him the message, which he recalled was signed '*Heinrich Himmler*', and he took it to Dietrich's chief-of-staff, Kraemer, just as Dietrich himself entered the room.

Kraemer read the telex first and then bent over the card table, 'supporting his head in his hands so that I couldn't see his face. He was deeply moved. It took some time before he could speak. Then he whispered, "And that is the thanks for everything we've done." Finally, Kraemer rose to his feet and pointed to his own armband. Harshly he said, "And that's staying where it is!'" Dietrich, just as moved and as angry as his chief-of-staff, decided at this stage of the withdrawal it would be no good to tell his divisional commanders what the Fuehrer had decreed. Besides, most SS divisions had taken off their armbands for security reasons when they moved from the Ardennes to Hungary. But to his immediate staff he complained bitterly: 'There's your reward for all you've done these last five years.'

Despite Dietrich's order that the Fuehrer's message should not be revealed to the Sixth SS Panzer Army, the news got out in a distorted form. It was rumoured that after Dietrich had received the Fuehrer's order, he said he would rather shoot himself than carry it out. Thereupon, he had ripped all his own medals off angrily, placed them in a chamber pot and had them forwarded to Hitler.

In fact, Dietrich felt that Hitler has been misinformed. With Kraemer's help, he sent an emissary to the Fuehrer HQ to explain the true situation in Hungary. On the next day, Himmler arrived in Hungary in his private plane. Apparently, he had been ordered to come to visit Dietrich by the Fuehrer. Once he arrived there, escorted by several tanks because he refused to come without an escort, he had begun to lie and bluster, telling Dietrich that he had done his best to stop Hitler sending the insulting order.

Dietrich, who didn't like Himmler, didn't believe one word. He had already heard through the SS grapevine that Himmler had not made a single objection back at the Fuehrer HQ. He treated his visitor with scorn, and after he had fled, together with his escort, back to the comparative safety of Woehler's army group HQ he told his staff: 'Himmler, the swine, lied from start to finish!' Still, he took no further steps.

Peiper could not rationalise like Dietrich. He called his officers together and told them angrily, 'Let's take a pisspot and put all our medals in it. Then we'll decorate it with the armband of the Goetz von Berlichingen Division.'

Peiper's comrades knew what their commander meant. The name of the 15th SS Panzer Grenadier Division 'Goetz von Berlichingen'[16] meant 'lick my arse' in German. But angry as they all were with the Fuehrer's decree, they prevailed upon Peiper to drop the idea. The chamber pot was not dispatched to Adolf Hitler.

But the die was cast. The end was near now, and even men like Peiper, who had idolised Hitler as a young man at his pre-war court, now broke with the Fuehrer. The Imperial Guard was about finished…

3. 'MY LIFE IS NOW IN YOUR HANDS'

On the morning of 24 April, four days after his last birthday, Adolf Hitler's daily briefing was interrupted by the appearance of one of his military adjutants, Captain Gerhard Boldt. He entered the underground bunker in Berlin, where Hitler would die.

'What is the matter?' Hitler asked.

Boldt replied he had just heard the Russians had launched a major attack westwards with two and a half million men, and it was clear that the Russians were heading for Berlin and *not* Prague as Hitler had anticipated. Already the Red Army had succeeded in breaking through the front of General von Manteuffel's Third Army.

Hitler weighed the information for a few moments before saying: 'In view of the great natural obstacle that the [River] Oder represents, this Russian success is simply the result of the incompetence of the German military leaders there.'

General Krebs, one of his advisers, attempted to defend von Manteuffel. He reminded the Fuehrer that Manteuffel's reserves, including a corps led by SS General Felix Steiner, had been diverted to help defend Berlin.

Hitler calmed himself somewhat and ordered that von Manteuffel should counter-attack on the morrow. His advisers agreed, and one of them suggested that Steiner with his corps should lead the counter-attack. Hitler flushed angrily and snorted: 'I have no use for these arrogant, dull, undecided SS leaders. Under no circumstances whatever do I want Steiner to be in command!'

The SS officers at the morning conference looked angry and uncomfortable. Ever since Dietrich's failure in Hungary and his decision, against orders, to give up the Austrian capital, Vienna, without a fight, the reputation of the Armed SS had sunk to zero at the Fuehrer's HQ. Several SS generals had been relieved of their commands, and before the week was out, Hitler would have his own brother-in-law, SS Divisional Commander Fegelein, shot for 'desertion'. To the SS officers present that morning, it was clear that the Fuehrer, for whom so many of their comrades had sacrificed their lives over the past six years, had abandoned his Imperial Guard...

But it was equally clear that the Imperial Guard was abandoning their Fuehrer, too. On that same afternoon, General Jodl arrived at Steiner's HQ. There Jodl told the SS General, who Hitler had commanded should have no part in the counter-attack: 'By the Fuehrer's order you must start the attack at once.'

Steiner argued that most of his men would be killed if he did attack, ending bluntly with: 'I don't want to do it.'

The discussion grew heated. Jodl's usually pale, cunning face flushed angrily. Suddenly, the door opened and their argument was interrupted by an aide, who informed Steiner that one thousand Hitler Youths and 5,000 pilots had just been posted to his corps.

Jodl grabbed at the news like a dying man clutching at a piece of driftwood as the water threatened to drown him. 'Mobilise them for the attack!' he suggested.

Steiner sneered. 'Yes, all those pilots with a little iron cross dangling from their collars. *No!* They are all untrained. They'll be slaughtered by the Ivans.'

Jodl gave in. In disgust he flew back to Hitler's HQ.

Now it was the turn of Hitler's senior military adviser, Field Marshal Keitel, to attempt to get Steiner to attack. A few hours later he arrived at the SS General's HQ and also urged Steiner to give the order to attack.

Steiner was embarrassed by Keitel's plea. Never in German military history had a German field marshal humiliated himself like this. Still, he faced up to the Reich's senior soldier and said: 'No, I won't do it. This attack is murder. Do what you want with me.'

And that was that. Keitel's face fell, then he shrugged and gave up. The Armed SS, once Hitler's most loyal troops, were no longer under his or anyone else's control. Now his SS formations were fighting for naked survival – with one exception…

One day before that fateful meeting with Steiner, General Mohnke, who had commanded the *Leibstandarte* during the Ardennes offensive, led his little command to their last battle – *by tram*. With 2,000 men, made up of the *Leibstandarte*'s guard battalion and new recruits, he had used the Berlin tramway system to bring them from their barracks outside the German capital to Hitler's underground bunker. Here Mohnke went to report personally to the Fuehrer, who told him that he was now in charge of the defence of the bunker and the surrounding area.

'General Mohnke,' Hitler said, 'you are a professional soldier and you already wear the highest award a German soldier can win on the field of battle. My life is now in your hands. We have known each other since 1933. As soldier to soldier, I have one last request to make as I now give you command of *Zitadelle*.'[17]

Mohnke, a man of few words who didn't wear his emotions on his sleeve, waited.

'Frankly, I had hoped to be able to remain alive and in Berlin at least until 5 May. There are historical reasons.' He paused but did not explain what those historical reasons were. 'However, under no circumstances can I risk being captured alive. Whenever you feel the military situation to be such that you can no longer hold for more than twenty-four hours, you must report to me in person. I shall take the consequences. This is a personal request. It is also an order.'

Mohnke, who had known Hitler ever since he first joined the *Leibstandarte* back in 1933, said nothing. Instead, he saluted and marched out to where his men, both old hares and teenage 'green-beaks', waited for his orders. They were simply: '*Dig in… take cover… don't draw fire!*'

Now where the 'asphalt soldiers' in their black uniforms had so often pounded the tarmac as they goose-stepped behind their bands, the survivors of the *Leibstandarte*, dressed in shabby field grey, most of them without the traditional jackboots (for the German Army was running out of leather), prepared to defend their Fuehrer to the last…

–

The first attack on the *Leibstandarte*'s positions among the smoking brick rubble of the capital of that empire that Hitler had boasted would last a thousand years came on Friday, 27 April. That morning, Mohnke received an urgent report from one of his outposts that the Russians had broken through at dawn. Now they were assembling a large force of tanks at the Potsdamer Platz for an assault on the bunker itself.

Already on the *Leibstandarte's* outer perimeter, the defences were crumbling. There an NCO, Georg Schmidt, was trapped in an office block, together with a comrade who was badly wounded and two elderly *Volkssturm* [Home Guard] men. Down below there were Russians swarming everywhere, but so far not one of them had looked up at the second floor, where the surviving Germans were hiding, pale with apprehension.

But Sergeant Schmidt was an old hare. He kept his nerve. Soon he knew the Russians would come storming up the stairs, and then he and the other SS man would be shot out of hand. 'Hastily,' he recalled long afterwards: 'I tied two office curtains together and fixed them to the smashed window. Outside, the Russians were beginning to approach the building. Somebody fired a burst and they went to ground – for a few moments. I ordered the two old boys to take advantage of the respite. Creaking and groaning, they abseiled down, using the curtain. A moment later the two of us followed. And it was just in time. For already we could hear the rattle of the Russian tank tracks as they moved into the attack. We ran like hell!'

Mohnke, who had fought Russian tanks in the East, thought the enemy was making 'a bad blunder... Their tanks were highly unmanoeuvrable, blocked by rubble and were sitting ducks in this classic street-fighting situation.

'Even young boys and old men, or women for that matter, armed with bazookas and heroic despair could get at them from point-blank range, usually under fifty metres, often from a cellar to the middle of the street, twenty metres or even less.'

After the first wave of tanks were stopped – burning, smoking wrecks, with their crews sprawling out of the turrets, dead or dying – the Russians tried again. This time they escalated the horror. In front of the tanks, they herded civilians, men, women and children, or propped them trembling with fear on the tank decks. In this way they hoped to stop the defenders firing. They were mistaken. Now it was war to the knife. The bazookamen, hidden in the rubble on both sides of the street along which the Russians advanced, did their best. But it was no use. As tank after tank shuddered to a stop, engine blazing or with a track severed, there were dead men, women and children everywhere.

And that was the end of the Russian tank assaults on the defenders of the *Zitadelle*. For the rest of that long, terrible Friday they contended themselves with pounding the SS positions with long-range artillery. And in the street the dead civilians lay sprawled out in the crazy postures of those done violently to death, their sightless eyes staring up at the unfeeling sky…

By Sunday, 29 April, it was a week since Mohnke had taken over the defence of the bunker area and he was exhausted. That night he turned in after midnight, but slept very little. For at dawn the phone at his bedside rang and awakened him rudely. It was SS Sergeant Misch, who had been in his company back in 1939 in what now seemed another age. Misch said: 'General, the Fuehrer wishes to see you alone in his quarters. Please come over immediately.'

Exhausted as he was, Mohnke knew he could not ignore a call from the Fuehrer. Still, before he went, Mohnke wanted to know Hitler's mood, so he said: 'Sergeant, as an old *Leibstandarte* hand, please tell me the unvarnished truth. What temper is the Fuehrer in? Is he as down in the dumps as he was last evening? And who else is there?'

Misch, who worked on the switchboard in the bunker, replied: 'The boss is now in a calm and relaxed mood. No one else is with him. I don't think he has been able to sleep this whole long night. Twice within the last hour he has come out to chat with me. Just a moment ago, he said he wanted to have a talk with his old friend Mohnke. He told me to ring you up.'

Ten minutes later, Mohnke was on his way, reminding himself that a week ago, Hitler had said he wanted to be informed when all hope had vanished. He needed twenty-four hours' notice, it appeared, to make his own plans, whatever they might be. Now Mohnke realised that time was near. His survivors (for the *Leibstandarte*'s losses were high) were still holding the Potsdamer Platz area. But that was about all. One more concerted Soviet attack and that would be that. And tomorrow was 1 May, the greatest holiday in the Soviet calendar. More than likely, the Russians would attempt one last assault on that 'holy' day.

Misch received his old company commander and told him, as the guards snored away on all sides (for these days they drank all the time in the bunker): 'The boss told me he wants to receive you informally in his bedroom.'

Mohnke nodded his understanding and then went into the Fuehrer's bedroom. He found Hitler perched on the edge of his bed, clad in a black satin dressing gown over his striped pyjamas. Hitler moved promptly to the one chair and indicated that the SS General should sit on the bed.

Swiftly, Mohnke filled in the Fuehrer on the situation above ground, noting that Hitler's left arm was trembling badly. Hitler took in all the bad news, showing no reaction. Indeed, to Mohnke he appeared amazingly calm.

Then he fell silent. It was an awkward, heavy silence, which embarrassed Mohnke. Although he was not a very sensitive man, he felt he had to say something to break the tension, so he said: 'My Fuehrer, as a soldier speaking to another soldier, true to my oath to you, I no longer can guarantee that my exhausted, battle-weary troops can hold for longer than one more day. I now expect a frontal, massed-tank attack tomorrow at dawn, May the first...' He hesitated a moment, then added, 'And you know what May the first means to the Russians.'

'I know,' Hitler said softly. 'Let me say that your troops have fought splendidly, and I have no complaints.' This was the first time Hitler had praised his black guards since the failure in Hungary and Mohnke was pleased despite the gravity of the situation.

'Too bad, really,' Hitler mused. 'I had sincerely hoped to make it until May the fifth. Beyond that date I have no desire to live.'

The date again puzzled Mohnke. He could not know that Hitler had become a great admirer of Napoleon, who had died on 5 May 1821 on St Helena. In the years of his defeats, Hitler had come to sympathise with the great Corsican, feeling that they had both been betrayed by their own people.

But it was Hitler's last words – 'I *have no desire to live*' – which really startled him. Did they mean the man he had served so long, the man who had conquered nearly the whole of Europe, was going to do away with himself?

Two days later, Hitler and his new wife, his ex-mistress Eva Braun, were dead in the fetid, stinking bunker, which was crowded with hundreds of wounded. There, among the Party functionaries, those 'golden pheasants', as they had once been called so contemptuously by the average German, the mood had sunk to zero. Some tried to blot out the nightmare by heavy drinking. Drunken men and women reeled down the dimly lit corridors everywhere, waving their bottles, singing and cursing. Others found relief in copulating, hidden away in the darker corners of the bunker. One woman secretary took on a whole line of men, squatting in Hitler's emergency dental chair.

Some, however, were determined not to go down with the sinking ship. There was still a kind of rump government in existence at Flensburg on the North German peninsula of Schleswig-Holstein. There, it was hoped, this last German government under the leadership of Admiral Doenitz might be able to do a deal with the Western Allies. With a bit of luck, they might be able to save their skins, after all.

Thus it was that on the evening of Tuesday, 1 May, with Berlin dying above their heads, General Mohnke called a conference of all the senior officers in the bunker, plus several important civilians. For several hours, he lectured his audience on the terrible events of the last week. Then he told his listeners: 'The news that the Fuehrer is dead … must be kept from the troops until at least ten p.m. Panic and chaos must be avoided at all costs. General Weidling [the overall battle commander for the whole of the capital] has ordered active fighting to cease at eleven, whereupon all German troops must be prepared to break through the Red Army's iron ring now closing around Berlin.'

There was a murmur of agreement from his audience. They knew how dangerous such an undertaking would be; but they reasoned, too, that they knew the capital better than the Ivans, the population was on their side, and they'd catch the victorious Russians off guard.

Mohnke noted their reaction and said: 'We must attempt this in small battle groups, probing for weak links wherever we can find them… I regret that I have no better information than some of you have about the battle situation in several of the outer boroughs of Berlin. Battle groups will simply have to play it by ear, probing to find their best march route. No provision can be made for any rear guard. We *are* the rear guard!'

His listeners knew what that meant. Anyone, man or woman, wounded or unwounded, who decided to stay behind in the bunker would be abandoned to his fate; and that fate was definitely going to be terrible…

By now Mohnke had some seven hundred soldiers left of his original 2,000 – and they were exhausted. Yet they responded with renewed energy when their officers informed them they were going to break out of the death trap of Berlin. Each breakout group would be limited to a couple of score men, under the command of a seasoned officer, and most of these groups would take with them important civilians, male and female, who had volunteered to make the attempt.

In the group commanded by Mohnke himself, there would be an ex-ambassador, an admiral, Hitler's last two female secretaries and twenty-one-year-old Else Krueger, who had been the secretary of Hitler's 'brown eminence', the power behind the throne, Martin Bormann. These women were dressed in Army field-grey uniform, complete with jackboots and steel helmets, and were probably given pistols too. For the whole group, civilian and soldier alike, was armed with pistols, machine pistols and grenades. Mohnke reasoned their luck wouldn't hold out for ever. Somewhere along the planned escape route they'd probably bump into the Ivans; and if they did, he intended to make a fight of it...

The first obstacle was the stretch of the Wilhelmstrasse they would have to cross before they came to the underground station at Kaiserhof, for their intention was to use Berlin's underground system (which Mohnke knew intimately) for as much of their escape as possible. As the escapers emerged from the bunker, they could see that the square was bathed in lurid crimson flame, which outlined everything. There was also the angry snap-and-crackle of small-arms fire, as if a fight was going on somewhere close by.

For a couple of minutes, Mohnke, cocked pistol clenched in his sweaty fist, surveyed the scene. It looked very exposed – and risky – to him. But he concluded that the small-arms fire was directed at some other party. He decided to risk it.

'*Los*,' he hissed, and waved his pistol.

His party needed no urging. Crouched low, arms going like pistons, they dashed across the littered square in groups of four and *slid* down the remains of the staircase of the Kaiserhof underground station (the long artillery duel had pounded it to rubble).

Down below, everything was pitch-black. But Mohnke sensed that there was someone down there. Dare he shine a light? he wondered. In the end he summoned up enough courage to switch on his flashlight. To his relief it wasn't the Russians. It was hundreds of civilians and soldiers cowering there in the darkness in scared apprehension. Mohnke breathed a sigh of relief and then ordered the civilians to get out of the way. His party had to press on.

Now holding some candles aloft, the little group started to make its way down the underground tunnel towards the Friedrichstrasse station. *Leibstandarte* NCO Kurt Schmidt remembered long afterwards: 'From somewhere water had partially flooded the tunnel, so we had to balance our way along the rails themselves. Our flickering candles threw our shadows on the sloping walls in giant relief and all the time we could hear the scuttling of the rats as they got out of our way. It was very eerie down there, I can tell you, while above our heads the Ivans finished off what was left of Berlin.'

About dawn the party reached the Stettin underground station and chanced climbing to the surface. 'But almost immediately,' Schmidt recalled, 'we received fire from our left. Then a mortar opened up and mortar bombs came howling down savagely. Several of us were wounded before we dodged back into the shelter of the ruins.'

Schmidt himself helped a couple of the wounded into a nearby cellar, where some friendly civilians attended to them and gave him a cup of ersatz coffee. Little did he know that it would be the last cup of coffee, ersatz or otherwise, he would drink for several years. For he fell asleep over it – he was completely exhausted by the events of the past ten days. When he awoke, he found himself facing a group of Russians busy pulling off his wristwatch and marriage ring. He was a prisoner-of-war…

While Schmidt slept, the rest pushed on, dodging back into the underground railway system as the best means of avoiding the Russians. But the next obstacle that Mohnke encountered was not the Ivans, but a couple of burly

German members of the Berlin Municipal Transport Company, both armed with rifles and carrying lanterns like medieval nightwatchmen.

They were guarding a huge steel bulkhead, which barred any further progress, and 'were surrounded by angry civilians, imploring them to open', as Mohnke recalled after the war. 'They kept refusing. One of them clutched a giant key. When I saw this ridiculous situation, I ordered them to open the bulkhead forthwith.'

The two guards refused, quoting some obscure standing order. Then to add insult to injury, one of them produced a book of regulations and started quoting from it, while the mob muttered threateningly. It was German bureaucracy gone crazy.

As the officials rattled on about how the steel bulkhead had to be closed after the last train every night (although no trains had run through the underground system for a week), Mohnke wondered just what he should do. 'We were armed, of course … and I feel that we might just have made our escape had we been able to follow my original plan to the letter. I sat for long hours in Soviet captivity quietly cursing myself for my strange hesitancy at this critical moment. Perhaps there is no rational explanation.'

But Mohnke had been raised in the 'strictest Prussian tradition', in which orders had to be obeyed, however stupid. Besides, in a way, he had 'a lingering respect for the eccentric devotion [to duty] of the two guards'. So instead of forcing the bulkhead to be opened, he and his party turned and retraced their steps to the Friedrichstrasse station, where they crawled up the splintered woodwork and twisted girders back to the surface.

Dying Berlin was now stretched out in front of them, and although the fugitives could not spot a clear frontline, they could see the Russian artillery positions – which was some indication of the way they should *not* go. Mohnke snapped an order to his group, which was now down to twelve people, and they started to run across a narrow bridge in single file. The General expected to be shot at any moment; they made excellent targets. But nothing happened. 'Again it was deathly quiet. Only the ghosts of shadows, sometimes real, sometimes imagined, lurked in the streets leading to the quays on both sides of the river [the Spree, which they had just crossed].' It seemed, ruined and dying as it was, Berlin already been abandoned to history.

–

But there were terrible things happening that night, as Mohnke's group tried desperately to escape. About two in the morning, they started to skirt the famed La Charité Hospital, which Mohnke knew had already been captured by the Russians. What the General did not know just then was that the Ivans had looted the hospital's supply of medical alcohol and were reeling drunk, intent on looting and rape; and it didn't matter one bit whether their victims were patients in bed or nurses actually still working in the operating theatre in spite of the chaos all round them. As one of Mohnke's men put it later: 'I had been in Russia and knew that there were two sides to this ugly story, atrocity followed by counter-atrocity. Still, it is not a pretty sight to see a terrified, naked woman running along a rooftop, pursued by half a dozen soldiers brandishing bayonets, then leaping five or six storeys to a certain death.'

It was that sight that convinced Mohnke that whatever happened to him, he *must* ensure at all costs that the women in his party should reach safety. He could not let them suffer the same fate as that poor dead woman…

That night the fugitives had many adventures. They viewed a last battle; saw SS men who could not speak a word of German battle with the Ivans (the last SS man to win the Knight's Cross of the Iron Cross was, ironically enough, a Frenchman); escaped capture by a hair's breadth several times; watched glumly as hundreds of German soldiers prepared for surrender by destroying their weapons. There was no *Goetterdaemmerung*, as Hitler had expected, after all. Most of the German defenders of Berlin would surrender tamely to the Russians at dawn. It would be only those foreign renegades, French, Belgian, Dutch, Russians, etc., seduced into the SS by Goebbels' propaganda of a 'Greater Europe', who fought to the bitter end.

By now it was first light and Mohnke decided it was time to find cover for the day. For he was determined not to surrender with the rest but to continue the breakout, although he and his surviving fugitives were totally exhausted. Now they started to bump into other groups that had fled the bunker and together they set off for a well-known Berlin brewery in the Prinzenstrasse, Brauerei Schultheiss, Patzenhofer.[18]

The brewery was in good shape. Although it had been used as a public air-raid shelter throughout the war, it had never suffered a hit during the years of bombing. Neither had it been touched in the Battle of Berlin. Now, with the spring sunshine flooding the big courtyard, the rank and file of the escape parties decided to enjoy a sunbathe. Meanwhile the officers retreated to the deep cellars filled with shining brass brewing vats, to decide what to do next.

It was about this time that several hundred civilians, men and women, plus soldiers began to flood into the brewery to seek refuge there. Drinking started, as the newcomers broke into the great kegs of potent beer. Several women grew drunk and hysterical, and threw themselves into the arms of the drunken German soldiers. Group sex took place all over the brewery's top floor.

While all this was going on above, General Mohnke, utterly weary and despondent by now, discussed with his surviving officers what they should do. He told them the truth about Hitler: that he had not died heroically at the head of his troops, but had committed suicide, together with his former mistress, Eva Braun. He then suggested they should try to escape from the brewery individually before the Russians stormed it.

One of his listeners, a Berliner who belonged to the *Luftwaffe* and not the *Leibstandarte*, showed more initiative than the SS. He said he knew a way out and volunteered to take out the three secretaries, including Else Krueger, Bormann's young secretary, through the Russian lines and out of Berlin.

Eagerly, Mohnke accepted the offer. Within minutes the four of them vanished. In due course, the secretaries would manage to board a refuge train heading west, disguised as 'French re-patriates' – ie, French women who had been forced to work for the Germans. At some stage of the long journey, the Russians flung them off the train, but the British train commander smuggled them back on board again. Thus it was that Else Krueger survived. She was one of the few to do so. Today, over forty years on, she remains one of the handful of eye-witnesses of the last hours of the *Leibstandarte* in Berlin: an old lady in deep cover in, of all places, a brick semi-detached in the suburbs of Cambridge...

Sometime later, Mohnke gave up. His nerves were stretched to the utmost and he was exhausted. He asked for a volunteer to contact the Russians and accept the surrender of what was left of the *Leibstandarte* in the shattered capital of that 'Thousand-Year Reich' which had lasted exactly twelve years, four months and four days. Tamely, his officers accepted they were going to be delivered into the hands of their arch-enemies, *die Untemenschen*, the Russians.

But not all the members of the *Leibstandarte* were prepared to accept defeat and surrender so easily. Twenty-four-year-old Lieutenant Stehr had been in the 1st SS Division ever since he was a teenager. He had fought in the Ardennes, then in Hungary, where he had been severely wounded in the hip. It was thought he would never be fit again for front-line duty, and he was sent back to Berlin for treatment. For two months he had lingered in hospital, but when he heard Mohnke's detachment of his old division had been alerted to defend his beloved Fuehrer, he had discharged himself from hospital and hobbled to join the battle.

Now for hours he had been crying that they should all commit mass suicide – a kind of *Heldentod* (heroic death) – a suitable Germanic way out, rather than surrender to the hated, degenerate Russians. The group's doctor, Captain Schenk, had tried to convince him that it would be a worthless gesture. Besides, Stehr had a young wife and two children to live for. To no avail. As Mohnke started to burn his secret documents before surrendering, a single shot rang out. Stehr had blown his brains out rather than give in.

As Dr Schenk recalled long afterwards: 'Stehr was the last to carry the swastika banner high, the waves now engulfing him, the loyal retainer on his way to Valhalla … It was all so long ago, but somehow, even today, I feel that this blue-eyed young man had a sense of loyalty and fidelity far greater than that of the higher-ups to whom he had sworn eternal fealty. Albeit in a senseless fashion, he was true in his way to what he called his "creed".'

There were few left in that first week of May 1945 still prepared to die for that creed.

4. 'ALL OUR PATHS LEAD INTO AN UNCERTAIN FUTURE'

Die Leibstandarte SS Adolf Hitler was fleeing!

It had retreated before. In Russia, back in 1943, and in the Ardennes one year later. But those had been orderly, disciplined retreats, conducted successfully with the men's hopes high that there was a future and all would work out well in the end. But now the man whose name the division bore was dead in Berlin, Germany had been defeated on all fronts and there was no hope left. Now all they could do was flee, each day bringing new terrors and fresh defeats.

For two months they had been on the run. They had fled Hungary, then Czechoslovakia. Now the *Leibstandarte* was fleeing through Austria, struggling ever westwards. And always the Russians were just at their heels, harrying them relentlessly, each new skirmish fuelling their fears of what would happen to them if they fell into the hands of the Ivans. It was said that if the Russians didn't shoot you out of hand, then they would emasculate you (for Hitler's Praetorian Guard would never be allowed to spawn a new *Leibstandarte*) and dispatch you to years of hard labour in their dreaded Siberian gulags.

Already this unreasoning fear had panicked their predecessors along this same route. In that terrible first week of

May 1945, the teenagers of the once proud *Hitler-Jugend* SS Division, which had held up a whole British army before Caen for weeks, had snapped at the sight of a *single* Russian tank. Hundreds of them had broken ranks and run. Later, when order had been restored, it was found that fifteen men had been crushed to death in the panic and scores seriously injured. Behind them a lone Russian lieutenant had stood in the turret of his T-34 tank, laughing his head off at the sight of 6,000 SS men fleeing before one single tank.

But the fugitives' fear of the Russians was overwhelming and total. Now the only hope that the average member of the *Leibstandarte* dared cherish was that they might be allowed to surrender to the Americans. For by now both the US Seventh Army and the US Third Army, which the *Leibstandarte* had once fought against in the Ardennes, were deep inside Austrian territory, heading for the River Enns. After five years and eight months in combat, the division, which had prided itself on being the best in the whole wide world, was pathetically eager to lay down its arms to those 'cardboard soldiers', as they had once called them contemptuously – *die Amis*. Already it was known along the grapevine – through 'latrine rumours', as they were called in the soldiers' slang – that another SS division, *Hohenstauffen*, had been able to surrender successfully to the Americans of Patton's Third. Its commander, General Stadler, had walked into the HQ of the Third's 71st Division, to be met, as he recalled after the war, 'By an icy stillness… None of the many American officers present said a word; instead they all stared at me, as if I were from another planet.'

However, luck had been on the SS division commander's side. Suddenly, one of the American officers had broken the heavy silence, with 'Hello, General Stadler, how are you?'

For a moment Stadler had been puzzled. Then he recognised the *Ami*. He had been captured by the *Hohenstauffen* in the Ardennes. Later he had been exchanged for two of Stadler's battalion commanders captured by the Americans.

Now he told his fellow officers how well he had been treated by the SS. As a result, the march into captivity of the *Hohenstauffen* had gone very smoothly indeed. Would the *Leibstandarte*'s surrender be as smooth?

But it was not only the Russians and mountainous terrain that were a thorn in the flesh of the retreating SS men. Their onetime comrades, the Austrians, were too. Suddenly the nation that had produced the Fuehrer (Hitler had remained an Austrian citizen till 1928), Eichmann, the executor of the 'final solution', and Kaltenbrunner, the head of Himmler's dreaded police *apparat*, now discovered it was an 'occupied' country. The Austrians had seemingly forgotten they had received the Germans and their native son with open arms when the Reich invaded the country in the late thirties. Now, with the war virtually over, Austrian resistance movements were springing up on all sides.

Thus it was that as the first group of SS passed through the Austrian city of Graz, they were received with cheers and cries of 'Come back soon, boys!' A few hours later, other groups were met with boos and threats. On all sides the old red-and-white flag of the Austrian Republic started to appear. Sniping broke out from upper-storey windows. The SS replied, although some of them were Austrian themselves. Now it appeared that German was fighting German!

Jochen Peiper, bringing up the rear with his handful of remaining tanks (instead of leading the division as he had done throughout the war) was sick at heart. His whole world was falling apart. In the long years of imprisonment to come, he would often wish he could have died in Berlin, 'fighting to defend the Fuehrer. Instead I was condemned to face these traitors and turncoats and the complete breakdown of everything I had believed in since I had been a kid in short pants...'

General Kumm, the divisional commander, had no time to waste on what might have been in Berlin. The Fuehrer was dead. His concern was the safety and the future of what was left of his division. For, unknown to Peiper and the rest of the officers in that first week of May, Kumm was engaged in a race.

Due to a major Allied security blunder, a top-secret document, ICS 1060, had fallen into German hands back in March 1945. This document outlined the Allied decisions reached at Yalta in February 1945, which included how Central Europe would be split up by the victorious Allies at the end of the war. It also covered the zones of occupation in both Germany and Austria and, in the latter case, it stated that the demarcation line between the Russians to the east and the Americans to the west would be the River Enns. Whatever the state of the German defence, the Americans would *not* cross the river. This meant that everything to the east of the River Enns would come under Soviet jurisdiction.

Kumm, who knew some of the details of the captured top-secret document, realised that he and his division would have to reach the Enns at least twenty-four hours before the Russians. This would give him time to negotiate with the Americans. For if the Russians beat him to the river line, he would not have a chance in hell of getting his division across. The *Leibstandarte* then might well suffer the same terrible fate as that of those two unfortunate cavalry divisions that had been trapped in Budapest – wholesale slaughter.

It was for this reason that he had put his best officer – Peiper – to bring up the rear and hold off the Russians in a series of hard-fought skirmishes, while he withdrew the rest of the division out of the line, urging them to move westwards with all possible speed.

Thus, by a strange irony of fate, Kumm was attempting to fight one enemy while, at the same time, doing his utmost to surrender to another! The man he chose to deal with the Americans was a tall, elegant staff officer, *Standartenfuhrer* Neumann, whom he sent – together with a regimental doctor, Dr Weit, and a runner – ahead of the division to make contact.

As the former recalled long afterwards: 'We soon met the advance elements of the 71st US Infantry Division. They promptly relieved us of our watches and other personal items before sending us on to the town of Steyr. Here we encountered an American colonel who remembered the *Leibstandarte* from the fighting in the Ardennes and thought we were a good combat organisation. He was of the opinion we should cross the Enns demarcation line as soon as possible.'

Colonel-General Rendulic, commander-in-chief of the German Army Group South, who was already in Steyr as a prisoner-of-war, thought differently. The Austrian commander-in-chief (for he had been an Austrian officer before he was absorbed into the German *Wehrmacht*) told the SS emissary: 'We should surrender to the Russians where we were at that moment.' An American colonel intervened, as Neumann recalled, 'and asked Rendulic if this was his honest opinion. Rendulic said it was.'

Neumann was disappointed, but said nothing more. A little later he was called in to see another American colonel, who was bent over a map of Austria. Neumann asked him when the bridges across the Enns would be blown up to stop the SS crossing into the American zone. The Americans did not give him a direct answer. Instead, he ran his finger along the course of the river on the map, stopping at each bridge. Finally, his finger stopped at a bridge north of Ternberg. As it did so, he gave the SS Colonel a piercing, significant look.

Neumann got the message, or so he thought. All the other bridges would be blown up or barred. The one north of Ternberg would not. The Colonel was offering him a way of escape for the *Leibstandarte*. In due course, Neumann would discover he had guessed right. When he and others of the division reached the bridge at Ternberg, they would find to their satisfaction that the Americans had 'forgotten' to blow it up.

Now the van of the *Leibstandarte* was reaching the American demarcation line, where the SS quickly had their watches, pistols and cameras removed and were dispatched into the prisoner-of-war cages. They would be the lucky ones. There were still plenty of the division's units in contact with Russians, trying to protect the *Leib-standarte*'s fleeing columns, now swollen with hundreds of civilians and stragglers from other units.

Almost till the very last moment, *Standartenfuhrer* Peiper kept on fighting, though now some of his men were mounted on horses instead of those massive Tigers and Panthers, which had so terrified the Western Allies back in 1944, for now the division was virtually out of fuel and men mounted on horses were much more useful in the mountains than tanks.

These mounted SS men's tactics were simple but potentially suicidal. They would wait in hiding in the mountains until the point of the pursuing Russian unit would make its cautious appearance. Then, while their remaining six cannon plastered the surprised Russians, they would charge in, whooping like Red Indians attacking a wagon train, and attempt to kill or wound as many of the Russian officers and NCOs as possible. They knew that, while the average Russian soldier was hardy and brave, his organisation usually fell apart when the officers and NCOs were knocked out. Day by day, Peiper's losses mounted, and the lean, hard-bitten officer grew increasingly bitter. Now all he wanted was for this impossible struggle against overwhelming odds to end – come what may.

By this time General Kumm of the *Leibstandarte* had also met Army Commander General Rendulic in the presence of his American captors. It was obvious that the Austrian officer had taken an intense dislike to the SS, and the *Leibstandarte* in particular. Perhaps, Kumm told himself, the Austrian was trying to disassociate himself from the SS in order that he might have a future in postwar Austria. Whatever his reasons were, he told Kumm categorically that the *Leibstandarte* must stay on the eastern bank of the Enns and surrender to the advancing Russians.

Angrily, Kumm snorted that not a single soldier under his command would surrender to the Russians. Indeed, now he was prepared to fight to the last bullet rather than give in to the Red Army. With that, Kumm left the US headquarters to return to his own HQ. Here he gave out his last order of the war. He commanded that the division should break up, after destroying all heavy weapons and equipment. Just as it had once done in the 'cauldron of blood' at Falaise, small groups of the division under the command of officers would attempt to cross the Enns any way they could. If they managed it, they could surrender to the Americans. But there was no compulsion to do so, he stressed. Anyone who wanted to take the risk could try to make his way home, without going into imprisonment...

It was a difficult choice for most of them to make. They had become so used to orders and military organisations that they could not conceive of a civilian world in which they had to make their own decisions. In the end, most of them concentrated on crossing the Enns and postponed worrying about what might happen next.

The group led by Colonel Hansen, that blond giant who had once looked as if he had just stepped out of an SS recruiting poster, was typical. Hansen and his men headed for Steyr and managed to find an ancient stone bridge intact across the river. But there was a catch. The Americans guarding it refused to let him cross. The GIs of the 71st Infantry Division had had relatively little combat experience, and Hansen decided he could risk challenging them. Although he had only a couple of tanks left, he ordered them to the front of his stalled column. There they trained their massive cannon on the awed GIs.

The bold gesture did the trick. Without a single shot being fired, Hansen's men crossed the Enns, breathing sighs of relief as they did so. For the Russians were only just behind them up the road. But the confrontation on the bridge had exhausted what was left of Hansen's boldness and daring. As the dreaded American *jabos* started to circle menacingly over their heads, Hansen started to lead his men tamely into the waiting US cages.

Hansen's was one of the few orderly surrenders. Now discipline in the Praetorian Guard began to break down as the rattle of the pursuing Russian tanks grew ever nearer. Men threw away their equipment and refused to obey the orders of their officers and NCOs any longer. It was every man for himself. They rushed the Enns. At one place they found a hanging rope and wood bridge, which should have been crossed by one person only at a time. But they were panic-stricken and did not heed the advice of their officers. Several score men tried to cross. The ropes frayed and finally broke. The bridge tumbled to the racing, ice-cold waters of the river below, carrying with it the doomed SS men.

In another spot, scores of men crossed only to find their further progress was barred by a steep cliff overhanging the water. Lieutenant Leidreiter was one of the many who decided he'd tackle the sheer cliff face. 'I had seen one of our companies which had been massacred by the Russians in 1941. I certainly was *not* going to fall into Russian hands. So making my way through the divisional vehicles which were burning on all sides – our people had set them on fire as a last act of defiance – I set about the dangerous climb. The whole cliff face was dotted with soldiers, civilians too. The wife of one of our NCOs who had been killed in action attached herself to me and my group. So we climbed in the darkness, our progress hindered on all sides by the equipment which those before us had thrown away. The naked rock bit cruelly into our hands and every now and again we'd hear a shrill scream of horror as some poor swine lost his grip and went hurtling down to his death below. Once we came across a bunch of horses in a little clearing. Someone had got them this far and then abandoned them. Now they were freezing and starving to death. Others had tried to get down the cliff by themselves. But they had fallen in the darkness and were now hanging suspended in bushes from the cliff face. Their legs were usually broken and now they were simply waiting for the relief of death, whinnying piteously all the time. It was a night of terror and sudden death. I shall never forget it – or that damned cliff.'

After finally conquering the cliff, Leidreiter decided he'd try to reach Germany. The *Leibstandarte* no longer existed. Why go voluntarily into American imprisonment? He enlisted the aid of the dead NCO's wife. She was Austrian and she knew the area. But the two of them had not gone very far when they bumped into a patrol of Americans in a Jeep. They told the SS officer, who spoke some English, that the *Leibstandarte* was going to be sent from the prison cages to London. There, Hitler's former black guards would be employed in clearing up the ruins left by the recently ended V-1 and V-2 campaign against the city.

Leidreiter thought differently. 'I felt London could wait a little longer for me. I still had some food and we were nearly out of the mountains now.' So as soon as the Americans busied themselves rounding up the many SS stragglers pouring out of the woods all around in answer to the loud-hailer demand to surrender, he quietly sneaked away...

It was on that same day that the fugitive had another strange experience that made a lasting impression on him and which, in a way, symbolised the fact that the old *Leibstandarte* had vanished for ever.

Moving out of a small wood, he was abruptly confronted by a full colonel of the SS, complete with pistol and with the Knight's Cross still dangling from his throat. The Colonel, who was all alone, appeared to be lost and slightly dazed.

When he approached the strange figure, who seemed not to have noted that the war had been lost and the days of wearing tin were over, he recognised him. It was Max Hansen, who had somehow become separated from the group he had led across the Enns.

Feeling a little awkward, Leidreiter clicked to attention and saluted for the last time before asking hesitantly what might happen to the men of the *Leibstandarte* now that they were in American hands.

Hansen, his eyes set on a far horizon known only to himself, replied that the other ranks would be sent home, but that the NCOs and officers would remain in the POW cages.

Leidreiter did not quite believe the Colonel, but he respected him. 'All the rest of us, whether we were making a break for it or tamely going into the *Ami* camps, had salvaged some piece of personal property to see us through the hard times undoubtedly to come – a blanket, a coat, some shaving tackle… Not Hansen. He began as a soldier, devoid of personal possessions, and he was going to end as one.'

A few minutes later, he set off to find the Americans and give himself up. Leidreiter watched him go, 'erect, proud, shoulders squared, as if he were about to inspect his regiment, a man with a date with destiny…'

Little did he know what that destiny was going to be.

That same day, one-legged SS General Bittrich, commander of the corps to which the *Leibstandarte* had belonged, assembled his remaining staff in a meadow near the cages into which they would all soon disappear. General Bittrich, who had beaten the 1st British Airborne Division at Arnhem the year before, did not pull his punches. He told his listeners what to expect in the bitter years to come.

'Comrades,' he barked, as the waiting Americans watched, 'all our paths lead into an uncertain future. Before us we have imprisonment, perhaps even exile. I'd like to thank you for your fighting spirit, your loyalty, your admirable discipline, which I ask you to maintain in the dark days ahead.

'For years to come, perhaps for decades, we will not hear our national anthem again. The words "Germany" and "Fatherland" will mean little in the coming age. But in our hearts, we must treasure those concepts for the generations to come in the hope that they will be granted freedom and a better fate. *Comrades, long live Germany, our Fatherland!*'

With tears in his eyes, General Bittrich limped to the waiting car that would bear him into captivity.

The trial of the *Leibstandarte* could commence…

5. 'THEY WERE YOUNG PEOPLE WITH A HOT HEART'

General Kurt Meyer, once known as 'Panzermeyer', was the first of the *Leibstandarte*'s old hares to have to face up to the harsh realities of a defeated Germany. Perhaps he had thought, as many of them did, that the war would end like some nineteenth-century conflict – with grave, dignified ex-enemies shaking hands before the vanquished warrior handed over his sword to depart with his shoulders squared in gallant adversity.

But there were no Waterloos or Gettysburgs in 1945. In the past few months some highly unpleasant details had come to light about Hitler's vaunted 'Thousand-Year Reich'. Names like Buchenwald and Belsen loomed large. There was horrified talk about human bodies being boiled down for soap, lampshades made of human skin, terrible experiments carried out on living subjects, mass murder by the million. And the men who had run those death camps had worn the same silver runes as the fighting warriors of the *Leibstandarte*.

Thus it was that on a foggy morning in November 1945, Panzermeyer was taken from his cell in the London prison-of-war cage, handcuffed and driven in a closed van to Croydon Aerodrome. Nobody explained where he was going, but as his transport began to fly eastwards and he spotted the Channel below, the prisoner made an accurate guess as to his destination. He was returning home.

A shouting, shoving crowd of photographers and pressmen were waiting for him when his plane landed, but unsmiling armed Canadian officers pushed their way through them to where Panzermeyer waited on the tarmac. The German prisoner saluted. His greeting was not returned. Instead, one of the Canadian officers, Captain W. Scott, attached one link of the prisoner's handcuff to his own wrist and jerked hard. Panzermeyer was forced to move. Moments later he was confined to the bowels of a smelly armoured car and being driven fast to the jail at the Canadian Army HQ. in a former German naval signals school in the little northern German township of Aurich.

Here, a confused and not a little apprehensive Panzer-mayer was thrust into a cell, which had been specially prepared for him. But the prisoner had little time to accustom himself to his new surroundings. Five minutes later the cell door was flung open by a jailer and he was dragged out into another room.

Colonel R. Clark of the 4th Winnipeg Rifles was waiting for him. Without any formalities being exchanged, Clerk informed Panzermeyer why he had been transferred so suddenly from London to Aurich: he was going to be tried as a suspected war criminal. Then the Canadian read out the two charges against him, which concerned the shooting of Canadian prisoners in Normandy back in the summer of 1944.

Minutes later, his warder had clicked the handcuffs back on Panzermeyer's wrists and he was being led back to his special cell, with Colonel Clark's last words ringing in his ears, 'You will be tried by a Canadian court here on 10 December 1945.'

The ordeal had begun…

Otto Skorzeny was the next old hare of the *Leibstandarte* to find out that the Western Allies could be vindictive; were not prepared to kiss and make up. Back in the summer of 1945, 'the most wanted man in Europe', as Eisenhower was now calling him, had twice offered to surrender to the Americans. But the American victors didn't seem one bit interested in the offer. Finally, in despair, he had driven down from his hiding place, dressed in full uniform and armed, to surrender – only to find the Americans had never heard of him.

In the end, someone in authority realised just who Skorzeny was and things changed dramatically. Immediately, half a dozen soldiers jumped on the scar-faced warrior. He was forced to strip and was searched in a very thorough – and humiliating – fashion. That done, he was pushed into a Jeep with a sergeant holding a machine pistol to his head and driven at top speed to Salzburg, escorted by armoured cars.

Here the press were waiting for him, as he was pushed into the conference room, his hands tied behind his back. The 'Skorzeny legend' was already growing by the minute. 'Skorzeny certainly looks the part,' the female correspondent of the *New York Times* gushed afterwards. 'He is striking in a tough sort of way: a huge powerful figure. The "Beast of Belsen"[19] is something out of the nursery in comparison.' Then for the sake of her female audience, she added as an afterthought: 'He has blue eyes.'

A British reporter present thought: 'It was best to keep Skorzeny with his hands manacled behind his back. When he was given a cigarette, it was lit and he had to have the ash shaken off.'

Despite his bonds, Skorzeny, a born showman, quite enjoyed the whole business, especially as someone suggested that he had really intended to kill Eisenhower, the Supreme Commander, during the Ardennes battle. That certainly added to the legend.

He would not have been so pleased if he had been able to read the comment the *New York Times* made the following day: 'Handsome, despite the scars that stretched from ear to ear, Skorzeny disclaimed credit for leading the mission to murder the Supreme Commander.' But there was no mistaking the journalist's own belief. Skorzeny was as guilty as hell; he really had intended to kill Eisenhower back in December 1944!

In due course, Skorzeny was charged. The indictments were massive. They ranged from the alleged slaughter of one hundred American prisoners during the Battle of the Ardennes, to the use of American uniforms during combat by men under his command and the planned assassination of General Eisenhower.

At the time that Panzermeyer was being sent to trial in northern Germany, Skorzeny was being arraigned in Number One Courtroom in the former German concentration camp of Dachau in the South... One by one the old hares were being apprehended and charged, for the victors wanted their pound of flesh. In the United States, in particular, they were attempting to place war on a legal footing. There it was maintained that anyone who started a war and helped to keep it going was little better than a criminal who would have to pay for his 'crime', especially if that person happened to be the loser. But one could not punish the whole German nation, some eighty million people in the heart of Europe, could one? All the same, a culprit had to be found.

The SS, and, in particular, Hitler's own Praetorian Guard, provided that culprit. The SS, in their black uniforms and gleaming jackboots, with their scarred faces under rakishly titled caps adorned with that silver death's head, were easily identifiable. They were the murderers. Ever since 1933 they had been Hitler's hired killers. No one in the Allied camp seemed to pause and consider that there was a difference between some forty-year-old *Herr Doktor* who for years had been conducting inhuman experiments on living prisoners in the concentration camps, and some seventeen-year-old callow kid conscripted into the Armed SS in the last months of the war. Now the SS had become the alibi of the nation. There were good decent Germans, millions of them – *and* the SS!

But of all the SS formations and their commanders who were now being arraigned for war crimes, no formation would have a more publicised 'show trial' than the *Leibstandarte SS Adolf Hitler.*

'As the world of the barbed wire closed about us,' as Jochen Peiper, the main defendant at what was now known as 'the Malmedy Massacre Trial', recorded afterwards, 'we were like children who had lost their mother overnight. We had been brought up under the clear rules of the front and we weren't capable of understanding the new rules of the game ... Our innocence was boundless. The state had taught its youth only how to handle weapons. We hadn't been trained in how to handle treachery. Yesterday we had been part of the Greater German Army. Today we were scorned and avoided, surrounded by the howling mob as the whipping boys of the nation.'

In the years to come, Peiper and his fellow accused, Dietrich, Kraemer, Knittel and all the rest of the old hares, would learn just how innocent they had been in that glorious summer of 1945...

Peiper's first real indication that he was not going to be regarded as an ordinary prisoner-of-war came in August 1945. That month he was taken to a US Army interrogation centre, where he was cross-examined by a 'Mr Paul', who turned up later in the trial as 'Lieutenant Guth', which was probably his real name.

Mr Paul made it clear to Peiper that his first investigation of the prisoner's record had presented 'a surprisingly favourable picture' of him. Although he had at one time been Himmler's adjutant, he was the only one of Himmler's staff to have preserved his 'personal integrity'. Mr Paul knew all about his military record, too, and Major McCown's report on the events in La Gleize had shown him in 'a very favourable light'.

However – Mr Paul paused and looked solemn – there was the matter of the Baugnez Crossroads. The whole American nation had been enraged when they heard of the Malmedy Massacre, as the US press called it. They had demanded revenge then and they demanded it still. Somehow, they had got hold of Peiper's name and now he was generally regarded in the States as the 'Murderer of Malmedy'. Indeed, Peiper was the most hated man in America and the 'US soldier's public enemy number one'.

Paul then suggested that as Peiper's life was already forfeit – the press had prejudged him – he should show that he knew how to lose and take the blame for the Baugnez Affair on his own shoulders.

After a while, Peiper said: 'I am prepared to take the responsibility on myself, Mr Paul – on one condition. That not one of my subordinates should be tried on the same charge.'

Mr Paul said he would consider the suggestion and went away, obviously well pleased that he had managed to get Peiper to plead guilty right from the start.

Thereafter, the weeks passed for Peiper in solitary confinement, while Mr Paul and his associates prepared the case, not only against Jochen Peiper, but against his superiors, including Dietrich, and his subordinates, down to a sixteen-year-old private and an eighteen-year-old who had lost a leg.

Sometime in the autumn of 1945, Peiper was taken out of his lonely cell, introduced to the officer who would successfully have him condemned to death, Colonel Burton Ellis, a former Californian divorce lawyer, and then taken under heavy guard to a nearby small town.

Here, Ellis ordered Peiper to get out of the car. Together with his escort, he was walked over to where four American soldiers were standing. They were some of the survivors of Malmedy – Lary, Ford, Ahrens and Dobyns.

Ellis waited expectantly as the four stared at the skinny German in his shabby *Wehrmacht* uniform devoid of badges of rank. As Peiper wrote later: 'I was confronted with the American survivors of the Malmedy crossroads. Without success' – which was not surprising, as Peiper had been several kilometres away when those terrible events at Baugnez took place.

Ellis knew this, too, of course. But he was determined to make a name for himself in a case that would have worldwide impact. Thus, he did not hesitate to employ tactics that were no advertisement for US justice or the US Army, in order to prove the guilt of the defendants, and Peiper in particular.

Throughout the latter half of that year, some 1,100 members of the *Leibstandarte* were interrogated. Of these, several hundred who were suspect or might have some use as witnesses for the prosecution were imprisoned in a modern jail near Stuttgart. Each prisoner was placed in a separate cell, often blacked out twenty-four hours a day. They were allowed no contact with the outer world, no legal advice, no exercise period, not even a visit from a priest.

When the Junior Senator from Wisconsin, the infamous Joseph McCarthy, who would first make his name with the case, heard this, he exploded: 'And you [John Kind, one of the guards at the prison] knew there was some sizeable number of Protestants, Catholics – or Jewish boys! I understand that there was no chaplain assigned to these boys!' *Jewish* SS men – the mind boggles.

Later, the McCarthy remark occasioned some amusement, but there was nothing funny about the treatment of the non-Jewish SS men of the *Leibstandarte* in the winter of 1945-46. They were subjected to near torture and the third-degree tactics employed by US police in that era. Beatings were commonplace, as were bribes. In return for offers of smaller sentences, food, better treatment for their families outside – some were threatened that their families' ration cards would be taken away from them, a virtual death sentence that winter – prisoners were talked into testifying against the main defendants. One such turncoat was twenty-one-year-old Max Hammerer, who was later sentenced to death. On oath, he stated afterwards: 'I had never seen a prison from inside before. As soon as I was admitted, accusations, curses, threats rained down on my head from all sides until I was totally confused. Soon I became a willing tool in the hands of my interrogators. If I said "yes" it became "no" and I had to write down "no". First Lieutenant Perl [a member of war crimes' investigation team] dictated my statement and, whether I wanted to or not, I had to write what Perl thought was right, although I knew it was wrong. That is how my statement came about… It is completely untrue and isn't mine, but that of the interrogation officer.'

Another prisoner, ex-SS Corporal Heinz Friedrichs, was led hooded into an underground cell. When he was freed from the hood, he was almost blinded by a bright light shone directly into his eyes. By narrowing his eyes, he could just make out some men sitting at a black-draped table decorated with a crucifix, with a noose swinging back and forth behind it. A priest entered (in fact, one of the interrogation team) and the cross-examination commenced.

Lieutenant Perl, the first interrogator, snapped, 'So you are Friedrichs. We've been waiting for you a long time. You can say what you like, but we know you shot them down left and right.' He clicked his fingers.

Friedrichs was terrified out of his wits and didn't know what to say. But (according to his own sworn statement) Perl and his companion, a civilian called Harry Thon, began to beat him up as he protested: 'I haven't killed any prisoners … If I had I would regard it as my duty to pay for it.'

They stopped beating him and Perl said: 'All right, let's tackle something else.' Leaving the Malmedy affair, he accused Friedrichs of killing two American prisoners at Stoumont, near La Gleize. Again the prisoner denied the charge and was beaten up, with Perl shouting at him red-faced with apparent anger, 'If you want to protect your officers, then you'll hang with them! But if you tell us everything we want to know, you'll be back with your parents in a couple of months.'

Friedrichs continued to protect his innocence and Perl calmed down. He said: 'A democracy like America is not interested in killing a young man like you. But if you persist, we'll put you in front of a court and have you hanged within twenty-four hours.' Thereupon he turned to Thon, who had begun to threaten he would have the ration cards of Friedrichs' parents withdrawn first thing in the morning, and said soothingly: 'Just one moment, Mr Chief Prosecutor. Perhaps Friedrichs is prepared to confess?' Friedrichs wasn't. So he was slapped about again until finally he broke. As he swore on oath later: 'After they had treated me like that for an hour or so, until I could hardly stand, I confessed to the untruth with which they accused me. I didn't care any more. In my apathy I wrote down everything they told me to. I had to write down a statement which was dictated to me by a first lieutenant I didn't know. This statement was used as the only piece of evidence against me in the Malmedy case...'

So it went on and on in the midst of a beaten, starving Germany. By the end of April 1946, the investigation team preparing the case for the prosecution had obtained seventy-one sworn statements from members of Peiper's battle group confessing to having shot some twenty individual American prisoners or Belgian civilians, and admitting to the murder of approximately *nine hundred American soldiers and civilians.*

–

Fittingly enough, the trial of the *Leibstandarte* was held at Dachau, in those dreary wooden huts that had once housed one of Nazi Germany's oldest and cruellest concentration camps. On the morning of 16 May 1946, Court B was crowded as never before. Movie cameras whirred. Flash bulbs exploded. Newspapermen joshed for position. Slowly the accused were led by the tall, immaculate military policemen in their white helmets.

A couple of them hobbled in on crutches – they had lost legs in the fighting since that December. But most of them were pale and trim in *Wehrmacht* uniforms, on their chests a large black number on a white cloth to aid better identification, for there were seventy-four of them from Battle-Group Peiper, including its commanders, and three SS generals, Dietrich, Kraemer, his former chief-of-staff, and Priess, commander of the corps to which the *Leibstandarte* had then belonged.

The first day was taken up with a recital of charges against the prisoners. '*Lined up against a wall and mown down by a machine gun… skulls beaten in by rifle butts… taken into the garden and slaughtered in cold blood…*' On and on the litany of horror and death went, while Peiper, his lean face a mixture of burning hatred and resentment, mouth twisted, stared above the heads of the court as if he wanted nothing to do with his accusers or his men, so many of whom had become traitors and turncoats in these last months.

The verdicts were a foregone conclusion. The media had prejudged the *Leibstandarte* killers and the US Army wanted revenge for Malmedy. Desperately, their chief American defender, Colonel Everett, who was risking his reputation in taking their case (he would spend some 40,000 dollars of his own money in their defence by the time it was all over), fought back the best he could. But he was hampered by the fact that he had few resources to find new evidence and defence witnesses; and all the time Ellis, for the prosecution, kept pulling new witnesses out of the hat, who testified that their superiors had actually ordered them to kill prisoners.

Here and there, Everett, a gentle, softly spoken Southerner, was able to dent the prosecution's case. He managed to find the parish priest at La Gleize, for instance, who testified that the SS had not shot a single American prisoner there despite the allegations of the prosecution's turncoat witnesses. Major McCown, whom the prosecution alleged had virtually collaborated with Peiper, came from the States at his own expense to testify on Peiper's behalf. At La Gleize, at least, there had been no second 'Malmedy Massacre'.

But these were limited successes. For the only witnesses produced regarding the happenings at the Baugnez crossroads were those of the prosecution. Everett knew nothing of those other witnesses of what had happened there on that fateful December afternoon; and he had not the resources to discover that there were any.[20]

On 15 July 1946, after a long recess during which Everett worked feverishly – and failed – to find new evidence to defend his clients, the cameramen and journalists were back in the court. For this hot summer's day was the day of the verdicts.

One by one, the defendants were brought before General Dalbey, the president of the court, and read their sentences. On average, he passed a sentence every two minutes – and each was heavy. Fleps, who had admitted firing the first shot at the Baugnez crossroads, was sentenced to death by hanging. Knittel, whose reconnaissance battalion had, it seemed, caused so much mayhem and murder in the Ambleve valley, received the same sentence.

On and on the General droned in English, with the interpreter translating his grim words into German. In just over an hour, forty-three of the accused from the *Leibstandarte* were sentenced to death. Another twenty-two were given life imprisonment, while a further four received twenty years' hard labour. Time after time the interpreter repeated the same frightening words, '*schuldig... schuldig*' (guilty) and the sentence '*Tod durch erhangen*' (death by hanging).

Then it was Peiper's turn. A few days before, he had written what he believed was his last letter to Everett, stating that his men were 'the products of total war, grown up in the streets of scattered towns without any education. The only thing they knew was how to handle weapons for the Reich. They were young people with a hot heart and a desire to win or die according to the motto – 'my country right or wrong'. When you see those defendants in the dock today, don't believe them to be the old Combat Group Peiper. All my old friends and comrades have gone before. The real outfit is waiting for me in Valhalla.'[21]

Now, as Peiper was brought in, there was no emotion on his pale, emaciated face. The hatred, the resentment, the disgust had vanished, and if he was scared that he, too, would soon be sent to Valhalla, his expression did not reveal it.

Softly, the interpreter translated General Dalbey's words into German: '*Tod durch erhangen*'. But Peiper did not need his services. He had understood already.

Quite clearly, in a voice audible to the back of the court, he said, '*Danke*' and turning smartly, as if on parade, he left...

By the time most people in the States were waking up, it was all over. The 'Malmedy Massacre Trial' was history. In the late editions of the US papers that July day, journalists would be quoted as saying: 'Because the conscience of humanity has not quite been stilled ... the world reaches out for a concept of international law. The Nazi philosophy of ruthlessness and its policy of frightfulness as an end in itself stood at the bar of judgement and were found guilty.'

Back at Dachau, a triumphant Colonel Ellis told a pack of noisy journalists eager for his story: 'They – the SS – showed no more emotion than if they had been eating a meal. They marched in, snapped to attention, listened to their sentence and then, doing an about-face, marched off.'

Die Leibstandarte SS Adolf Hitler was dead at last...

6. 'HE WHO EATS WITH THE DEVIL NEEDS A LONG SPOON'

The years passed.

In Canada, Panzermeyer was released from life imprisonment and sent home to West Germany, where he would soon be pardoned and become a passionate advocate of the rights of former SS men. That other old hare of the *Leibstandarte*, Otto Skorzeny, decided he could wait no longer for the slow process of Allied justice to release him.

On 27 July 1948, he stowed away in the luggage compartment of his old adjutant's car and escaped from the camp where he was being held prisoner. Dying his hair bright blond and in civilian clothes, he crossed the mountains into Austria and from there he went to Spain to start a successful career as an engineer. Some said, however, that his main interests lay in arms smuggling and assisting a mysterious SS underground organisation, *die Spinne* (the Spider), which allegedly smuggled old SS comrades wanted by the Allies out of Europe to the safety of obscure South American banana republics. A lot of sensation-hungry journalists and novelists believed the story. It made good copy, and in the fifties and sixties Skorzeny and his Spider continued to provide the background for a number of novels and movies on the subject.

By 1948, when Skorzeny made his escape, Peiper and twelve others of the old *Leibstandarte* still continued to wear red jackets at Hitler's old prison at Landsberg[22]. A red jacket indicated to the ever-watchful guards that the man wearing it had to be specially watched for he was under sentence of death. All it needed was confirmation from the American commander of their zone of occupation and the particular 'red jacket' would be quietly taken away one early morning and hanged by the neck.

But the American zonal commander did not give that final order.

Over on the other side of the Atlantic the debate still raged on the validity of the Dachau court's findings. Year after year the executions were postponed, while high-ranking politicians such as President Eisenhower and Senator McCarthy became involved in the fight for the lives of the 'Landsberg Red Jackets'.

In 1951, after Peiper and the rest had been under sentence of death for five long years, they were told that their sentence had been commuted to imprisonment for life.

In rare good humour, Peiper wrote to Everett, who was now back in the States working as a civilian lawyer:

> *'We have received a great victory and, next to God, it is from you that all our blessings flow. In all the long and dark years you have been the beacon flame for the forlorn souls of the Malmedy boys, the voice and conscience of the good American and yours is the present success against all the well-known and overwhelming odds. May I, therefore, Colonel, express the everlasting gratitude of the red-jacket team as well as of all the families concerned.'*

That afternoon, as far away in Landsberg her father took off the hated red jacket for the last time, Peiper's ten-year-old daughter Elke returned home from school to find her mother 'beside herself with excitement'. She asked her mother what was the matter and her mother cried, '*Papa ist heute begnadigt worden*' – 'Papa was pardoned today.'

Many years later, Elke Peiper recalled: 'Suddenly I realised for the first time that he would not be hanged after all... that one day he would be coming home to us...'

But that was not to be yet. Dietrich was released, as were most of the others. But Peiper and six of his comrades were still kept in prison, despite mounting pressure from outside in the newly created Federal Republic of West Germany. By now the details of just how rigged the original trial at Dachau had been were common knowledge and demands came from all sides to have the remaining prisoners released. To no avail. The survivors of the *Leibstandarte* were not going to get away with it that easily.

Another year went by, and another. The outside world began to forget Peiper and his comrades. West Germany was experiencing its 'economic miracle' and trying desperately to forget its recent past. The scramble for the 'hard mark' was uppermost in most people's minds. In the winter of 1952, Peiper wrote a long essay for a book on the SS to be edited by an old comrade – 'the ugliest man in uniform I have ever seen', as Patton had once described General Hausser. It began as if its author were twice his actual age:

> '*In this lonely cell sits a war criminal on a stool and dozes. On his door the sign says "Life" and on the calendar the date is October 1952. The stove*

sings, the spider is looking for new winter positions
and autumn is shaking the cell windows with a
rough hand.'

But Peiper's resentment and bitterness about his fate soon
crept through:

'Thirteen years now separate me from my wife, my
birthday celebrated five times as a man sentenced
to death and now before me the eighth Christmas
in jail. Really a sunny youth I've spent! One
wouldn't treat an animal that badly...

'The news which managed to penetrate our cells
from outside was not exactly calculated to make
the manner of dying any easier. We learnt that we
belonged to a criminal organisation and that we
had served an unjust state...

'During the war our divisions [those of the
SS] were regarded as particularly stable in times of
crisis. In the jails of the world we have proved just
how steadfast we are. Let us hope that one day our
children will say we were not meaner than our fate
and that even in our Diaspora we contributed to the
idea of reconciliation and the European movement.
I salute all who have remained free in prison!'

The essay was a moving piece of writing and it showed
that Peiper was well aware of the important events of the
time – the new European movement and the Cold War.
But, in essence, it was the work of an embittered man who
felt out of step with the age in which he lived – Peiper
knew well that most sons of SS were frantically trying to
forget in 1952 that their fathers had ever belonged to that

criminal organisation – and who was not resigned to the life of a jailbird.

Another two years passed. Then in 1954, Peiper's sentence was reduced to thirty-five years' imprisonment. That meant he would be seventy-six if he managed to survive till the end of his sentence. It must have been a bitter blow to the prisoner.

Finally, fortune smiled on Peiper. In the third week of December 1956, he learned that the West German parole board had recommended his release in the early new year. He would be discharged to the town of his choice, where he would have to report to the police weekly and not leave the place without prior permission. Thus, at the age of forty-three *ex-Standartenfuhrer* Jochen Peiper of the *Leibstandarte SS Adolf Hitler* was released, the last member of the division in the West to be freed. He emerged into a new world, a Germany that wanted nothing to do with men with his kind of past.

He started off washing cars at the Porsche factory, which had once built the Panthers he had led down the fiery trail he had blazed across Europe. But although he had become very introverted in prison, he still possessed that drive and dash that had made him the youngest regimental commander in the whole of the SS. 'I decided to get on the steeplechase for money,' he stated, and within a short time he had worked his way up to become manager of Porsche's American sales.

But the past would not leave him alone. The local grammar school refused to accept his son – 'We don't want the son of a war criminal here,' the headmaster was reported as saying.[23]

Then a picture of Peiper in John Toland's book on the Battle of the Bulge, published in 1958, led an

Italian to accuse him of being involved in war crimes in Northern Italy. The local public prosecutor's office launched an inquiry. Hundreds of former members of Peiper's battalion at the time (1943) were cross-examined, and in the end Peiper was cleared of any guilt.

Even so, the many 'guest workers' employed by Porsche refused to work with him, innocent or not. He moved from Porsche to Volkswagen, but it was the same thing all over again. The Italian guest workers there threatened to go on strike if Peiper continued to be employed by the company. Again, Peiper was forced to leave. In the end, he managed to find a job with a well-known magazine- and book-publishing firm, Auto, Motor und Sport Verlag in Stuttgart.

But now he was losing any remaining faith he might have had in his fellow Germans and the rat race for money – that 'holy D-Mark', as he called it bitterly. He started to make plans to leave the country once and for all, like so many of his surviving comrades of the *Leibstandarte*. This was not his Germany, and as his daughter said after his murder, 'He had had good reason to have lost his faith in his fellow human beings.'

In 1959, he purchased a small plot of land in the French village of Traves at the fringe of the Jura, some 150 kilometres or so from the German border. There, over the next year, he had a wooden house built. It had its rear to the steep bank of the River Saone, with thick patches of trees to the left and right, but with an unrestricted view over the fields to the road to its front. No drive or real path led up to the lonely house, and in due course the only indication that there was some kind of dwelling there would be the overhead electricity cable that looped its way over the undergrowth and trees. It was in an ideal defensive position, though at the time he had the house built, Jochen Peiper had no idea he would ever be called upon to do battle again.

In 1972, after being granted a five-year EEC residential permit by the local French prefect, Peiper left Germany for Traves for good. 'The only people I took my leave from,' he said later, 'was the tax office and the only gap I left behind was the garden gnome I removed from the vase of flowers in my office.' Dropping his bitter cynicism about all things German for a moment, he confided to a friend that he hoped one day he and his wife would stand like 'a double oak on the bank of a river, unharmed by the failure of our society and economy which is bound to come'.

Thus '*l'Allemand*', as he was called in the tiny village, settled at his house – number thirteen; Peiper had never been superstitious. Besides, most of his adult life he had been unlucky anyway. There he earned his living by translating books on military subjects into French and German, supplementing his service pension. The Peipers kept to themselves, though as the local burgomaster would tell the press afterwards: 'Everyone knew him and what he had been. But he didn't do any harm to anyone.'

At first his wife, Sigurd, did not like the village or village life after the years she had spent in German cities. But gradually it began to grow on her. As she wrote to her son shortly before her own death: 'The move, the different way of life, a strange new way of life – these were all a radical change for me … But as the months passed, I grew more and more accustomed to Traves … Pa and I became so happy and carefree, making plans for the future, enjoying every new day.'

But there was going to be no future for Jochen Peiper. Whatever plans his wife Sigurd had made – or might make – they were all doomed never to reach fruition…

—

On Bastille Day 1976, they came for him.

All that blazingly hot summer, with the meadows around Traves burned yellow and the farmers feeding bananas to their cattle for lack of grass, Peiper had been receiving threats. It is now known that Honecker's East Germany had been feeding information about Peiper to the French Communists in order to sour the new entente between West Germany and France.

In June French Communists appeared in the village and started handing out pamphlets to the locals. These stated: 'A war criminal lives among you, an SS man. *Peiper out!*' Overnight great white swastikas were painted on village walls and on the roads leading to Peiper's house.[24]

Now Peiper started receiving anonymous phone calls threatening, 'We'll set fire to your house. On 14 July, we'll murder you,' and ordering him to leave before that date. Peiper dug his heels in, knowing he would receive no support from either French or German police. After all, he was an embarrassment to both their governments.

On 21 June, the French Communist newspaper *L'Humanite*, giving East Berlin as its source of information, published full details of Peiper's record, publicising the fact that a known German war criminal was living in a French village with the agreement of the French authorities. *L'Humanite*'s account was followed by a flood of others, none of them very accurate, which mentioned Peiper in the same breath as Himmler and Eichmann.

Time was running out, and Peiper knew it. He sent Sigurd back to Germany. But he insisted he would stay in France until his permit expired in 1977. He was not prepared to make a run for it. Instead, he armed himself with an old American revolver and borrowed a shotgun from a French neighbour. Thus prepared, and guarded by his two dogs, *ex-Standartenfuhrer* Peiper of the *Leibstandarte* was ready for his final battle...

Bastille Day 1976 came to an end at last. In Paris, undoubtedly, they would still be dancing in the streets, as tradition demanded. But the farmers of Traves had to be up early on the following morning to tend to their animals. Besides, most of them were glad to remove their clothes and find some relief from the burning heat of that 14 July. Heatstroke had taken its toll amongst the pig stock, and on the nearby *autoroute* heading for Dijon, tourists were driving in their underwear and bikinis. *Mon Dieu*, they groaned as they fell into bed, gorged on rich food and good wine, what a heat!

Peiper spent the evening with a German neighbour, one of a score or so who had a summer place in Traves. Herr Ketelhut offered to stay with him in case there was an attempt to carry out the threat to kill him. Politely, the sixty-two-year-old Peiper refused. He said, 'I won't be bullied ... They can shoot me if they wish, but I'm not going to allow them to beat me into a cripple. If they come, I shall defend my home!'

With that, Ketelhut, the last man to see Peiper alive, took his leave. It was nearly midnight.

Sweating and stirring uneasily in their hot beds, a score or so of the villagers of Traves were awakened by a series of loud bangs just after midnight. A couple padded barefoot to their windows to see what had occasioned the noise.

But there was nothing to be seen. They returned to their rumpled beds, complaining about unthinking people who still continued to let off fireworks when the Bastille Day celebrations were over. Some folk had to get up early in the morning to go to work. A few recognised the sounds for what they were. Firmly they turned round in their beds and faced away from their windows.

At two-thirty precisely on that morning, a motorist raised the alarm. Driving down the little road past the church that led out of Traves, he had seen flames rising from beyond the woods. The timber out there was bone-dry. If something was not done quickly, he knew the whole damned place would be on fire.

Minutes later, the heavy-handed voluntary firemen of the village had tumbled out of their beds, hastily grabbing their polished helmets and laying out their hoses as they stumbled across the field to the site of the fire. The captain gave the order to turn on the water. Nothing happened. Someone had slashed the hoses!

So while they fussed and fumed, and tried to call the brigade at the nearby town of Vesoul – later it was reported that the telephone lines had been cut, too – number thirteen burned merrily as Peiper's neighbours stood back impotently, fearing the worst. For there was no sign of its owner, Jochen Peiper.

Dawn arrived early. With it came the detectives from Vesoul and later from Dijon. Immediately, they set about searching the smouldering charred wreckage. Soon, they knew, the press would be descending upon them, for already the alarm had gone out – and before this day was out every major newspaper in the world from *Pravda* to the *New York Times* would be reporting the strange events in this remote village.

Swiftly, they found the crude, unexploded petrol bomb on the blackened grass outside the wrecked house and concluded correctly that number thirteen had been set on fire by a petrol-bomb attack. But where was Peiper? Moments before they found the blackened lump that had once been a human being, they came across a shotgun – it had been fired – and one of Peiper's dogs, whimpering piteously near a tree, with a bullet wound in its side.

The body was a charred, unrecognisable mass without features, shrunk by the intense heat to a length of exactly sixty centimetres. Next to it was Peiper's watch and thirteen boxes of exploded ammunition. Later it was discovered at the autopsy that the corpse had traces of smoke in its lungs, which indicated that the victim had still been breathing when the fire was started. *But was it the body of Jochen Peiper?*

For a few more days the more sensational papers throughout the western world had a field day, as neither Sigurd Peiper not the three French specialists who examined the blackened torso were able to say with certainty that the corpse was Peiper's. Some papers said the whole business had been stage-managed by unnamed Nazis. Peiper had known Europe was too hot to hold him anymore. Therefore, the feigned attack had been the cover he needed to disappear to the jungles of South America, just as Martin Bormann, Eichmann and Dr Mengele had done before him. The charred corpse was a plant. Others maintained that Peiper had fought off his attackers, killed one of them and then fled. Another story had it that the German Baader-Meinhoff terrorist gang had liquidated Peiper and that this really was his corpse.

The local detectives, who believed that the attack was the work of French people from the region, plodded on with their inquiry, though only half-heartedly. After all, Peiper had been a war criminal and a member of Hitler's own Praetorian Guard, the *Leibstandarte*. They interrogated several local youths. In the end, one of the youngsters did confess to the crime. But when it was discovered that he was an arsonist, one of those barn-burners always found in country areas and known to be psychologically unstable, the youngster was released.

In the meantime, Peiper's dentist in Munich had identified the jaw taken from the corpse. It matched Jochen Peiper's dental records. There was going to be no new life with a new identity in South America for Peiper. He had been murdered at Traves all right, dying as an old man as he had lived when young – with a weapon in his hands...[25]

–

Thus, the last of the *Leibstandarte*'s bold commanders passed from the scene. Peiper epitomised the daring, the self-sacrifice and arrogant ruthlessness of those young men who had once flocked so eagerly to that evil, crooked-cross banner.

They had had their great days, all of them. There had been years of victory after victory; when they had been the scourge of Europe, seemingly unbeatable. But right from the start they had been doomed – all of them. Back in 1933 on that torch-lit square in Munich, they had sworn 'obedience to death' to the monster who would ruin Europe. That oath had ruined them. They had remained obedient to death. To the very end they refused to see just how evil Hitler and his 'New Order' were. Just as time and fate had once selected them to be the supreme heroes of Hitler's Reich, later they were chosen to become the alibi of a nation: the guilty men who had fought a war of conquest, which Germany had lost.

In a post-war West Germany, which feared and denied any connection with the Nazi past, they would be the ones who continued to pay the price for their youthful hubris – even when they were white-haired old men in their dotage. Even in 1990, attempts are still being made in the British Parliament to bring the eighty-year-old General Mohnke to trial for his alleged part in the massacre of the British prisoners at Wormhout in 1940...

One day after it was officially announced that the charred body found at Traves was indeed that of *ex-Standartenfuhrer* Jochen Peiper, a West German newspaper headlined its account of the killing with an old German proverb. Probably the paper's editor thought this the best way of symbolising for his readership what really had been the fatal flaw of Peiper and all those others who had served with him in the *Leibstandarte*. The proverb was: '*Wer mit dem Teufel isst, braucht einen langen Lojfel*' – 'He who eats with the Devil needs a long spoon'.

It was as good a summary as any of what Peiper and the rest had failed to do. They had eaten at Adolf Hitler's table and had not distanced themselves from him when they found out how evil he really was. Even when Hitler had scorned and spurned them in the end, they had still remained loyal.

After the war they had been forced to pay the price of that failure. It was disgrace, dishonour and ultimately – in Peiper's case – sudden, violent death.

SOURCE NOTES

PART ONE

Chapter 1

R. Lehmann, *Die Leibstandarte* Vol IV (Munin Verlag Osnabruck, 1979).
P. Carroll, *Sie Kommen* (Ullstein, 1968).
L. Farago, *Patton* (Obolensky Press, 1969).
F. Winterbotham, *Ultra Secret* (Weidenfeld, 1974).

Chapter 2

Lehmann, *Die Leibstandarte* Vols I–III.
J. Weingartner, *Crossroads of Death* (University of California Press, 1979).
Interviews with Colonels Peiper, Frey, Bremer and Skorzeny.

Chapter 3

O. Bradley, *A General's Life* (Simon & Schuster, 1984).
Lehmann, *Die Leibstandarte* Vol IV.
C. Whiting, *Papa Goes To War* (Crowood Press, 1990).
Carroll, *Sie Kommen*.
BBC War Reports (Collins, 1945).
Interview with Herr X, Peiper's radioman.

Chapter 4

Lehmann, *Die Leibstandarte* Vol IV.

C. Wilmot, *The Struggle for Europe* (Collins, 1964).

W. Gorlitz, *Model* (Ullstein, 1972).

J. Johnson, *Fighter Ace* (Corgi, 1970).

D. Flower, *Anatomy of Courage* (Cassell, 1960).

Chapter 5

D. Hamilton, *Monty* (Hamish Hamilton, 1986).

K. Meyer, *Panzermeyer-Grenadiere* (Schildverlag, 1973).

Carroll, *Sie Kommen*.

Gorlitz, *Model*.

M. Shulman, *Defeat in the West* (Ballantine, 1968).

R. Martin, *Papa Goes to War*.

The GI War (Little Brown, 1967)..

Whiting, *Papa Goes to War*.

W. Trees and C. Whiting, *Die Amis Kommen* (Triangel Verlag, 1978).

Personal interviews with men of the 99th and 106th US Infantry Divisions.

PART TWO

Chapter 1

C. Whiting, *Massacre at Malmedy* (Leo Cooper, 1971).

Interview with Skorzeny Shulman, *Defeat in the West*.

Bradley, *A General's Life*.

Chapter 2

Whiting, *Malmedy*.

Lehmann, *Die Leibstandarte* Vol IV.
Interview with Colonel Peiper.

Chapter 3

Whiting, *Malmedy.*
Crimes de Guerre (Liege, 1945).
Weingartner, *Crossroads of Death.*
Hamilton, *Monty.*
J. Giles, *The Dammed Engineers* (Houghton Mifflin, 1970).
Lehmann, *Leibstandarte.*
Whiting, *Papa Goes to War.*

Chapter 4

Lehmann, *Leibstandarte.*
J. Gavin, *The Road to Berlin* (Ballantine, 1968).
Shulman, *Defeat in the West.*

Chapter 5

Lehmann, *Leibstandarte.*
Whiting, *Malmedy.*

Chapter 6

C. MacDonald, *Ardennes* (Department of the Army, 1965).
J. Toland, *Battle* (Ballantine, 1960).
Lehmann, *Leibstandarte.*
Farago, *Patton.*

PART THREE

Chapter 1

Lehmann, *Leibstandarte*.
J. Toland, *Battle* (Ballantine, 1960).
R. W. Thompson, *Men in Battle* (Collins, 1945).
C. Whiting, *Skorzeny* (Ballantine, 1970).
Personal interviews with Skorzeny and Caspary.

Chapter 2

Lehmann, *Leibstandarte*.
J. Toland, *The Last Hundred Days* (Random House, 1968).

Chapter 3

J. P. Donnel, *The Berlin Bunker* (Dent, 1977).
Correspondence with E. Krueger.
E. Ziemke, *Battle for Berlin* (Pan, 1968).
Lehmann, *Leibstandarte*.

Chapter 4

Lehmann, *Leibstandarte*.
H. Stoeber, *Die Sturmflut und das Ende* (Munin Verlag, 1972).
W. Tieke, *Im Feuersturm letzter Kriegsjahre* (Munin Verlag, 1973).
Toland, *The Last 100 Days*.
Personal interview with Colonel Peiper.

Chapter 5

Interview with Colonel Peiper.

Interview with H. Le Joly and M. Bodarwe.

C. Whiting, *Massacre at Malmedy* (Leo Cooper, 1971).

Meyer, *Panzermeyer-Grenadiere*.

W. Trees and C. Whiting, *Entscheidung in St Vith* (Doepgen Verlag, 1979).

Chapter 6

Correspondence with the former E. Peiper.

P. Hausser, *Waffen SS im Einsatz* (Schutzverlag, 1958).

Interview with Colonel Peiper.

Stern Magazine, *Aachener Volkszeitung*, etc, July 1976.

Notes

1. SS marches, clear the streets. The assault columns are ready. Death is our comrade in battle. We are the black hordes.

2. One, two, three – a song.

3. Jagd bomber.

4. A pun on his name, Hans Kluge. King means clever in German.

5. F. Schoenhuber: *Ich War Dabei*. Langen Muller, Munich.

6. Everything passes, Everything goes. After every December there is always a May.

7. Lieutenant Bouck, now a doctor of medicine, wrote his account personally to Peiper after he came out of prison.

8. Up to 1919 this area of Belgium belonged to Germany. In accordance with the terms of the Versailles Treaty, it was then ceded, with its mainly German-speaking population, to Belgium. After Belgium's capitulation in 1940, the area again became German, its citizens German.

9. To the author in 1970.

10. Canned meat nicknamed 'old man' because it was reputed to be made from the corpses of dead old men, in thick green pea soup.

11. The GIs' name for Place Pigalle.

12. Persistent rumour has it that General McAuliffe used a much earthier word than 'nuts', but it was cleaned up by the division's PR man.

13. Bastogne – 'Nuts City', as it calls itself today – has made quite a bit of money over the past five decades from this legend, but at first the locals were equally as puzzled by the reply. They thought that the answer somehow referred to the annual nuts fair held in the place before the war.

14. Patton had already been involved in one scandal of this nature when men of one of his divisions – the 45th Infantry – shot a couple of score Italian POWs in Sicily in 1943. The men blamed Patton's aggressive speech to them just before they had gone into action for the cold-blooded killings.

15. Budapest is divided into two parts by the River Danube – Buda and Pest.

16. Goetz von Berlichingen was a surly medieval knight in a play by Goethe. In it he told the Bishop of Bamberg to 'lick my arse'. Over the years the name 'Goetz von Berlichingen' thus became a polite euphemism in German for that insult.

17. The code name for the bunker area – Citadel.

18. For those interested in such things, it still exists, selling its excellent beer.

19. SS Major Josef Kraemer, the commandant of Belsen Concentration Camp.

20. What was thought to be the body of Madame Bodarwe, minus one leg, was found in a German border village after the war. While the trial was being conducted, Henri Le Joly was in prison in Antwerp, and Pfeiffer, the boy who had been at Baugnez, wisely returned to his village and kept quiet about what he had seen.

21. The slightly awkward style of the letter to Colonel Everett is explained by the fact that Peiper wrote it in English.

22. After his abortive putsch of 1923, Hitler was imprisoned there for a year and a half.

23. Today that son, an engineer, is an American citizen living in the United States.

24. For those interested in such things, they can still be seen in Traves, though much faded.

25. The file on the Peiper murder is still open at police HQ at Dijon. Since 1976, however, there have been no further arrests or any new leads. Peiper was – and is – a source of political embarrassment for both the French and West German governments. Their policy' is to let sleeping dogs lie.